The United States and Venezuela

The United States and Venezuela
RETHINKING A RELATIONSHIP

JANET KELLY AND CARLOS A. ROMERO

ROUTLEDGE
New York   London

Published in 2002 by
Routledge
29 West 35th Street
New York, New York 10001

Published in Great Britain by
Routledge
11 New Fetter Lane
London EC4P 4EE

Routledge is an imprint of the Taylor & Francis Group.

Printed in the United States of America on acid-free paper.

10 9 8 7 6 5 4 3 2 1

Library of Congress Cataloging-in-Publication Data

Kelly de Escobar, Janet.
  The United States and Venezuela: rethinking a relationship / Janet Kelly & Carlos A.
Romero.
    p. cm. — (Contemporary inter-American relations)
  Includes bibliographical references and index.
  ISBN 0–415–93184–3 (hardcover)——ISBN 0–415-93185–1 (pbk.)
    1. United States—Foreign relations—Venezuela. 2. Venezuela—Foreign relations—United
  States. I. Romero, Carlos A. II. Title. III. Series.

E183.8.V3 K45 2001
327.73087—dc21   2001019761

CONTENTS

Authors carry around many books in their heads, and most of them never get written. This book would not have come about without the energy and imagination of Jorge Domínguez and Rafael Fernández de Castro, who led the project to write a series of volumes on the bilateral relations between the United States and a group of countries in Latin America and the Caribbean. Recognizing the need for studies that would avoid the charge of bias toward one side or another in bilateral relations, they invited us to join our minds and write a single book about the United States and Venezuela that would incorporate the separate visions that spring from our different backgrounds, languages, and perspectives. We accepted the challenge and now offer the result to our readers in the hope that our effort will contribute to their understanding. Each of us has tried to put ourselves in the shoes of the other, see the same relation from a different standpoint, and analyze U.S.-Venezuelan relations with a sympathetic view to both countries. Our objective is to clarify the present and see into the future, but we base our view on the longer trends of history and the "big events" of the recent past, in particular the breakdown of the Cold War system and the emergence of new concerns with globalization, international justice, and the growing role of international institutions as the rule-makers at the start of the twenty-first century.

We have benefited greatly from the support of Jorge Domínguez and Rafael Fernández, and their respective institutions, the Weatherhead Center for International Affairs at Harvard University and the Instituto Tecnológico Autónomo de México (ITAM). The Ford Foundation gave its vote of confidence to the project and enabled the entire group of authors of this and the nine additional books on other countries and areas to meet together several times over the course of the project to exchange ideas, widen horizons, and help one another to place our ideas in a broader context. We thank our own institutions for the time we devoted to the project, sometimes at the expense of our colleagues and often with their help and stimulus, and hope that our effort meets the expectations of these and many others who helped us along the way.

Janet Kelly
Instituto de Estudios Superiores de Administración (IESA), Caracas
Carlos A. Romero
Instituto de Estudios Políticos, Universidad Central de Venezuela
May 2001

The transition from authoritarian rule to constitutional government.

The continentwide economic depression of the 1980s and the subsequent shift toward more open market–conforming economies.

The end of the Cold War in Europe.

The transformation of relations with the United States.

Each of these major events and processes was an epochal change in the history of Latin America and the Caribbean. More striking is that all four changes took place within the same relatively short time, though not all four affected each and every country in the same way. They became interconnected, with change on each dimension fostering convergent changes on other dimensions. Thus at the beginning of the new millennium we witnessed an important transformation and intensification in U.S.–Latin American relations.

This book is part of a series of ten books on U.S. relations with Latin American and Caribbean countries. Each of these books is focused on the fourth of these four transformations, namely, the change in U.S. relations with Latin America and the Caribbean. Our premise is that the first three transformations provide pieces of the explanation for the change in U.S. relations with its neighbors in the Americas and for the changes in the foreign policies of Latin American and Caribbean states. Each of the books in the series assesses the impact of the epoch-making changes upon each other.

The process of widest impact was the economic transformation. By the end of 1982, much of North America, Western Europe, and East Asia launched into an economic boom at the very instant when Latin America plunged into an economic depression of great severity that lasted approximately to the end of the decade. As a consequence of such economic collapse, nearly all Latin American governments readjusted their economic strategies. They departed from principal reliance on import-substitution industrialization, opened their economies to international trade and investment, and adopted policies to create more open market–conforming economies. (Even Cuba had changed its economic strategy by the 1990s, making its economy more open to foreign direct investment and trade.)

The regionwide economic changes had direct and immediate impact upon U.S.–Latin American relations. The share of U.S. trade accounted for by Latin America and the Caribbean had declined fairly steadily from the end of World War II to the end of the 1980s. In the 1990s, in contrast, U.S. trade with Latin America grew at a rate significantly faster than the growth of U.S. trade world-wide; Latin America had become the fastest-growing market for U.S. exports. The United States, at long last, did take notice of Latin America. Trade between some Latin American countries also boomed, especially within subregions such as the southern cone of South America, Venezuela and Colombia, the Central American countries, and, to a lesser extent, the Anglophone Caribbean countries. The establishment of formal freer-trade areas facilitated the growth of trade and other economic relations. These included the North American Free Trade Agreement (NAFTA), which grouped Mexico, the United States, and Canada; the Mercosur (southern common market), with Argentina, Brazil, Paraguay, and Uruguay; the Andean Community, whose members were Bolivia, Colombia, Ecuador, Peru, and Venezuela; the Central American Common Market (CACM); and the Caribbean Community (CARICOM). U.S. foreign direct and portfolio investment flowed into Latin America and the Caribbean in large quantities, financing the expansion of tradable economic activities; the speed of portfolio investment transactions, however, also exposed these and other countries to marked financial volatility and recurrent financial panics. The transformation in hemispheric international economic relations—and specifically in U.S. economic relations with the rest of the hemisphere—was already far-reaching as the twenty-first century began.

These structural economic changes had specific and common impacts on the conduct of international economic diplomacy. All governments in the Americas, large and small, had to develop a cadre of experts who could negotiate concrete, technical trade, investment, and other economic issues with the United States and with other countries in the region. All had to create teams of international trade lawyers and experts capable of defending national interests, and the interests of particular business firms, in international, inter-American, or subregional dispute-resolution panels or "courtlike" proceedings. The discourse and practice of inter-American relations, broadly understood, became much more professional, less the province of eloquent poets, more the domain of number-crunching litigators and mediators.

The changes in Latin America's domestic political regimes began in the late 1970s. These, too, would contribute to change the texture of inter-American relations. By the end of 1990, democratization, based on fair elections, competitive parties, constitutionalism, and respect for the rule of law and the liberties of citizens, had advanced and was still advancing throughout the region, albeit unevenly and with persisting serious problems, Cuba being the principal exception.

Democratization also affected the international relations of Latin American and Caribbean countries, albeit in more subtle ways. The Anglophone Caribbean is a largely archipelagic region long marked by the widespread practice of constitutional government. Since the 1970s, Anglophone Caribbean democratic governments have rallied repeatedly to defend constitutional government on any of the islands where it came under threat and, in the specific cases of Grenada and Guyana, to assist the process of democratization in the 1980s and 1990s, respectively. In the 1990s, Latin American governments also began to act collectively to defend and promote democratic rule; with varying degrees of success, they did so—with U.S. support—in Guatemala, Haiti, Paraguay, and Peru. Democratization had a more complex relationship to the content of specific foreign policies. In the 1990s, democratization in Argentina, Brazil, Uruguay, and Chile, on balance, contributed to improved international political, security, and economic relations among these southern cone countries. Yet democratic politics at times made it more difficult to manage international relations over boundary or territorial issues between given pairs of countries, including Chile and Peru, Colombia and Venezuela, and Costa Rica and Nicaragua. In general, democratization facilitated better relations between Latin American and Caribbean countries, on the one hand, and the United States, on the other. Across the Americas, democratic governments, including the United States and Canada, acted to defend and promote constitutional government. Much cooperation over security, including the attempt to foster cooperative security and civilian supremacy over the military, would have been unthinkable except in the new, deeper, democratic context in the hemisphere.

At its best, in the 1990s democratic politics made it possible to transform the foreign policies of particular presidential administrations into the foreign policies of states. For example, Argentina's principal political parties endorsed the broad outlines of their nation's foreign policy, including the framework to govern much friendlier Argentine relations with the United States. All Chilean political parties were strongly committed to their country's transformation into an international trading state. The principal political parties of the Anglophone Caribbean sustained consistent long-lasting foreign policies across different partisan administrations. Mexico's three leading political parties agreed that the North American Free Trade Agreement should be implemented, even if they differed on specifics, binding Mexico to the United States and Canada. And the Bush and Clinton administrations in the United States followed remarkably compatible policies toward Latin America and the Caribbean with regard to the promotion of free trade, pacification in Central America, support for international financial institutions, and the defense of constitutional government in Latin America and the Caribbean. Both administrations acted in concert with other states in the

region and often through the Organization of American States. Democratic procedures, in these and other cases, served to establish the credibility of a state's
foreign policy, because all actors would have reason to expect that the framework
of today's foreign policy would endure tomorrow.

The end of the Cold War in Europe began following the accession of Mikhail
Gorbachev to the post of general secretary of the Communist Party of the Soviet
Union in 1985. It accelerated during the second half of the 1980s, culminating
with the collapse of communist regimes in Europe between 1989 and 1991 and
the breakup of the Soviet Union itself in late 1991. The impact of the end of the
U.S.-Soviet conflict on the hemisphere was subtle but important: the United
States was no longer obsessed with the threat of communism. Freed to focus on
other international interests, the United States discovered that it shared many
practical interests with Latin American and Caribbean countries; the latter, in
turn, found it easier to cooperate with the United States. There was one exception
to this "benign" international process. The United States was also freed to forget
its long-lasting fear of communist guerrillas in Colombia (who remained powerful and continued to operate nonetheless) in order to concentrate on a "war"
against drug trafficking, even if it undermined Colombia's constitutional regime.

This process of the end of the Cold War also had a specific component in the
Western Hemisphere, namely, the termination of the civil and international wars
that had swirled in Central America since the late 1970s. The causes of those wars
had been internal and international. In the early 1990s, the collapse of the Soviet
Union and the marked weakening of Cuban influence enabled the U.S. government to support negotiations with governments or insurgent movements it had
long opposed. All of these international changes made it easier to arrange for
domestic political, military, and social settlements of the wars in and around
Nicaragua, El Salvador, and Guatemala. The end of the Cold War in Europe had
an extraordinary impact on Cuba as well. The Cold War did not end the sharp
conflict between the U.S. and Cuban governments, but the latter was deprived of
Soviet support, forcing it thereby to recall its troops overseas, open its economy
to the world, and lower its foreign policy profile. The United States felt freer to
conduct a "Colder War" against Cuba, seeking to overthrow its government.

Two other large-scale processes, connected to the previous three, had a significant impact on the international relations of the Western Hemisphere. They
were the booms in international migration and in cocaine-related international
organized crime. To be sure, emigration and organized crime on an international
scale in the Americas are as old as the European settlement that began in the late
fifteenth century and the growth of state-sponsored piracy in the sixteenth century. Yet the volume and acceleration of these two processes in the 1980s and
1990s were truly extraordinary.

One effect of widespread violence in Central America and in Colombia, and of
the economic depression everywhere, was to accelerate the rate of emigration to

the United States. Once begun, the process of migration to the United States was sustained through networks of relatives and friends, the family-unification provisions of U.S. legislation, and the lower relative costs of more frequent international transportation and communication. By the mid-1990s, over twelve million people born in Latin America resided in the United States; two thirds of them had arrived since 1980. The number of Latin American–ancestry people in the United States was much larger, of course. In the 1980s, migrants came to the United States not just from countries of traditional emigration, such as Mexico, but also from countries that in the past had generated few emigrants, such as Brazil. As the twentieth century ended, more people born in Latin America lived in the United States than lived in the majority of the Latin American states. The United States had also come to play a major role in the production and consumption of the culture of the Spanish-speaking peoples, including music, book publishing, and television programming. These trends are likely to intensify in the twenty-first century.

Had this series of books been published in the mid-1970s, coca and cocaine would have merited brief mention in one or two books, and no mention in most. The boom in U.S. cocaine consumption in the late 1970s and 1980s changed this. The regionwide economic collapse of the 1980s made it easier to bribe public officials, judges, police, and military officers. U.S. cocaine supply interdiction policies in the 1980s raised the price of cocaine, making the coca and cocaine businesses the most lucrative in depression-ravaged economies. The generally unregulated sale of weapons in the United States equipped gangsters throughout the Americas. Bolivia and Peru produced the coca; Colombians grew it, refined it, and financed it; criminal gangs in the Caribbean, Central America, and Mexico transported and distributed it. Everywhere, drug traffic–related violence and corruption escalated.

The impact of economic policy change, democratization, and the end of the Cold War in Europe on U.S.–Latin American relations, therefore, provides important explanations common to the countries of the Americas in their relations with the United States. The acceleration of emigration and the construction and development of international organized crime around the cocaine business are also key common themes in the continent's international relations during the closing fifth of the twentieth century. To the extent pertinent, these topics appear in each of the books in this series. Nonetheless, each country's own history, geographic location, set of neighbors, resource endowment, institutional features, and leadership characteristics bear as well on the construction, design, and implementation of its foreign policy. These more particular factors enrich and guide the books in this series in their interplay with the more general arguments.

As the 1990s ended, dark clouds reappeared in the firmament of inter-American relations, raising doubts about the "optimistic" trajectory that seemed set at the beginning of that decade. The role of the military in the running of state agencies and activities that normally belong to civilians rose significantly in Colombia, Venezuela, and Peru, and in January 2000 a military coup overthrew the constitutionally elected president of Ecuador; serious concerns resurfaced concerning the depth and durability of democratic institutions and practices in these countries. Venezuela seemed ready once again to try much heavier government involvement in economic affairs. And the United States had held back from implementing the commitment to hemispheric free trade that Presidents Bush and Clinton both had pledged. Only the last of these trends had instant international repercussions, but all of them could affect adversely the future of a Western Hemisphere based on free politics, free markets, and peace.

This Project

Each of the books in the series has two authors, typically one from a Latin American or Caribbean country and another from the United States (and, in one case, the United Kingdom). We chose this approach to facilitate the writing of the books and also to ensure that the books would represent the international perspectives from both parts of the U.S.–Latin American relationship. In addition, we sought to embed each book within international networks of scholarly work in more than one country.

We have attempted to write short books that ask common questions to enable various readers—scholars, students, public officials, international entrepreneurs, and the educated public—to make their own comparisons and judgments as they read two or more volumes in the series. The project sought to foster comparability across the books through two conferences held at the Instituto Tecnológico Autónomo de México (ITAM) in Mexico City. The first, held in June 1998, compared ideas and questions; the second, held in August 1999, discussed preliminary drafts of the books. Both of us read and commented on all the manuscripts; the manuscripts also received commentary from other authors in the project. We also hope that the network of scholars created for this project will continue to function, even if informally, and that the website created for this project (www.itam.mx/organizacion/divisiones/estgrales/estinter/americalatina.html) will provide access to the ideas, research, and writing associated with it for a wider audience.

We are grateful to the Ford Foundation for its principal support of this project and to Cristina Eguizábal for her advice and assistance throughout this endeavor. We are also grateful to the MacArthur Foundation for the support that made it possible to hold a second successful project conference in Mexico City. The Rockefeller Foundation provided the two of us with an opportunity to spend four splendid weeks in Bellagio, Italy, working on our various general responsibilities in this project. The Academic Department of International Studies at ITAM hosted the project throughout its duration and the two international conferences. We appreciate the support of the Asociación Mexicana de Cultura, ITAM's principal supporter in this work. Harvard University's Weatherhead Center for International Affairs also supported aspects of this project, as did Harvard University's David Rockefeller Center for Latin American Studies. We are particularly grateful to Hazel Blackmore and Juana Gómez at ITAM and Amanda Pearson and Kathleen Hoover at the Weatherhead Center for their work on many aspects of the project. At Routledge, Melissa Rosati encouraged us from the start; Eric Nelson supported the project through its conclusion.

Rafael Fernández de Castro
ITAM

Jorge I. Domínguez
Harvard University

OFTEN, A VENEZUELAN WILL MEET AN AMERICAN WHILE visiting the United States and find that the first question asked of him will be: "And what language do they speak down there?" Most Americans are surprised to learn that Venezuela is so close to their country, perhaps because it sounds exotic, or perhaps because they confuse it with faraway places like Argentina or Chile. They might remember that Venezuela has oil but know nothing of its delicious coffee and world-class cacao. Of course, Americans are not more ignorant of the outside world than are Venezuelans—neither would probably get very far if they had to converse together about Paraguay or Bolivia, not to speak of Slovakia or the Sudan. It is just that the United States is relatively well known by its neighbors in Latin America because of the large role it plays in their lives and in the destinies of their countries. Yet even among Latin American countries, Venezuela ranks behind Brazil or Mexico or even Argentina and Chile in the American imagination, despite the fact that its oil might seem to put it second only to Mexico in terms of its strategic importance to the United States. Why the low level of interest and knowledge?

Several arguments could be used in order to give an answer to the question of why this relationship tends to maintain a low profile, with few exceptions. Faced with the repeated question posed by some Venezuelans as to why Washington does not give signs of seeking a special relationship with the country, some knowledgeable people from within political, academic, military, and business circles often comment that: "In Venezuela, nothing ever happens."[1] Another frequent observation made throughout many years of close relations was that, to a great extent, Venezuela had achieved fundamental objectives in relation to American ideals and goals—its democratic system, the successful integration of Venezuelan oil into the U.S. market, the Pentagon's influence on the National Armed Forces, and the presence of the "American way of life," which is felt more strongly than in much of Latin America. Historically, there were few factors of stress in the U.S.-Venezuelan relation, and thus the American government simply did not have much to worry about during the postwar years when Venezuela was ultrastable and the rest of the Latin American region looked comparatively violent and chaotic.

Four premises were at the base of bilateral relations from the last years of the 1950s up to our days, although these premises, as we shall later see, are being questioned today.

The first premise assumed the Venezuelan government's traditional position on the strategic importance of the country within the hemispheric context as a trustworthy partner and supplier of oil; second, the idea of the historically exceptional condition of the Venezuelan case as compared with other countries of the region (a partner with political and economic stability) was taken for granted; third, relations were characterized by the predominance of cooperation over conflict in both countries' dealings with each other; and fourth, the predominance of bilateral issues in U.S.-Venezuelan relations simplified the nature of contacts between them by not involving other issues on both countries' regional and global agenda. These four premises reflect a high level of stability over the last fifty years, accompanied by two historical facts: Venezuela has not been subjected to the United States' political, military, or economic sanctions over the period, and it has been able to mark the limits of its bilateral commitment without compromising a more independent stance on other international matters.[2]

Venezuela, in spite of its asymmetric relationship with the United States, holds a fundamental place in this superpower's hemispheric interests, just as the United States forms a vital part of the international environment in which Venezuela operates. The facts that Venezuela has consistently been one of the primary sources of imported oil to the United States and at times even the top-ranked supplier, that it is ranked as the nineteenth global country in trade with Washington, and that Venezuelan democracy was long a model for other Latin American countries were enough to explain the close and friendly relationship that developed over time. Even so, relations with the United States have inevitably passed through some difficult moments as a consequence of the plurality of interests and identities peculiar to Caracas's foreign policy and of its activist vocation as reflected in Venezuela's diplomatic stances, which have sometimes come up against limits set by the United States, mostly at international forums and in multilateral organizations. Within this framework, Venezuela has maintained at least one constant attribute among the objectives of its foreign policy: that of appearing to the United States as a safe ally, enhanced by the strategic importance of oil and and the moral value of its democracy.

Relationships with the United States are intense from the Venezuelan perspective, although naturally much less so from Washington's standpoint. The local economic elite aims its business toward the United States. Fifty percent of Venezuela's world trade is transacted with its northern neighbor; imports to

Venezuela from the United States make up around 45 percent of total imports; the government-owned oil company Petróleos de Venezuela (PDVSA) invests in the United States and establishes strategic alliances with North American corporations. U.S. banks play a vital role as depositories for Venezuelan private funds and as lenders to investors. In the same manner, the Venezuelan military sector's training and institutional culture is imbued with strong American influence; its political sector has traditionally had a good relationship with American elites, and those in the general public on the whole express their wish for a good bilateral relationship. The only exception to this general rule would perhaps have been found in some of Venezuela's cultural elites, where European attitudes and nationalistic leanings generated some distrust of the United States, much as they have done in many developing countries.[3]

In strategic matters, with the economic importance of oil, Venezuelan heads of state have been careful to offer to their North American counterparts favorable conditions for a safe alliance, positioning Venezuela both as an intermediary with third parties and as a moderate ally and cooperative actor within the regional environment.

Although it is true that on a strategic level Venezuela has been able to reach a stable relationship with the United States, on specific issues some problems have arisen, mainly relating to American postures regarding new issues on the international agenda. Venezuela has felt frustration when observing unilateral positions adopted by Washington in some regional political crises and has some views different from those of the United States on economic issues. The uncertainty of trade restrictions, the problem of the foreign debt service, the concentration of the assets of Venezuelan citizens placed mostly in the United States all give rise to concern. The fact that the United States holds first place in the list of countries importing products from and exporting to Venezuela sets a most complex basis for cooperation when conflicts do arise.[4]

Over the course of the 1990s, new complexities began to affect relations between the United States and Venezuela. The bilateral nature of their contacts increasingly came under the pressure of global rule-making. Latin America itself made a new push for integration, creating new intermediaries such as the Andean Community, of which Venezuela is a member. At the same time, the United States began to conceive of a hemispheric bloc that would transform the North-South system of the Americas. In Venezuela, political conflict and change contributed to call its traditional diplomatic stance into question as the country began to seek a wider range of partners in the post–Cold War environment. The coming to power of the government of President Hugo Chávez in 1999 seemed to mark a turning point, even a breaking point, whose meaning should be examined in the context of the long-term history of U.S.-Venezuelan relations. The Chávez government, in office for a year and a half at the time of the writing of this volume, announced its intention to change Venezuelan foreign policy, seeking to escape from what it perceived as excessive American dominance of world politics. While it is still too early to evaluate the full meaning of such a shift or even to predict its results, this attempt on Venezuela's part will be analyzed with a view to determining how much is truly new and how much is really a continuation of traditional positions.

This book seeks to explore events since the beginning of the 1990s in a historical context and to analyze the way in which both global and local issues began to create a new relationship between the two countries under study. Many of the changes under way belong to trends throughout the world that naturally come to intrude on the relations of the United States with its many partners. Others respond to the particularities of developments in Venezuela and in Latin America, where the drive for development and autonomy generates new tensions as countries adapt to the ebb and flow of history.

ONE

THE PAST IS PRELUDE: HISTORICAL BASES FOR U.S.-VENEZUELAN RELATIONS

A<small>N UNDERSTANDING OF THE PRESENT REQUIRES KNOWLEDGE</small> of the past, especially in international relations, where collective memories of far-off events often color perceptions for many years. Such memories may be piecemeal, half-forgotten, and even wrong, but nevertheless exert tremendous power over the way nations react to one another. Nations remember ancient slights or perceived injuries and wax nostalgic over moments of solidarity. Images are often more important than reality. This chapter reviews the history of relations between the United States and Venezuela, with the aim of revealing those crucial moments that left their mark on the collective consciousness of each country and continue to affect how they see each other and judge each other. What emerges is the story of two countries that began their common history of independence with shared hopes, gradually drifted apart, and then came together again in the twentieth century as their interests converged, but with a much more complex and unequal relationship.

Venezuela's oil economy and search for democracy created a special relationship that later yielded to other forces: Venezuela's own desire to achieve greater autonomy, and broader events that reduced the nature of Venezuela's exceptionalism in the eyes of the United States. That special relationship also eroded as a result of insufficient attention to the task of watering and pruning. To a certain extent, Venezuela took its friendship with the United States for granted and never developed its opportunity to ground it in specific actions such as the promotion of a good lobbying organization or a network of connections that would be useful when strains inevitably appeared.[1] Equally, the United States tended to take for granted that Venezuelan democracy would also work well and repeat its traditional patterns. In reality, forces weakening the domestic political system in Venezuela increased slowly but surely without their being taken seriously abroad. By the 1990s, turbulent events within Venezuela would reverse some of these images and lay the groundwork for significant changes.

Parallel Lives: The First New Nations

Venezuelan children learn that the United States was the first country in the Americas to gain its independence and write a Constitution to define the rules of the republic. They see Venezuela as champion of independence in the Southern Hemisphere, and they are proud of their own leader, Simón Bolívar, who led Venezuela and other Latin American countries to independence from Spain after a long war. Washington and Bolívar are the heroes that link the historical traditions of both countries. Spain had been weakened during its own war with Napoleon Bonaparte at the beginning of the 1800s, leading people in Caracas to declare independence in 1811 when it appeared that there was a power vacuum in the mother country. Bolívar was the hero who led diverse groups in what today makes up both Venezuela and Colombia to gain their freedom from the Spaniards in 1821, and he also played an important role in the liberation of other nations in the Andean region. Unfortunately, the union of Venezuela and Colombia in 1821 in what was called "Great Colombia," or "La Gran Colombia" did not produce a peaceful or stable solution, so in 1830, Venezuela and Colombia separated, and Venezuela wrote its first Constitution, which owed much to the U.S. example, although it was later replaced by others that would serve the interests of the successive and unstable governments of the next one hundred years. Because of their common birthright as countries born of the first wars for independence in the Western Hemisphere, we can say that the United States and Venezuela are linked in parallel lives as the "new nations" that, together with other countries in the Americas, set out on a common adventure two centuries ago.

The United States and the Venezuelan War for Independence

Even in the heady period of the fight for independence, however, the United States sometimes assumed a more distant stance than Venezuelans would have liked. In a first phase, Venezuela-U.S. relations were framed in a context of mutual understanding. Even before the declaration of independence in 1811, trade between the Spanish colony and important American seaports such as Boston, Philadelphia, and Baltimore was active and Venezuela's future patriots admired the ideas of free trade and democracy coming from the North.[2] Francisco de Miranda, one of the leading patriots of the war for independence, looked for the support of the American government when he tried to invade Venezuelan territory in 1806, five years before independence was declared in Caracas. The autonomous Junta of Caracas, which was a sort of provincial council, had expelled its Spanish governor in 1810 and sent two emissaries to the United States in order to convince the American leaders of the patriotic cause. They failed in their mission, and in 1811 the United States hesitated to recognize Venezuela officially after the formal declaration of Venezuelan independence on July 5th.

Venezuelans felt disappointed and betrayed by American neutrality through-out the long war that would not end until ten years later. Within this short period, the United States matured in its own foreign policy. The War of 1812, in which England had tried to reassert its power over the United States, had sensi-tized Americans to the danger that the European powers would continue to meddle in their affairs. Furthermore, European interests in Latin America might also become a threat. In 1822, the United States finally recognized the independ-ence of Gran Colombia. Only a year later, President Monroe declared to the Europeans his famous doctrine that proclaimed "any attempt on their part to extend their system to any portion of this hemisphere as dangerous to our peace and safety." He said furthermore: "The political system of the allied powers, is essentially different . . . from that of America. . . . "—thereby suggesting a spe-cial commonality with the new Latin American republics. In 1834, the United States recognized the independence of Venezuela from Gran Colombia and signed a commercial treaty, although four years had gone by since the proclamation of the Venezuelan Constitution in 1830 and the unification of the country as the Republic of Venezuela under President José Antonio Páez.[3]

The Nineteenth Century: Divergent Lives

The common struggle for independence would connect the destinies of Venezuela and the United States as two countries striving for autonomy from the European colonial powers and for development as successful members of the international community of states. However, while the United States quickly attained an impressive position in the world, both economically and in terms of power, Venezuela faced greater problems in reaching its goals as a sovereign and inde-pendent country. Where the United States enjoyed democracy based on its own colonial traditions and on the guarantees of its long-lived Constitution, as well as economic success and opportunities for its citizens, Venezuela stumbled in its efforts to establish stability, equality, and economic security. The nineteenth cen-tury in Venezuela was marked by the repeated disintegration of the state, civil wars that substituted one faction for another, and an economy constantly ham-pered by political disorders and dependent on the export of a few basic products. Some Venezuelan leaders managed to maintain order for a while, but internal rivalries always came to the fore. This was no environment for integrating the population and creating open educational systems or civil infrastructure; by the end of the century, the country was fairly exhausted by its own conflicts. By 1900, the United States had firmly established itself as a world power, while Venezuela was still subject to the danger of intervention from abroad. Their rela-tions were friendly but somewhat intermittent.

From the 1830s to 1860s, Venezuelan affairs generated little international interest, but unofficial relations with other countries began to grow with the presence in Venezuela of adventurers, traders, and observers, all in search of a better life in tropical lands. José Antonio Páez (president, 1830–1835, 1838–1843, and 1861–1862), the leader of the new Republic of Venezuela, became an authoritarian strongman in Venezuela and dominated its politics for some thirty years. He was well regarded by the American governments in the years in which he was either in power or struggling to restore order in the face of uprisings by rival "*caudillos.*"[4]

The United States maintained a pragmatic policy toward Venezuela, extending diplomatic recognition to each Venezuelan government in turn. In those days, of course, democratic performance was not a criterion determining relations with other countries. Only a small portion of the world at that time aspired to democracy, while the United States tended to see itself as exceptional. Under the circumstances, it could hardly condition its diplomatic relations according to whether or not a country was democratic. This distinction would be developed only in the twentieth century and even today is subject to the realities of international power politics.

An issue that marred the positive relations between the United States and Venezuela during the period was the controversy in the late 1850s over Isla de Aves, an island rich with guano (valuable bird-droppings) over which Venezuela finally guaranteed its control as a result of an arbitration decision presided over by the Queen of Spain in 1865. Overall, the nineteenth century represented a time of balance in the relations between the two nations,[5] perhaps because both countries had turned inward to deal with their domestic problems. Venezuela suffered from a civil war over the issue of the power of the central government versus the provincial powers in the period, just as the United States almost split in two in its own Civil War. The difference lies in the fact that Venezuela's internal conflicts would not be resolved until the beginning of the next century, while the United States emerged from the Civil War as a nation with a clear vocation as an industrial power and as a future world leader.

A second stage in the relations between Venezuela and the United States developed in the period from the 1860s to 1908, when the relative difference in power came into evidence. By that time, the United States was not just a friendly neighbor anymore. In fact, it had become a regional power and increasingly a world economic power eager to assume its place on the international stage. In that role, the United States supported Venezuela in a boundary dispute with Great Britain over Venezuelan claims to a section of the British Guyana territory and as early as 1887 pressured London to accept an arbitration decision. In 1899 a court of arbitration decided in favor of Venezuela at least in part, although Venezuela would later maintain an unrecognized claim over a large swath of what is now the independent country of Guyana to its east, with little likelihood of an international settlement in its favor. (Contemporary Venezuelan maps always indicate this region as the "reclamation zone.")[6] The case provided an opportunity for the United States to flex its muscles at a time of growing confidence, even jingoism, especially when Secretary of State Richard Olney sent a defiant note to Great Britain in 1895 that went far beyond the Monroe Doctrine's stricture that had limited itself to warning against additional European colonization in the hemisphere.

During the same year as the arbitration court's decision, Cipriano Castro took power in Venezuela after a successful revolution in 1899.[7] Castro's arrival to power coincided with an economic crisis, the fall of world coffee prices, a costly external debt, and a banking crisis. In addition, Castro was involved in a tax dispute with an American company, the New York and Bermúdez Company, and refused to pay Venezuela's external debts. In the meantime, Germany, Italy, and Great Britain were demanding immediate recognition of their debts and blockaded Venezuelan seaports, which was considered to be a shameful state of affairs in Venezuela, whose very sovereignty was threatened by the Europeans. The United States pressured Castro to settle with the foreign governments and signed a protocol in 1903. In part, however, the United States had taken sides with Venezuela against European intervention in the Americas, in keeping with the precepts of the Monroe Doctrine. From the Venezuelan point of view, of course, one foreign power was displacing another. The European countries would never again constitute a threat to Venezuela, but the United States would clearly be the dominant outside influence henceforth.

Castro left Venezuela at the end of 1908 because of chronic health problems. Juan Vicente Gómez, Castro's comrade in arms and vice-president of the Republic, was left in charge of the presidency and within a few days seized power with the tacit approval of Washington, where Castro had always been seen as difficult, particularly when it came to Venezuela's external debts. In February of 1909, Gómez signed the Buchanan Protocol, in which Venezuela recognized its debts and allowed the return to free trade. A new and third era in the bilateral relations had just started.

In the midst of the turmoil of the final period of his predecessor, General Juan Vicente Gómez took control and committed the country to putting its financial affairs in order and to unifying under a single national authority, eliminating the anarchy of local leaders, or *caudillos*, who had often gone their own way, ignoring the central government or, worse still, defying it. His long period of control, generally considered a dictatorship, lasted from 1908 until 1935 under his presidency or that of others subservient to him. Despite the nondemocratic nature of the Gómez period, the restoration of order marked the start of the modern era in Venezuela and the beginning of stability there, as well as the initiation of a long and difficult struggle to gain autonomy, to catch up with the more developed countries in terms of wealth and income, and to take a place among the respected members of the international community based on internal security and external strength. But democracy would have to await the next generation that succeeded the death of General Gómez. Ironically, Venezuela and the United

States began the nineteenth century with similar aspirations, but by the beginning of the twentieth century, the United States had transformed itself into a more powerful country that might also threaten the autonomy of Venezuela. Relations between the two countries would thereafter be marked by the constant interplay of the links that bind two friends with common ideals and of the tensions that separate two countries with very unequal weight in the international balance of power.

Twentieth-Century Issues

Oil: Common Interests and Ground for Conflict

Had it not been for the discovery of oil in Venezuela, signaled by the first gusher that sprouted in 1914 bolstering the long dictatorship of Juan Vicente Gómez that would last until 1935, perhaps Venezuela and the United States would not have developed the close relationship they have had since then.[8] The very specialness of the relation forged by the United States' historic interest in assuring safe supplies of oil has been both the bane and the blessing of their contacts throughout the twentieth century. Venezuelans have always expected that Americans would recognize their privileged status as loyal associates and have sometimes felt unappreciated and distraught that, at times, the United States has treated them without distinction. This might not have been the case during major wars in Europe or elsewhere, when the Venezuelan oil card came into play more importantly, but in normal times, and especially since the diversification of sources of energy that followed the oil crisis of the 1970s, Venezuela has sometimes slipped into a lower position in American priorities.

Oil has linked Venezuela and the United States in many ways that go beyond the mere export of hydrocarbons to the north. Venezuela's location just across the Caribbean from the tip of Florida, close to the sea routes of supply to the Gulf of Mexico and to the eastern ports of the Atlantic, always made it possible to travel easily to and from the United States. American oil companies settled in early there, and there is little doubt that Texans quickly found themselves at home in the oil fields around the Lake of Maracaibo, where they established towns for their personnel that provided all the comforts of home. While Venezuelans often griped about these enclaves as unintegrated "colonies" of the foreign oil powers, they also became a part of the system. Most employees were locals, and many began to learn the business and form part of the corporations themselves. They gained a taste for American culture, from baseball to university education. As young Venezuelans studied in Oklahoma and Texas in order to make their way in the oil industry, their attachment to American values came to influence the worldview of the educated classes. Perhaps their parents had studied French and looked to the old continent, but they spoke English and vacationed in Miami and New York. Venezuela became, perhaps, the most "American" of South American countries.[9]

The importance of these cultural links, which would contribute mightily to cementing the U.S.-Venezuela relationship, also generated some problems. Not everyone in Venezuela participated in the deepening of the connection between the two countries; in fact, most of the Venezuelan population was left out. The oil industry that penetrated so much of the geography of the country, stretching from Maracaibo in the west all the way to the Atlantic in the east of Venezuela, actually employed a relatively small portion of the labor force, some 40,000 people by the 1970s, in a population of 20 million. Those connected directly to the industry constituted an elite, with home financing and pensions and good schools for their children. The rest of the population, while it benefited from the ample income that permitted the government to operate practically without collecting taxes from the citizenry, felt a vague distrust of the foreign companies and of their countries of origin. They suspected that their government was not sufficiently independent of foreign pressures and that perhaps they were seen as not much more than a sort of oil "colony," or enclave, by the Americans and other foreign investors.

Most Venezuelans were not in a modern economy at all; rather, their lives had not changed much since the rough-and-ready days of the traditional agricultural economy of the nineteenth century. Politicians increasingly played on this sense of dependence and sought public support for increasing their demands for taxes and other contributions from the foreign owners of the oil industry in Venezuela. This tension began to mount particularly in the 1940s, when World War II increased the relative importance of Venezuela as a supplier and when democratic forces raised new expectations after the death of General Juan Vicente Gómez.

Oil also created deep problems in Venezuelan society, which led later critics of the system to blame it for multiple ills. From the very start, oil bred corruption, as the government of General Gómez treated it as its personal asset, distributing concessions to friends, who would later sell their rights to foreign investors at a great profit.[10] More than one family fortune was built in Venezuela in this way, and thus some wealthy families would thereafter suffer a certain suspicion. In those days, the most important investors were the Standard Oil Company from the United States, as well as the British-Dutch giant, the Shell Oil Company. With the Standard Oil Company came other Rockefeller interests, whose stamp is still visible today in agribusiness and telecommunications, long after the nationalization of the industry in 1976 and long after the Rockefellers themselves sold out to local investors.

Thus, the Venezuelan-U.S. relationship has been marked by the existence of common interests and a certain conflict whose roots are in the asymmetry of their relative power. This was best expressed during the 1970s by a Venezuelan writer, Carlos Rangel, in a book called *The Latin Americans: Their Love-Hate Relationship with the United States*.[11] This book expresses the mixed emotions of Latin Americans, who recognize their common ideals with Americans but also struggle with the urge to separate themselves, establish their own identities, and take a place in the world as sovereign and independent nations. This sometimes leads them to perceive slights and take offense when they are not given proper consideration and even to search for their own models for their economies, their societies, and their international relations. It means that relationships with the United States can be complicated indeed, and that conflicts can break out when they are least expected.

Latin America in U.S. Foreign Policy to 1945

Venezuela and the United States came to enjoy a special relationship in the twentieth century because of the intimate contact that American investment in the oil industry tended to generate. Nevertheless, the specialness of this link should not be exaggerated. In fact, the United States has usually tended to develop its relationships with Latin America according to a regional definition of its own goals. Perhaps only Mexico escapes from this tendency to group the Latin Americans, a natural difference for a country with a long common border with the United States, not to speak of the history of the development of the two countries, whose consolidation was even to lead them into a short conflict at the beginning of the twentieth century.

Like Venezuela, much of Latin America confronted difficulties in gaining political and economic stability after independence. The dominant tradition of the region was that of dictatorships led by strongmen, who were sometimes enlightened but who more often subjected their countries to arbitrary rule. The lack of ideological consonance marked the normal state of world affairs until recent years, so the United States necessarily had to adopt a pragmatic stance toward the Latins: if they confined their internal difficulties and conflicts to their own territory and collaborated with international schemes for trade and investment, the United States would treat them as diplomatic equals and not meddle in their domestic affairs. This was fine with Latin American rulers. In fact, the United States had little or no interest in such matters as long as its basic strategic aims were met. These could be summed up simply as a policy that kept external powers out of the American sphere, a policy called "strategic denial" by Hartlyn, Schoultz, and Varas.[12] Except when some particular interest, such as the Panama Canal or Cuba, would wake the United States to pursue its objectives directly, Latin America was mostly treated as a more-or-less homogeneous region, with common issues left to multilateral organizations such as the Pan American Union, founded at the end of the nineteenth century.

Although the Latin Americans were often taken for granted, the U.S. government discovered that they had minds of their own when they rejected a 1942 suggestion that they declare war on the Axis powers, including Japan and Germany. There were few takers for joining this particular crusade, although nations friendlier to the United States, such as Venezuela, did break off diplomatic relations with Axis powers in 1941, while Brazil and Mexico became belligerents. Indeed, Venezuela cooperated with the United States to preserve the flow of oil to the Allied powers and froze the assets of residents from Germany and other Axis nations.[13] After the war, the United States would make efforts to tighten up the inter-American system.

The United States was busy with its own affairs for most of the first part of the 1900s, what with the two world wars and the Depression of the 1930s. There had been a brief spurt of enthusiasm for Latin America after the end of World War I, when U.S. investors saw opportunities for expansion abroad. Trade increased, and with it credit and investment, but the surge was short-lived and sputtered out when a slump occurred in the prices of agricultural products at the beginning of the 1920s. American banks, which had made their first incursions into foreign lands during the period, faced difficulties due to the failure of their clients and they soon pulled back from the adventure they had begun. When the Great Depression took hold after the Crash of 1929, dreams of investment in Latin America were largely postponed. Indeed, U.S. investors would delay their massive involvement in Latin America far beyond the end of World War II. The Latin Americans were hardly in a position to do anything about the situation. They were accustomed to the presence of English investment in railroads, electricity, and banking; the French and Germans also had their beachheads in the region.

That Latin America found itself left to its own devices during the Depression and World War II had interesting consequences for thinking about development in the region. For the first time, local economies had to turn to producing goods they had formerly imported without difficulty. At the same time, National Socialist thought, especially in its period of relative respectability before the war, took root in Latin America, influencing leaders such as Juan Perón in Argentina as well as economic thinkers such as Alberto Adriani in Venezuela. Feeling abandoned and suffering from the widespread protectionism of the era, most Latin American countries began to adopt their own more closed economic systems, based on the principle that the state should create the conditions for industrial development and strategic strength.

In some countries, like Argentina, more inward-looking policy undoubtedly contributed to economic diversification as well to a relatively high level of industrial production. Other countries, including Venezuela, followed Chile's lead in creating government development corporations, whose role would increase in succeeding years. Chile had created CORFO (the Chilean Industrial Development Corporation) in 1939, and Venezuela followed suit with the creation of the CVF, the Corporación Venezolana de Fomento, in 1945.

The impulse toward protectionism fell short of full-fledged closure, however, and Latin America continued to play its part as responsible member of the international community, particularly during the 1930s, when the U.S. government proposed a return to trade openness through reciprocal trade agreements and when efforts were made to restore convertibility of currencies and resuscitate international economic transactions in general, which had been hard hit by the Depression and the global financial crisis of those years. For Venezuela, closure was never so great as elsewhere, however, because its oil supplies became even more important during World War II and its export earnings were thus protected from the chaos of the era.

Despite the hardships that affected other countries, the period from the death of General Gómez in 1935 until the end of World War II was very positive for Venezuela. Although Gómez's two successors, Generals Eleazar López Contreras (1935–1941) and Isaías Medina Angarita (1941–1945), were also military men, their intention seemed clearly to lead Venezuela slowly and carefully toward democracy. The country enjoyed a flourishing oil economy during the war, and it seemed that a new middle class was emerging and demanding the modernization of the country. This fit in well with the U.S. view of the future of Latin America, where President Franklin D. Roosevelt's "Good Neighbor Policy" had signaled as early as 1933 a welcome change toward putting relations with Latin American countries on a new footing of respect and equality. While U.S. intervention in the region did not disappear, the new approach was meant to counteract the hostility associated with terms sometimes applied to American actions in the past such as "dollar diplomacy" or the "big stick." In the 1940s, Venezuela's gradual evolution toward democracy fit in well with the American view that perhaps Latin Americans needed a more guided approach to democracy, given the fragile nature of their societies as well as the low educational levels of their populations.

While Latin American governments, often under the sway of military presidents, followed the nationalist impulse to use the state to stimulate industrial development in countries that had long depended on the export of agricultural products and natural resources, the statist strategy they adopted in economic policy found support as well in the ideology of the socialist Left in the region. With a limited industrial labor force, unions in Latin America were still relatively weak before World War II, but the attraction of socialism was strong for many intellectuals who often sought solutions in the model of industrial development of the Soviet Union. These ideas proved interesting to young students in Latin America who chafed under the ruling dictatorships of the day and who yearned to bring equality to nations where inequality was most severe and where, as they saw it, a few landowners controlled vast swaths of agricultural land and the poor faced exclusion from education and health services.

Educational differences constituted the biggest gap between North and South America at mid century and continue to do so even at the start of the twenty-first century. In any case, the stage was set in Latin America for the organization of new political groups, for the end of the passive acceptance of dictatorial rule, and for fresh approaches to the problem of economic development. In Venezuela, the first outburst of protest against authoritarianism came in the student uprising that created a new political force called the Generation of 1928, many of whose leaders would play a role in the democratic period after 1945, when a coalition of civilian and military groups overthrew President Medina Angarita.

Relations between the United States and Latin America until 1945 were, in summary, congruent in the essentials and characterized by mutual tolerance. The United States did not aspire to control all that went on beyond its southern borders; Latin Americans tended to mind their own business and hope that others would do the same. The United States tolerated dictatorships and democracies, free market economies and state-controlled ones. There was not much ideology in the balance as long as access to vital raw materials would not be in danger. In fact, there were virtually no difficulties in ensuring security of access, least of all in Venezuela, where military governments showed themselves happy enough to negotiate with just about all investors who promised to bring new capital into the country to develop oil fields, at least until 1943. In that year, Venezuela introduced an income tax law whose purpose it was to raise the take of the government from the oil industry. The income tax law was one of the first signs that thinking in the country was changing and that Venezuela was beginning to try negotiating for a better deal that would provide resources for national development. It was an announcement of winds of change.

Until the Cold War, then, North-South relations could be described as generally calm and mutually tolerant, although somewhat distant on the main continent of South America, where the security interests of the United States were not perceived to be affected. Perhaps for Panama or the Dominican Republic or Cuba, vitally located for the United States, the extension of tolerance was not the same, but for Venezuela and its neighbors in Latin America, distance guaranteed tranquil relations until 1945, when world politics would undergo a sea change, vastly altering mutual perceptions in the hemisphere.

Postwar Problems: Cold War Issues

It is easy to forget the bitterness of the Cold War, born not so much out of economic or ideological differences as from a crude power confrontation that divided Europe, pitted whole continents against each other, generated distrust even among friends, and converted the smallest conflicts into deep and serious ruptures. It might seem surprising that the worst dispute of the postwar period arose between allies of World War II, the United States and the Soviet Union, who had come together to make common cause against Hitler's diabolical regime. Indeed, the Soviet communist system only remittently seemed a direct threat to the United States before World War II, although it certainly appeared alien to American beliefs. After the war, however, when communism was combined with geographical expansionism in the heart of Europe, when another brand of communism was overtaking China, and when the awareness of the possibility of nuclear war shattered confidence throughout the world, rivalry between the Soviet bloc and the Western nations took precedence over other problems. What is more, many problems that had little intrinsic ideological content found their way into the Cold War debate.

Latin American countries, even though they were not directly involved in World War II, participated in the creation of the postwar system that produced the United Nations, the International Monetary Fund and the World Bank, and a host of other world organizations that exacted commitments by their members on many planes: strategic, economic, political, and social. These organizations had global scope, but the burgeoning Cold War gave birth to another set of regional alliances and accords that proposed to protect noncommunist areas through mutual assistance. Thus was born the Inter-American Treaty of Mutual Assistance in 1947 (usually called the Rio Pact and known in Latin American by its Spanish initials, TIAR), modeled on the North American Treaty Organization (NATO), which committed its members to a joint response should an attack be made against any one of them. While the Rio Pact called for mutual assistance, it also required nonintervention in the internal affairs of members according to the usual norms of international law. This clause would often be a bone of contention in the future, when the United States would tend to apply a very broad interpretation of what could be considered "internal." In 1948, one year after the signing of the Rio Pact, the countries of the Americas also created the Organization of American States (OAS), which would replace the rather dormant Pan American Union that had regulated the multilateral affairs of the region.

The essence of the Cold War was precisely that its major contenders no longer saw internal political or economic decisions as neutral for the international community. Where in the past, the economic system chosen by a country was its own business, now socialist policies might indicate that a country was moving into the communist camp.

A few examples from the history of Venezuelan-U.S. relations in the Cold War illustrate how the bipolarity of the international scene tended to invade all spheres of interchange between the countries. As we have seen, after the end of World War II, the United States began to worry about whether a given government, be it democratic or not, would take a strong and unequivocal anticommunist stance. This would be evidenced both in direct and indirect ways: that the economic strategy should be oriented to free markets and private property; that the rights of foreign investors should be protected; that the country should vote together with the United States in world forums like the United Nations; and that relations with the Soviet and later the Chinese blocs should be strictly limited to a necessary minimum.

The Cold War stance of the United States became so rigid that any action taken in defiance of U.S. positions, particularly if the action were to count on the support of some communist country, would necessarily imply that if you were not with them, you were "ag'in 'em," or, in other words, that you had crossed the line into the enemy camp. Everyone had to define himself as communist or anticommunist. Woe to the country that aspired to neutrality; only very large countries such as India could take that risk. Meanwhile, authoritarian regimes such as Somoza's Nicaragua or Trujillo's Dominican Republic found themselves protected from criticism as long as they maintained their anticommunist credentials.

How did Venezuela, a minor actor on the world scene, manage its role in the Cold War? Mostly by keeping a low profile and projecting its anticommunist orientation when necessary. For instance, just at the close of World War II, Venezuela was undergoing an important change of government, made possible by the decision of General Medina Angarita to promote a change to civilian government. Medina was a staunch ally of the United States, but the emerging opposition awoke some suspicions because young leaders such as Rómulo Betancourt had been involved in communist politics during the 1930s, much as other radicals had been during those years, even in the United States. But a smooth succession looked likely as the different political groups agreed on a compromise candidate. By one of those unfortunate flukes of history, the candidate who was to be designated as president by the Congress, Diógenes Escalante, suffered a mental breakdown, throwing the country into confusion, since no one else offered the neutrality and acceptability that Escalante would have done. Impatient for change, Betancourt and his party, Acción Democrática (AD), founded in 1941, joined with an equally impatient military group to overturn President Medina and installed a de facto government in 1945.

The new government immediately called for open and direct elections, a new constitution, and in general a rapid transformation and modernization of the country. While a new and liberal Constitution was approved in 1947 and the distinguished writer, Rómulo Gallegos, was elected president in that year, in fact the administration set up by Betancourt and the AD party took a radical turn, particularly on educational matters, that enraged conservative forces from the Catholic Church to the business elite. The military allies that had supported the original coup began to think that they would do a better job at governing, and soon overthrew president Gallegos in November of 1948, installing a junta that would turn into a dictatorship lasting until 1958. Despite its high-handed methods, lack of democratic principles, and disregard for human rights, this dictatorship under General Marcos Pérez Jiménez had no problem in gaining recognition from the American government. Commonly during the 1950s, the first requirement of a Latin American government in the opinion of the United States was that it be staunchly anticommunist, and the rule of Pérez Jiménez, for all its undemocratic faults, was both anticommunist and favorable to American business interests, especially oil interests.

By the end of the 1950s, the authoritarian model imposed by Pérez Jiménez began to lose domestic support. The leaders who had been exiled or silenced after the 1948 coup, including Rómulo Betancourt, had not been idle during the fifties and were ready to return as soon as the dictator faltered. By that time, the Cold War had reached great intensity in the U.S. worldview. Anticommunism became the only "politically correct" attitude, while Stalin's dictatorship fully revealed its uglier side; the Soviet Union put down revolts in Eastern Europe such as the Hungarian uprising of 1956; in 1957, the Soviets launched the first satellite, *Sputnik*, raising fears that they might overtake the United States in military technology; North Korea shot down an American spy plane: tolerance for fellow travelers on the communist road was nil in U.S. foreign policy.

The prospect of a return of Rómulo Betancourt to government in Venezuela might have been seen as a dangerous turn of events in Latin America in 1958, but by that time, he and his formerly radical allies were firmly in the anticommunist camp. Pérez Jiménez was ousted without much ado in a coup, and Betancourt assumed the positive image of democrat at a time when democracy was the exception in the region. As Fidel Castro took the opposite route in Cuba at about the same time, allying himself with an ever-skeptical Khrushchev, who had succeeded Stalin in the Soviet Union in 1953, Venezuela became an important bastion of freedom in an endangered Caribbean, especially after Castro backed a leftist guerrilla movement in Venezuela. Despite his personal distrust of Castro, however, Betancourt did not back direct American intervention in the island of Cuba, especially in the cases of the Bay of Pigs invasion of Cuba in 1961, supported by the U.S. government, and the events surrounding the crisis over the Soviet Union's placement of missiles in Cuba that provoked a serious Cold War conflict in 1962.[14]

During the 1960s, many Latin American countries were failing the democratic test, increasingly ruled by a variety of authoritarian governments, usually after military coups whose leaders often managed to procure U.S. neutrality by taking anticommunist positions. But a few countries like Venezuela and neighboring Colombia managed democratic transitions that enabled them to establish positive relations with the United States.

The AD government's development plans for Venezuela fit in well with President John Kennedy's project for promoting economic progress and democracy through the Alliance for Progress, such that Betancourt and Kennedy formed a friendship that sealed good relations with the United States throughout the 1960s. Experts from the Massachusetts Institute of Technology and Harvard helped plan new industrial cities; Peace Corps volunteers joined to strengthen schools and community organizations; American companies such as Reynolds Aluminum, General Motors, Ford, Bethlehem Steel, and United States Steel expanded investments in huge projects; oil production rose to new heights: in short, relations could not have been better in an era of optimism both in Venezuela and in the United States.

In diplomatic affairs, Betancourt and his government went so far as to outlaw the Communist Party and break off relations with Cuba, even at the risk of alienating some of his domestic allies. The so-called "Betancourt Doctrine" firmly expressed the Venezuelan position that diplomatic relations should be broken with any de facto government that was product of a coup d'état or corrupt elections.[15] The OAS condemned both the Dominican Republic in 1960 and Cuba in 1964 for intervening in Venezuela, and Venezuela had no diplomatic relations with Cuba until the 1970s, when the Christian Democratic president Rafael Caldera (1969–1974) began to develop the idea of "ideological pluralism" in Venezuelan foreign policy and experimented with sports diplomacy with Cuba. Caldera's successor, Carlos Andrés Pérez (1974–1979), opened diplomatic relations formally in 1974.

Perhaps the United States had no better friend in all of Latin America in the 1960s. This was not to say, however, that Venezuela ever allowed itself to be an unquestioning friend, especially when the principle of nonintervention was at stake. Betancourt's successor, Raúl Leoni (1964–1969), followed a line consistent with that of the former government but opposed the American invasion of the Dominican Republic in 1965, although without great fanfare and without letting this difference get in the way of excellent relations.[16] This would be the pattern of Venezuelan reactions to other similar interventions on the part of the United States, although as time went by, its opposition to U.S. intervention in the region would become more vociferous.

The Oil Card and the Troubles of the 1970s

On one front, the Betancourt government initiated a policy that would later tend to separate Venezuelan and American interests. In 1960, Juan Pablo Pérez Alfonzo, the minister of mines (later, energy and mines) traveled to the Middle East and discussed the possibility of forming a club of oil exporters with his Iranian colleague. Thus was born the Organization of Petroleum Exporting Countries (OPEC). Betancourt might not have been communist, but that had no bearing on his desire to ensure that Venezuelans extract the maximum benefit from their huge oil industry, which accounted for over 90 percent of export earnings and was the main external supplier of oil to the United States.

Discomfort with the international oil companies operating in Venezuela was always present, but U.S. actions also contributed to the emerging policy of wresting control from the powerful multinationals through a cartel of producers.[17] For instance, in 1958, the Eisenhower administration imposed quotas on imported oil in response to excess world production and low prices. But Canada and Mexico were granted preferential treatment, while Venezuelan exports to the United States began to fall.[18] Another goal was to require that the government receive at least 50 percent of oil profits and to see to it that privately held companies complied fully with its demands. Pressures mounted to guarantee the training and employment of Venezuelans in the industry and to create space for the creation of a new oil company under government control. The long-term objective aimed at eventually converting the industry into a national entity. In 1960, Venezuela established a government oil company to gain a foothold in the industry. It was resolved that no new concessions would be granted. Afterwards, in 1971, the so-called Reversion Law was approved by the Venezuelan Congress, programming the gradual phaseout of all foreign investments in the oil industry, whereby existing concessions would terminate on their conclusion, starting in 1983.[19]

Betancourt's philosophy with regard to the primacy of oil, summed up in his book *Venezuela: Oil and Politics*,[20] set the agenda of gaining control over oil produced in Venezuela for all the governments that followed him at least until the 1990s, including the Christian Democratic governments (under the Comité de Organización Política Electoral Independiente, or COPEI, the party that alternated in power for almost forty years with Acción Democrática). Of the foreign oil firms in Venezuela at the time, the two most important were Creole Petroleum Company (Exxon, an American company) and Shell Oil Company (British-Dutch), but many others participated, most of them based in the United States, so policies aimed at the international oil companies in general were perceived as policies that principally affected U.S. firms. Rafael Caldera's first COPEI government (1969–1974) also terminated Venezuela's adhesion to the Reciprocal Trade Agreement with the United States, which signaled Venezuela's growing sense of autonomy and its belief that it no longer needed a "special relationship" with the United States that would require alignment on all issues, such as trade. In fact, it exported little except oil to the U.S. and thus the trade advantages that were sacrificed gave little benefit to Venezuela.

This nationalist approach was congruent with the growing drive for autonomy throughout the Third World that reached its peak in the wave of expropriations of foreign companies of the 1970s, especially in mining and petroleum. But the United States at the time was plagued with multiple crises so intense that from today's perspective it might be difficult to capture the spirit of those years. The Vietnam War had upset domestic peace in the United States, with a frequency and ubiquity of protests between 1968 and 1972 that disrupted cities and universities to an unprecedented extent. While the Vietnam peace agreements were signed in early 1973, the Watergate crisis led to a continuation of internal conflict during 1973 and 1974 that tended to undermine President Nixon's authority and divert attention from what seemed like minor irritations in Latin America.

In the context of domestic conflict in the early 1970s, international events also combined to complicate things further. The Vietnam War had stretched the U.S. economy to the breaking point, generated inflation, and weakened the position of the dollar in international markets. The Nixon government had to devalue the currency in 1971 and 1973, a process that led to the breakdown of the Bretton Woods system of fixed exchange rates and to greater instability in world financial markets. The other striking event of the period was the third Arab-Israeli War, which broke out in 1973. That war had significant implications for the balance of power in the Middle East and signalled a new period of Arab solidarity. It also had unexpected consequences that would have lasting effects on Venezuela. As we have seen, oil-producing countries had formed OPEC in 1960, but their power to control the international oil market remained limited throughout the sixties. But the Arab-Israeli War led to the declaration of an embargo on oil sales by Arab producers that ended a long period of stability in prices, quickly quadrupled gasoline prices in the United States, and contributed to deep feelings of vulnerability there as citizens found themselves in long lines at the pump. Venezuela never joined its OPEC allies in the embargo and showed itself to be a secure supplier to the U.S. But the high prices for oil changed the country's perspective of its place in international affairs profoundly. Government revenues soared in all of the oil-exporting countries, and dreams of greatness took over. The rise in prices of the boom of the 1970s would continue, with some pauses, until 1981, as is seen in Figure 1.1. Venezuela saw an opportunity to speed up its own plan to take over the oil industry and take advantage of the relative reverse that the United States was suffering both at home and abroad.

The Arab-Israeli War of 1973 provided an opportunity for the emergence of OPEC power. High prices for oil transformed the possibilities of countries lucky enough to be blessed by large reserves. The nationalization of the Venezuelan oil industry was approved by Congess in 1975 and by then-president Carlos Andrés Pérez well in advance of the date programmed by the Reversion Law.[21] Venezuela became giddy with its good fortune and changed from a somewhat humble and frugal nation to an aspiring regional leader, dispensing aid to its neighbors and speaking the language of the New International Economic Order in which asymmetries with the developed countries—principally the United States—might come to be a thing of the past. Scotch whisky replaced domestic rum at social functions in Caracas, and government expanded immensely with its newfound wealth, since most profits on oil go directly to the government through taxes. Huge investments were made in large industrial plants under state control in steel, aluminum, and hydroelectric plants. In the United States, economists predicted the permanence of high oil prices and Americans became convinced that natural resources of all kinds were running out. Perhaps American hegemony was in danger.

Throughout the economic turmoil and even the nationalization of American companies in Venezuela in the oil and iron ore industries, good relations between the United States and Venezuela nevertheless persisted, although the Venezuelan government was clearly seeking to act as an independent country in the world

FIGURE 1.1

**Venezuelan Oil Export Prices
1958–2000**   *Source*: Petróleos de Venezuela, S.A. (PDVSA).

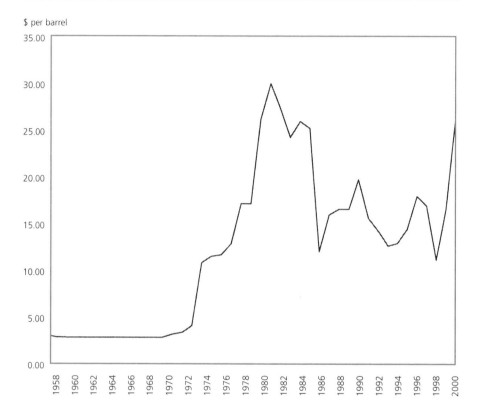

$ per barrel

arena and was also veering toward a much more statist model in its economy, with new laws that would limit foreign investment and favor domestic produc- ers. Carlos Andrés Pérez enjoyed his leadership role in organizing countries from "the South," a term that meant, in those days, all the developing countries and not just the Latin Americans. But Venezuela was scrupulous in keeping to the for- mal rules of the game. While a radical military government had attempted to nationalize Peru's oil industry without adequate compensation to the former owners, Venezuela negotiated the exit of foreign oil companies without a hitch, subscribing technical assistance contracts with the former concessionary firms that left everyone relatively satisfied with the outcome. Without doubt the gov- ernments of the 1970s no longer supported the American line unquestioningly, but in a continent that was constantly shaken by revolutionary movements and tempted by socialist solutions, Venezuela still stood out as a beacon of stability and democracy.

The efforts of President Carlos Andrés Pérez to assume leadership of the Third World, to bring Castro's Cuba into new organizations such as the Latin American Economic System (Sistema Económico Latinoamericano, SELA[22]) outside the traditional groupings led by the United States, and to break down the bipolar rigidity of the Cold War were made at a time when U.S. attention was focused elsewhere. From the fall of President Nixon in 1974, after losing a battle to prove his innocence against the onslaught of a merciless and public investigation, until the election of Ronald Reagan in 1980, U.S. foreign policy assumed a more passive posture that was tolerant of countries like Venezuela that respected democracy and maintained their general position within the anti-Soviet camp.

In the end, much of the disruption of the 1970s turned out to be temporary. Oil prices did not continue rising—over the long term they have fallen from their peak in real buying power, despite the fact that the nominal price has risen—and developing countries did not create a new international order.[23] Venezuela did not become a rich country and missed many opportunities to turn its oil wealth into real development. Its leadership in Latin America flagged even as its economy later sputtered. From today's standpoint, such aspirations sound a bit ridiculous or even sad, since we know that the great oil surge brought only temporary prosperity and that in 2000 the country's population enjoyed a lower per capita income than it had in 1974.[24] Yet Venezuelans cherish the idea that they can be world leaders and important players on the global playing field as well as significant actors with influence over the United States.

New Trends in U.S. Foreign Policy

Despite the low point of the mid-1970s in the United States, important changes had occurred that presaged the end of the Cold War. Most significant, perhaps, was the opening to China that U.S. National Security Adviser Henry Kissinger promoted within the Nixon government. This single act constituted a symbolic recognition that communism was not monolithic and that the United States was now interested in exploiting the differences among countries it had formerly portrayed to its own citizens as ideologically one, despite ample evidence to the contrary. Under President Jimmy Carter (1977–1981) in the United States, further changes marked foreign policy. Reversing the earlier view that as long as a Latin American government was anticommunist, it did not matter much what it did in its domestic affairs,[25] the Carter government began to put governments to the democratic test, withdraw its support from long-entrenched dictators, particularly in Central America, and cool relations with others, such as General Pinochet in Chile. One consequence was the loss of political equilibrium in Central America and the outbreak of civil wars in Nicaragua, El Salvador, and Guatemala, which contributed to the delayed development of these small countries and also to the greater maturity of their Latin neighbors, who for the first time organized themselves to mediate in favor of peace in Central America

through the so-called Contadora Group, in which Venezuela was an active partic-
ipant. The United States interpreted the leftist insurgencies in Central America
within its traditional policy of strategic denial that, in the context of the Cold
War, assumed all such movements as evidence of Soviet involvement within the
American sphere of influence.

Another consequence of the new approach would be that the commitment
under the Rio Treaty that prohibited intervention in the domestic affairs of the
countries of the region might not be so unambiguous to the extent that the quality of democracy within a country would henceforth affect relations between the
United States and Latin America. While Venezuela and the United States shared
a strategic vision that opposed Soviet and Cuban intervention in Central
America, for instance, they differed on the best tools to apply. The U.S. gave arms
support to the "Contras" in their campaign against the leftist Sandinista government in Nicaragua and at times even seemed to be willing to tolerate abuses of
human rights by governments under pressure from guerrillas, while Venezuela
avoided direct conflict, supporting moderates, negotiating with the Sandinistas,
and collaborating in peace efforts. Venezuela maintained the position that
American intervention in these local conflicts in Central America should be
interpreted as undue meddling in internal affairs, although the Christian
Democratic government of Luis Herrera (1979–1984) shared the U.S. preference
for nonsocialist solutions.

Consistency of principle is difficult to achieve in international relations.
Venezuela did not give its support to Great Britain during the Falkland Islands
(Islas Malvinas) War, when the British fought to retain control of the Falklands
against Argentina's failed attempt to take them over. In that affair, Venezuela
gave first priority to Latin American solidarity against a vestige of colonialism,
even though the Argentinian regime of the time was clearly undemocratic and
repressive of human rights. Venezuela also denounced the American invasion of
Grenada, supporting instead the search for political solutions to this Caribbean
island's crisis in 1983, although with the invasion's success, the issue was
dropped. In contrast to the U.S. chastisement policy toward Sandinismo in
Nicaragua,[26] Venezuela opposed American interventionism in that country but
supported newly elected Violeta Chamorro in 1990 when she beat the Sandinistas
at the polls.[27] Of course, the relative wealth and power of the United States grants
it options to intervene that Venezuela simply does not have.

By the 1980s, Venezuela's increasing economic problems made its interest in
hemispheric affairs less active in any case, and despite differences in terms of the
best means to achieve peace, fundamental agreement existed about the best outcomes. The oil boom had petered out, and a severe financial and debt crisis led to
concentration on how to solve those problems. AD president Jaime Lusinchi led
an inward-looking government that preferred exchange controls and state inter-

vention as ways to solve its difficulties.[28] Fresh approaches would have to await the decade of the 1990s, when the stage was set for a change not only in Venezuelan-U.S. relations but also in the shape of world politics.

Even before the formal end of the Cold War, usually associated with the disappearance of the old Soviet Union in 1991, U.S. policy had started to move away from its traditional stance of pure anticommunism, at least to the extent of paying more attention to the democratic character of regional governments as well as to economic issues. Cold War politics, which had become a sort of anti-Soviet version of the strategic denial of the nineteenth century, stressed that only those factors directly affecting America's perceived interests, particularly communist takeovers seen to represent the threat of influence from outside the region, would be considered worthy of action. Although some would like to forget the facts and certainly not all presidents shared the same vision, the United States held a view of Latin America mostly derived from a global strategy in which the Latin Americans were bit players.

President Nixon perhaps represented the last gasp of this cynical view of the final years of the Cold War period, as revealed in tapes of his private conversations in 1971:

> I think we should support whoever are our friends in the world. I think that the majority of Latin American countries . . . I wouldn't call them dictatorships, that's a horrible word, and it wouldn't sound good to Americans, but strong leadership is necessary. . . . (March 5)

Responding to criticism by Senator Frank Church of his maintaining good relationships with the military government of Brazil, Nixon said:

> What is he talking about? . . . We are going to get along with Brazil, because it is a friendly country; we are going to get along with any country that behaves well towards us. Our judgment about countries is not based on their [political] systems, but on what kind of relation they have with the United States. I don't give a fig for what that son of a b—— Castro does [in Cuba], the problem is what he does with us. (July 27).[29]

Significantly, President Nixon's intransigence toward his enemies would eventually lead to his own resignation.

Most of all, the United States wanted to ensure that there would be no more Cubas in Latin America, but as Fidel Castro aged and Cuba no longer seemed to be much of a model for its neighbors, this policy failed to serve as a guide for the future. The end of the Cold War and the corresponding end of a simplistic and Manichaean view of the world would open the regional theater to much more complex relations, although the asymmetry of power between the United States and its southern neighbors would continue to dominate the scene.

TWO

GLOBAL CHANGES AND RELATIONS BETWEEN THE UNITED STATES AND VENEZUELA

Is the world truly different now that the cold war is over? Is globalization really a new phenomenon that radically alters economic and political relations in the world? Has the United States changed its foreign policy toward Venezuela as it readjusts its worldview? And has Venezuela reacted to the variations on the world stage in such a way as to redefine its role or question its traditional stance toward the United States?

This chapter reviews the new factors that have characterized the world system of security and economic relations since the beginning of the 1990s and examines the forces that were brought to bear on U.S.-Venezuelan relations during the period, in order to detect trends that affect both the conduct of nations and their images of one another today. In fact, many of the issues that link the two countries continue to be the same, particularly on the economic plane, where oil continues to dominate as a key factor. Yet the breakdown of the Cold War opened a panoply of options in such a way that no country is now so clearly placed on one or the other side of a divide.

The strategic agreement that lasted for so long between the United States and Venezuela regarding the negative consequences of communist revolutions and of Soviet presence in the Latin American region, despite the tactical differences that appeared over time, began to yield somewhat to a more complex relationship in which alliances and divergences are less patterned and in which problems formerly considered secondary, such as trade and investment, become more salient. Local conflicts are more local since they no longer count as part of any East-West differences; trade and investment issues are more global, belonging now to the sphere of regional and multilateral organizations. American concerns have shifted to problems of the environment, human rights, and labor market problems; meanwhile, radical political change within Venezuela's democracy has brought new actors to the scene, with new concepts of that nation's foreign policy that can be seen as the logical extension of nationalistic trends that had been gathering force slowly over many years but that were stifled or relegated to minor status as long as the Cold War overshadowed them.

The Bases of Security

Security means something different for every country. The Cold War imposed a homogeneous concept on the world, born of European conflicts in the twentieth century in which territorial integrity dominated thinking. After attempts by Germany to rule the European continent and expansion by the Soviet Union into Eastern Europe, postwar leaders established a worldwide network of alliances whose chief object was to diminish the possibility that any member country should be invaded or otherwise controlled by another. Thus emerged the North Atlantic Treaty Organization (NATO), the Southeast Asian Treaty Organization (SEATO) and the Interamerican Reciprocal Security Treaty (known as TIAR or the Rio Pact) soon after the end of World War II. The Soviet Union likewise established its treaty for mutual security among its socialist allies. Paradoxically, these organizations have only rarely exercised an active role in protecting the security of their members, although some might argue that precisely because of their existence, countries hardly dared to attack or invade their neighbors in the old-fashioned way.

Conflict did not disappear in the postwar period. It just took other forms, often marked by civil war and ideological differences among local forces within sovereign nations, where the strictures against international aggression failed to distinguish clearly between the parties in order to decide who was the aggressor and who the victim. The most common characteristic of the times was the definition of these internal conflicts as struggles between communist and anticommunist forces, and there is some evidence that warring groups defined themselves in these terms so as to receive external support from either side in the Cold War. The war in Vietnam was perhaps the emblematic conflict of the 1960s and seventies in this sense, but the pattern repeated itself in multiple Latin American conflicts of lesser scale, where revolutionary opposition groups challenged but rarely toppled incumbent governments. While the Cold War lasted, the two sides took on communist and anticommunist ideologies; now that the Cold War seems to have ended, the victorious communists that came to control all of Vietnam hardly look different from their capitalist neighbors. In Latin America, former communists, socialists, and guerrillas could be found running quite orthodox governments.

For the United States, the end of the Cold War would lead to all sorts of reassessments of the U.S. place in the world. Was the world now just a "unipolar" entity in which the U.S. would be a single hegemon with good intentions, as Robert Kagan would argue in a provocative article called "The Benevolent Empire"?[1] Or, on the contrary, did the breakdown of the Cold War now mean a world of multiple powers and shifting alliances on different issues? Would the disintegration of the system of opposing blocs lead to the profusion of local wars or bring to the fore suppressed conflicts among different cultural systems, as Samuel Huntington persuasively argued in *The Clash of Civilizations and the Remaking of the World Order?*[2] Certainly the United States would tend to change the mix of its military strategy to prepare better for the kinds of conflicts in which it would now find itself. It would have to think about the realignment of regional blocs and its natural relationship with Latin America. It would have to pay attention to economic matters to make sure that the world would remain open to its goods and investments and continue as a source of raw materials. At the same time, those concerned with consolidating U.S. influence would have to deal with the natural temptation of domestic groups to turn inward now that external threats were supposedly reduced.

Views of the Cold War and Security in Latin America

In Latin America, the Cold War had often looked like someone else's conflict and its termination was seen as a welcome respite, although some also feared that the United States might focus its development concerns on the rickety economies of Eastern Europe and forget about its southern neighbors. With the important exception of Cuba, it had been difficult to find groups in Latin America that truly threatened to institute communist regimes allied to the Soviet Union or China. Latin America's long history of political instability and coups had not really changed much, except that during the Cold War, domestic conflicts in the region were defined externally as communist threats. Certainly, as in Central America, socialist insurgents such as the Sandinistas barely strengthened their cause by aligning themselves to Cuba or the Soviet Union, but it is not so clear that if the Cold War had not existed, the internationalization of local conflicts would have occurred. While a few border conflicts do come to a head from time to time, Latin America has the privilege of being an area practically free of war, where mutual assistance treaties tend to rust on the shelf from lack of use. With the disintegration of the Soviet Union, as Thomas Carothers has noted, the United States lost the basis for guiding its relations with the Latin American region, since even local conflicts would hardly call for external intervention.[3] Indeed, the United States undertook a collective revision of the meaning of security in the post–Cold War world.[4]

In Venezuela, the Cold War had limited domestic relevance, although it did move the United States to support the democratic regime when Marxist guerrilla movements threatened destabilization during the sixties. Leftist parties that had originally cooperated with the pact between Betancourt's Acción Democrática (AD) and the Christian Democratic COPEI party—including the Communist Party of Venezuela (PCV), the Unión Republicana Democrática (URD), and dissident splinter groups that left AD, such as the Movimiento de Izquierda

Revolucionaria (MIR)—retired their support for the government and formed a loose leftist opposition that had its radical counterpart in guerrilla groups that took arms against the regime, stimulating immediate U.S. sympathy and support for Betancourt. In 1962, both the Communist Party and the MIR were declared illegal. The guerrillas, for their part, felt solidarity toward Fidel Castro's revolution and presented themselves as an almost romantic alternative to Betancourt's pro-U.S. and anti-Castro stance.

While rebel groups were causing havoc in the 1960s promoting urban terrorism, labor strikes, and student revolts, Betancourt's government voted together with the United States in the Organization of American States (OAS) condemning foreign (Soviet) interference in the hemisphere. Attitudes toward the Cuban revolution were the litmus test dividing the government from the small beleaguered left. After the failure of two leftist uprisings in 1962, pro-Soviet movements shrank close to irrelevance and were reduced to rural bases, where they were definitively defeated by President Raúl Leoni's counterinsurgence tactics between 1964 and 1968. Inspired by the Prague Spring of 1968, former guerrilla leader Teodoro Petkoff moved into the sphere of European-style socialism, stressing antiauthoritarian values clearly distanced from Soviet leadership. He and other ex-Communists would found the Movimiento al Socialismo (MAS) in 1971, opening a space for a more moderate socialist party. The PCV was legalized again in 1969 and the MIR followed in 1973, although both remained on the margin of mainstream politics.

Venezuelan politics had become strictly centrist. The defeat of the radicalism of the Left reduced the danger of radical right-wing military reaction as well. As consensus over democracy took root in Venezuela, the United States showed little interest in Venezuela, simply because "nothing happened there." Venezuela's "exceptionalism" resided in the fact that it had become so peaceful. As the democratic regime strengthened and as oil income reduced the need for outside assistance, much of the apparatus of foreign aid and involvement by international organizations such as the World Bank (WB) or the Interamerican Development Bank (IDB)[5] disappeared. In the meantime, Venezuela, like other Latin American countries, began to define security in other terms. In various ways, politicians and military leaders increasingly adopted the view that security is more than safety from invasion.

Various factors contributed to the redefinition of security in Latin America and in Venezuela. On the one hand, the United States itself played a role. The collaboration among the military establishments of the region under the Rio Pact created frequent contacts among those charged with national security. Ironically, the Cold War promoted the idea that international security cannot be defined as the mere absence of international aggression. The United States had gone far beyond the Monroe Doctrine in considering that communism within Latin America threatened the region.[6] This idea spread to diverse countries, taking different forms. In the military dictatorships of the southern cone of Latin America, national security doctrine included the concept that dangers to the state could come in many forms, including domestic groups hostile to the regime, levels of social unrest that could stir up discontent, and even the presence of foreign companies whose power might permit them to undermine a government. The much-publicized role of companies like ITT, the International Telephone and Telegraph Company, in destabilizing the government of Salvador Allende in Chile at the start of the 1970s provided ample support for this view.

In Argentina, Brazil, and Chile, countries then dominated by military governments that attempted to direct all areas of society, the new doctrine of national security widely defined took root and spread to the rest of Latin America. In Venezuela, such ideas took on a somewhat different meaning, since the democratic regime established since 1958 clearly attempted to reduce the influence of the military in national life. Yet, in their new role as guardians of democracy, military thinkers also extended their concept of their responsibilities. The Constitution approved in 1961 explicitly subordinated the military to civilian authority in what Samuel Huntington calls a system of "objective control."[7] The two dominant political parties, AD and COPEI, agreed that a military dictatorship should never again threaten democracy in the country. At the same time, however, elements of "subjective control" grew in importance as military training sought to form soldiers fully imbued with democratic values, with the idea that military forces that share and understand the benefits of democracy would naturally come to support it.[8] This would turn out to be a double-edged sword in the 1990s in a way that, paradoxically, threatened to harm U.S.-Venezuelan relations.

A Broader Definition of National Security and Its Implications

Why would the acceptance of a broader view of national security generate problems between the United States and Venezuela in the 1990s? At first, during the intermittent period of domestic reform that lasted from 1989 until 1998, it seemed that Venezuela was putting aside its nationalism of the oil boom of the seventies and accepting a more modest role in international affairs. This occurred at the level of national politics, but contrary forces were developing within the military sector at the same time, manifested in two frustrated coups in 1992 and brought to fruition with the election of President Hugo Chávez in 1998, the very lieutenant colonel who had burst from the army ranks as leader of the first coup attempt six years before. He and his followers subscribed to the idea that Venezuela should be faithful to the Bolivarian ideal whereby the country should act as a progressive force on the world stage.

The amplification of the concept of national security, both in the United States and Venezuela, increases the scope of military activity in areas outside of traditional defense. Under the wider definition of security in Venezuela, the armed forces must guard against all sorts of phenomena that might weaken national strength and integrity. They began to think about economic autonomy, about basic civics education, and about poverty and social cohesion. The impact of a broader concept of national security can be seen particularly in the case of drug trafficking, which threatens national security in two ways. First of all, the financial power of drug mafias enables them to corrupt governments to ensure their protection from investigation and interdiction. Colombia, a country that produces large quantities of drugs, found its own government ever more threatened by guerrilla groups that finance themselves with money from the drug trade. Analyses of that insidious industry showed that the plague could easily implant itself in Venezuela far beyond the already troublesome fact that Venezuela was a convenient transit route for the drug cartels and that the porous Colombian-Venezuelan border provided ample opportunities for spillovers.

In the United States, the war against drugs would divert military attention from its traditional focus on armed threats to a new need to patrol its frontiers against drug shipments and even to extend its scope to limiting the drug trade at its source in Latin America. Secondly, the effects of drug consumption, particularly in the United States, threaten civil peace and the integration of youth into society. Outraged congressmen began to favor an enlarged role for the military in working with foreign governments. In Venezuela, antidrug efforts involve all parts of the military establishment, giving it a new objective but also generating mixed feelings about the long-term viability of the strategy of making war against the drug lords. What is more, pressures from the United States to join forces in a common antidrug policy awakened fears that such collaboration might be tantamount to undue American presence and influence in Venezuela and that it implied some weakness or incompetence on the part of the armed forces. This issue will be analyzed in greater detail in Chapter Six.

Another aspect of the wide doctrine of national security played a role in increasing the interest of military officers in influencing both domestic politics and international relations. In Venezuela, officer training came to include studies of the problems of economic and social development, for instance, and military officers found themselves charged with protecting the domestic peace. But an understanding of the goals of democracy and the aspirations defined by the Constitution—which was meant to deepen liberal attitudes among the armed forces—paradoxically generated criticism of the less-than-complete achievements of the regime. Younger officers started to notice that their own education exceeded that of their superiors and rankled when they perceived corruption in the higher ranks. They absorbed the teaching that they were the custodians of democracy, but some would come to the conclusion that democracy was not working as it should. Oil wealth was seen as a corrupting influence on the system, while the failed attempts by governments in the eighties to stabilize the economy awoke feelings of disgust among younger officers.

Such was the situation that moved Lieutenant Colonel Hugo Chávez and his comrades in arms to plan a coup that would turn the system on its head and reestablish, according to them, the true goals of a better democracy such as they understood it from their studies. On February 4, 1992, Chávez and Lieutenant Colonel Francisco Arias Cárdenas led a coup attempt to overthrow President Carlos Andrés Pérez with the idea of instituting a new civil-military government that would "refound" Venezuelan democracy. They failed in their attempt, but their daring revealed a deep dissatisfaction in the country that could not be quieted in the coming years. The core group of rebels had sworn allegiance to their common cause years before, so that their coup attempt must be seen as a rejection of the democratic system as it had developed over the years and not a simple action of the moment against a particular government. A second coup attempt on November 27 of the same year, led by Admiral Hernán Gruber Odreman and General Francisco Visconti also failed, but served to maintain the atmosphere of unease and expose the depth of political opposition to the Pérez government. These military officers sought out civilian allies and organized a wide net of supporters from varied disgruntled groups, including well-respected critics of the system from both the Right and the Left, mostly people who disdained the increasingly shortsighted and corrupt political parties that had dominated politics since 1958, AD and COPEI. With the coup leaders in jail or exile, the civilian elements fed popular discontent and promoted the ouster of President Pérez, who was finally impeached on corruption charges in 1993.

Politically, at least, those who led the coups were seen as popular heroes rather than disobedient soldiers, who claimed that they were defending the true objectives of national security. Hugo Chávez and his partner Francisco Arias were released from jail without trial by President Rafael Caldera two years after their imprisonment. Arias actually joined Caldera's government (much to the disgust of Chávez) and was thereafter elected governor of the populous Zulia state in December of 1995, but Chávez took to the campaign trail with his message that the democratic system established by the Constitution of 1961 was beyond repair and could be rescued only by radical change.[9] Further fumbling and economic mistakes made by the succeeding government of second-time president Rafael Caldera, combined with strategic errors by the other presidential candidates in 1998, would lead to the victory of Hugo Chávez at the polls in a resounding victory that would permit him to put his own theories of national security into action.

The Chávez approach to security and foreign policy certainly marked a new path in the international relations of Venezuela. His views reflected the very teachings he received during his officer training under the regime he came to despise. That education stressed the goal of national autonomy and the strengthening of the nation through the integration of the military in all aspects of society. Simón Bolívar, hero of the war for independence, was always a figure of admiration and study, and Chávez absorbed the cult of Bolívar to such an extent that the name came to represent the spirit of practically every important initiative. One of his first actions as president was to mount a major program, the so-called Bolivarian Plan-2000, that would send soldiers into the streets and towns to carry out tasks ranging from neighborhood improvement to selling subsidized food. The Education Ministry immediately set about changing textbooks to reinterpret the history of Venezuela since independence to infuse the national conscience with the conviction that radical change would be necessary to undo the injustices of the past, a task that would be possible only through revolutionary change. Premilitary training was incorporated in high school studies. (Obligatory study of Bolívar was already part of the program.) Chávez even insisted on changing the name of the country during the writing of the 1999 Constitution, so that it would henceforth be called the "Bolivarian Republic of Venezuela." The new Constitution would also explicitly bring the armed forces into politics by giving soldiers the right to vote. This was an important break with the old Constitution, which had sought to emphasize the absolute separation between the political and the military spheres.

The highly autonomous oil industry was purged of high executives who had seen PDVSA as a state-owned firm that needed to convert itself into a world-class multinational company; they were replaced by Chávez supporters who shared the view that the strategic industry of Venezuela should respond first to priorities set by the government, not always linked to pure business objectives. International security would be maximized by negotiating unofficially with guerrillas in neighboring Colombia, even at the expense of degrading relationships with the Colombian government. And Venezuela would seek to rearrange its positioning in the world by exploiting the disappearance of Cold War definitions, actively looking for deepened friendships in China, Europe, Cuba, and the Arab countries in an implicit declaration that the United States would continue to be an important point of reference for the country but its relative power would be counterbalanced by the multiplication of other contacts. Chávez began to devote considerable time as president of Venezuela to visiting other countries. Notable was the baseball game he organized in Cuba in which he himself was the opening pitcher for Venezuela and Fidel Castro the coach of the island team. Venezuela lost the game, but there was little doubt about the personal warmth between the two presidents, which would be reciprocated the following year in a return match in Venezuela.

Venezuelan-U.S. relations suffered during the 1990s as a result of the political upheavals that would culminate in the election of President Chávez. The U.S. government, whose own revised national security doctrine indicated that de facto regimes of both the Left and the Right in Latin America were to be interpreted as contrary to its interests, made it clear to Venezuela that it would view any anticonstitutional forms as motive for disapproval and even breaking of diplomatic relations. But when Venezuela managed to change presidents within the formality of the law using the constitutionally sanctioned process for impeachment of President Pérez, the United States adopted a more positive view of events. Relations took a difficult course again when President Caldera released Lieutenant Colonel Chávez from jail. At first it looked as if Chávez would continue to push for a radical antisystem solution, but in 1995 he declared his intention to pursue the presidency within the existing rules of the game. Chávez immediately started a campaign that failed to gain much attention at the beginning but began to take off, especially in 1998 as his opponents showed themselves to be weak candidates and the country discovered that Chávez was a powerful speaker and talented politician whose violent language condemning the traditional political parties found resonance among voters. It bothered some that the United States had denied a visa to Chávez as a coup leader who had threatened Venezuelan democracy, although others saw it as a political asset either to condemn Chávez as an unsuitable candidate or to make a martyr of him.[10]

The American policy of shunning him as a possibly antidemocratic leader certainly did nothing to reduce Chávez's natural tendency to distrust the government of the United States, fed by his close circle of civilian supporters who typically came from small leftist parties and circles that had long opposed U.S. policy in Cuba and distrusted American motives in the Southern Hemisphere. Chávez went on to win the presidency by a landslide in December of 1998. By that time the United States could assume his democratic sympathies, since he had gained power through the system, and a visa was immediately issued. But relations would remain somewhat strained despite the efforts of U.S. Ambassador John Maisto to calm the waters.

Interestingly, European governments, particularly Great Britain, initially accorded more friendly treatment to Chávez, who used this fact to minimize the importance of the snubbing he received from the United States. Later on, however, the Europeans would be more circumspect. Other Latin American governments were also wary, mixing friendliness with a cautious distance. Countries such as Argentina, Brazil, Chile, Peru, and Mexico were undertaking reforms in their economies and they did not need a new charismatic leader in Latin America questioning their "neoliberal" approach.[11] President Fernando Henrique Cardoso of Brazil perhaps exemplifies this behavior best. He and President Chávez began to work toward common economic goals and enjoyed good relations, yet Cardoso was also recorded by the press as describing Chávez as an "unconscious authoritarian," not exactly an epithet that his colleague would appreciate. The Colombian government had special concerns with the fact that the Chávez government seemed to be courting the friendship of guerrilla forces in its country, while the United States failed to receive much Venezuelan support for its efforts to put together a joint antidrug effort in the region.

While the United States defined its security in terms of the suppression of the drug trade, the control of illegal immigration, and the maintenance of democracy, Venezuela's security interests included some other considerations. Venezuela's long and largely unpopulated borders with Brazil, Colombia, and Guyana concerned governments worried by the weakness of its defenses and undefined borders. The United States normally takes little interest in these problems, with the significant exception of border violations resulting from drug and guerrilla operations on the Colombian border, mainly because of the possibility that the anarchy associated with these forces might spread to Venezuela.[12] On the other hand, Venezuela's long-standing resistance to outside intervention, now emphasized anew by Chávez, makes it prickly to suggestions that the United States act against the drug trade within its frontiers or that U.S. companies operate satellite bases in the disputed territory of Guyana. While the Chávez government could be expected to resist such suggestions, its position in favor of its own sovereignty and integrity followed closely the stance taken by the former governments of Carlos Andrés Pérez and Rafael Caldera.

By the end of the Cold War, security issues that mutually concerned the United States and Venezuela had changed. The issue of communism or socialism hardly existed. What is more, a government such as that of Hugo Chávez defied old definitions of what is favorable or contrary to American interests. The chief worry of the Venezuelan government was simply to be able to act without U.S. intervention in its internal affairs, especially at a moment when it proposed to write a new Constitution whose purpose would be to renew the whole democratic system.

For its part, the United States remained unsure about the meaning of the changes in Venezuela for its own vital interests. Would the new government continue to respect the traditional relation of secure oil supplies? Would military influence change the democratic orientation that had permitted friendly relations for so many years? How would the United States redefine its security interests in Latin America now that it could no longer distinguish between allies according to the Cold War credo? Would differences over how to deal with drug production and trafficking turn out to be the issues that would dominate and complicate relations between the United States and Venezuela? Would Venezuela have any success in its efforts to seek out new allies and counterbalance American influence? These questions state the problems that shaped Venezuelan-U.S. relations at the start of the new century.

Economic Shifts

Observers of the world scene often refer to the phenomenon of "globalization" as the novel characteristic of the international system in the 1990s. While there are divergent definitions for globalization, the concept refers generally to the process by which economic, social, political, and cultural relations are increasingly linked; where once countries seemed to go their own ways without much reference to what was happening in other countries, now trends seem to be worldwide, simultaneous, and irresistible. Like it or not, a financial crisis in Russia may result in a fall in Venezuelan steel exports to the United States, as Russian producers feverishly drop their prices in order to be able to pay their international bankers. Many have likened the force of globalization to the image of a butterfly flapping its wings in one corner of the globe, causing a chain reaction that translates into a hurricane on another continent. Meanwhile, others have noted that the interconnectedness of the world is hardly new. While it is undoubtedly true that McDonald's and American films are much more likely to be found in the remotest spots today, nevertheless the internationalization of investment and trade was well advanced by the end of the nineteenth century.

Paul Krugman is only the most recent of critic of the view that globalization is an entirely new phenomenon without historical precedents.[13] In the 1960s there was considerable ferment about the negative effects of the internationalization of world business, leading Europeans to intensify their efforts to integrate and to find a common answer to "The American Challenge." At the same time, Latin American countries were deepening their commitment to protectionism and import substitution in order to close themselves off from the "danger" of too much trade and investment from developed countries (and from one another as well). Kenneth Waltz tended to take the long view, noting, like Krugman twenty-five years later, that the march of internationalization and the decline in autonomy were perhaps exaggerated.[14]

Forces of Liberalization

Despite the controversy over globalization, there is something to the argument that by the 1990s, international forces were affecting economic (as well as social and political) relations between the United States and Venezuela in new ways. The world oil market had been changing since the brief era of the dominance of OPEC, and this inevitably altered Venezuela's perspectives. Economic troubles within Venezuela would generate pressures to put aside policies aimed at economic protection, and external events also tended to push the country toward new market-oriented policies.

The shift that would bring Venezuela to change its approach to the international economy did not occur as an isolated incident but rather as part of a larger world movement that slowly enveloped the globe. The ideological force of "neoliberalism" in Latin America first took root in Chile under the government of Augusto Pinochet, who remained in power from 1973 until 1990. In the developed countries, meanwhile, slow growth and economic stagnation pushed politicians to look for new ways of doing things. Stagnation was perhaps greatest in the United Kingdom, where interventionist policies associated with Labour

Party rule and with old-fashioned conservative social responsibility seemed to have run into a dead end. An abrupt change took place with the election of Margaret Thatcher in 1979, giving birth to a new free market trend. In the United States, Ronald Reagan based his own presidential campaign in 1980 on a promise to reduce government and give free rein to the market.

While the promise of reducing the size of government turned out to be more rhetorical than real in developed countries, the rhetoric itself finally began to take root in Latin America at the end of the 1980s. That Pinochet, the first liberalizer, represented free market thinking perhaps lowered the acceptability of such policies for some years, since many came to the conclusion that only a dictatorship could absorb the political cost of liberalization in Latin America, while models successful in developed countries generated doubts about their relevance and applicability. But the "lost decade" of the 1980s, in which many countries found themselves mired in debt and unable to invest and grow, led to experiments. Particularly in Mexico, after the financial crisis of 1982, things began to change, and the incipient success of the few justified reforms for others. One by one, Latin American governments implemented reformist programs to open up their economies and profoundly change their relations with the outside world.

Venezuela, Argentina, Peru, Bolivia, and later Brazil and others adopted similar policies from the late 1980s into the 1990s. The United States fully supported liberalization as in its own best interests, but Latin Americans came to see it as in their interest as well. Within this framework, a new consensus emerged, often called the "Washington Consensus," which recommended economic opening with a reduction in the role of government, economic integration, an international agenda including economic and trade issues, the internationalization of goods, services, and other economic factors, and the strengthening of civil society.[15] International organizations, particularly the IMF, the World Bank, and the Interamerican Development Bank, gave unstinting support to these changes throughout the period.

Venezuela embraced the new view with enthusiasm after the election of President Carlos Andrés Pérez in 1989, but the country never managed to accept fully the implications, and the Pérez government did not achieve its goals in all the areas it strived to reform. Pérez had been a great defender of Third World unity to oppose the economic hegemony of the United States and other developed countries in the 1970s, but now he had come to embrace the virtues of the market and abandoned the old ideas developed in the Economic Commission for Latin America of the United Nations (ECLA, also known as CEPAL by its Spanish initials) that recommended more state intervention and protectionism. Unfortunately for the president and his team of young technocratic ministers, the rest of the country resisted the Pérez reforms that called for privatization, commercial liberalization, and the ending of a host of domestic subsidies that were bankrupting the states.

The political resistance to President Pérez took advantage of the stress of the reforms, particularly the high inflation that accompanied the end of subsidies and a large devaluation of the currency, to condemn his government for impos-ing an unwanted and inhuman neoliberal model. This strategy, combined with parallel attacks on Pérez including the coup attempts of 1992, would lead to his impeachment and a winning campaign by Rafael Caldera, the aging statesman who sensed popular rejection of economic liberalization and built his campaign position in 1993 on his promise to roll back much of what had been done, par-ticularly with respect to privatization and the newly implemented tax on value added (VAT).

In effect, a matrix was commonly conceived in which various elements would converge: on the one hand, "an economic development strategy based on free markets, foreign investment and export-oriented aims,"[16] a government able to achieve "a successful opening and economic modernization (measured in terms of an integral development and not only of growth or macroeconomic stability) together with a consolidation and even a deepening of the democratic system (measured in terms of popular participation, representativeness of rulers and law-makers and transparency and stability.) . . . "[17] This change of paradigm in development strategies was and is conceived by a qualified majority of decision-makers and analysts as a virtuous process, where one observes the deepening of economic interdependence and transnationalization, the link between the coun-tries' foreign policies and trade policies and the quest for a sustainable development. A consequence of the shift to the global approach would be the multilateral treatment of many issues formerly considered internal matters.[18]

New Responses to Globalization

The internationalization of agendas creates complications for countries little accustomed to negotiating policies outside of the domestic arena. As one Venezuelan involved commented: "The current variety of issues and forums fea-turing all countries' external economic relations may be seen, at first sight, as a disorderly mixture complicating the identification of priorities, preventing the monitoring and evolution of results, both in the capital cities as in the interna-tional or regional organizations and whose only visible results are the unmanageable calendars of meetings and commitments of all kinds."[19]

The job of managing international relations becomes exceedingly complex, with the mixture of issues as diverse as evaluating the meaning of the financial markets' volatility, of foreign debt, of world contraction and recession, of the Asian crisis, of internal fiscal deficits, of disguised protectionism, of specific exchange, fiscal, labor, and environmental policies in national societies, of gener-alized corruption, of the hurdles against free competition, of the so-called global psychology (the ever-growing trend in the countries toward financial panic, as the result of rumors, financial investments' volatility, and the careless handling of information), of the practical reach of international regimes in the regulation of state conduct and the critical role of technology.[20]

Two problems emerge from the global shifts described. First, countries must adjust to the international economy, resulting in an inevitable tension from contradictions between that adjustment and internal needs.[21] Second, the actors in the world system undoubtedly come to the table with varying levels of power and capabilities. Global formulas and rules for international relations tend to homogenize policy and create problems for countries that do not quite fit the standard model. It is not clear how to satisfy the demand for justice within this context.[22]

Venezuela and the United States do not fully share a common opinion about their own relations and how to satisfy both the demands of a global set of rules and the particular orientations of each country. Many incidents reveal this difficulty and its persistence. As we have seen, Venezuela seeks at times to escape from the dilemma of globalization by insisting on its own sovereignty and right to go its own way. Venezuela's tendency to favor national over international approaches has been a constant in its history,[23] perhaps strengthened by the relative autonomy that oil income bestows on the country. President Caldera, facing a major banking crisis and attack on the currency in 1994, reverted to the isolationist route, hunkering down and putting on stiff exchange and price controls that would tend to rebuff investors and detain the liberalization process that President Pérez had initiated. But the cost of cutting off the country came to create more problems than it solved, such that Caldera practically reinstituted Pérez's policies in mid-1996. But this was not the end of domestic discontent. Within a short time, Hugo Chávez, now free from prison, would take up the complaint against neoliberal policies and promise, yet again, to institute a different system that would protect the country from the negative aspects of globalization.

An important alternative to globalization stressed by practically all Venezuelan leaders since the 1960s is regional or Latin American integration through associations such as the Andean Community (originally called the Andean Pact when it was founded in 1969[24]), the so-called G-3, comprising Mexico, Colombia, and Venezuela and formed during the liberalization period of the second Pérez government, the Latin American Free Trade Association (LAFTA, a wider and looser agreement of Latin American states agreed to in 1967), and Mercosur (which groups the southern cone of South America and Brazil and was born of the convergence of liberalizing tendencies in those countries in the 1990s).

The Andean Community represents the most important effort by Venezuela to achieve the benefits of liberalization within a regional context. The Andean Community achieved few results in its first years, being used by its members more for protection from third countries than as a real liberalizing force. It declined until the confluence of forces in the 1990s gave it a new lease on life as internal barriers were dropped and a more open policy was adopted toward trade and investment with the rest of the world. Trade between Colombia and Venezuela intensified greatly, as did cross-border investment. As Table 2.1 indicates, Colombia's share of Venezuelan trade soared in the first half of the 1990s. In general, this and other regional integration schemes developed apace without blocking the simultaneous growth of trade with the United States.

It was to be seen whether the Chávez government would continue to support Venezuela's commitment to regional integration and economic opening with the rest of the world. President Chávez's frequent diatribes against neoliberalism and globalization indicated that he might turn back, but his exaltation of the values of Latin American solidarity, especially with the Andean nations linked by their common hero of independence, Simón Bolívar, also suggested that he might support further deepening of integration. On the other hand, Chávez promised a nationalist economic strategy that differed substantially from that of his neighbors and seemed to hark back to the traditional inward-looking approach. Even less did his rhetoric suggest much interest in extending his principles of solidarity to relations with developed countries, nor with the United States in particular. Despite his sometimes tough words, however, many did not expect Chávez to be able to go entirely his own way when he took over the presidency in February 1999, precisely because the world market and the commitments of the country under diverse treaties allow only slight margins of freedom to national governments.

Shortly after assuming the presidency in 1999, Chávez showed his more protectionist colors without, however, denying the general principles of regional liberalization or widening world commercial and investment flows. One notable action was his closing of the Venezuelan border to truck traffic with Colombia (goods would have to be transferred to trucks of the other country), ostensibly based on security problems caused by guerrillas in Colombia, but convenient for those who opposed competition from that country. Interestingly, a similar dispute would dog U.S.-Mexican relations, because the United States imposed similar restriction on Mexican trucks.

From the U.S. point of view, world economic shifts presented no fewer challenges. At the start of the 1990s, many in the United States argued that the country had entered a long decline and that the rest of the world would overtake it. Japan had surged as the premier Asian power, and the other "tigers" increasingly competed on terms threatening American markets. Europe looked to be consolidating its own union that could exclude the United States to some extent. A sensation of stagnation contributed to the defeat of President George Bush by Bill Clinton in the elections of 1992.

A variety of happy circumstances combined to put the United States back on the route to growth and confidence at about that time. Canada, Mexico, and the United States signed the North American Free Trade Agreement (NAFTA) in 1994, a first step in hemispheric integration that the United States put up as a model that could eventually be extended to all of Latin America. But such global relationships did not awaken fears only in developing countries. U.S. presidents from Reagan to Clinton also faced congressional opposition from representatives of regions that saw themselves as vulnerable to competition. Meanwhile, Venezuela and many of its neighbors saw such an extension of NAFTA as dangerous to the weaker countries of Latin America, replicating the problem of asymmetric power imbalances. This "threat" would act as a stimulus to Venezuela to strengthen its ties in South America so as to face any negotiations with the United States in a united group.

The grand paradox of globalization is that resistance to absorbing international effects, be they in labor, trade, finance, or culture, occurs in all countries, not just in the weaker ones. At the same time, neither Venezuela nor the United States seems to recognize the limits imposed by domestic factors in the other country and assumes instead that the other is stubborn or unfeeling in its negotiations. The media in both countries act as transmitters of all of these factors, often influencing people's perceptions about what is going on. Sophisticated or well-financed groups also know how to influence the press itself, and well-meaning journalists often have trouble providing a truly objective picture of this complex globalized world.

Trends in Trade and Investment

To what extent do patterns of trade and investment between Venezuela and the United States reflect the shifts in the world system? The twin forces of globalization and liberalization act to increase world trade and investment in general as a portion of economic activity and to generate greater diversification. Lower communications costs and more open markets multiply the opportunities open to all countries. While some complain that the post–Cold War world is one ever more dominated by the United States, the evidence is that, at least in the economy, diversity is more and more the rule.

Trade Relations

Over time, real changes have occurred in trade that reveal two contrary forces: on the one hand, strategies on the part of the Venezuelan oil industry undertaken by Petróleos de Venezuela to improve its positioning in world markets altered the flows of exports, and on the other hand, efforts to bolster regional integration also produced important results, as can be seen in Table 2.1.

The United States continued to be the number one trading partner of Venezuela. The data show that trade relations between Venezuela and the United States increased proportionately in the twenty years from 1976 to 1996, dropping back again by 1999.[25] Large variations occur as a result of the volatility of the price of oil, Venezuela's chief export. The persistent purchase of imports from the

United States tends to reinforce further the conclusion that Venezuela, despite its announced intention of achieving greater economic independence, is first and foremost a country tied economically to the United States. At the same time, important changes occurred in Venezuela´s relations with its Latin neighbors. Most striking is the increase in both imports and exports from Colombia resulting from the free trade arrangements of the Andean Community. At the same time, imports to Venezuela from Brazil, Mexico, and other Andean partners increased significantly in the nineties, displacing to some extent sourcing from the United States and Europe, particularly in manufactured goods from these countries. Even so, 61 percent of Venezuelan imports from the United States are manufactured goods.[26] Overall, if any conclusion can be drawn from the figures, the 1990s intensified regional trade as a result of the rationalization of sourcing from local partners.

While oil dominates Venezuela's exports, nonpetroleum exports tended to grow somewhat during the 1990s, reaching $4.8 billion in 1997, and falling somewhat in the following years as the bolivar became increasingly overvalued and the economy slumped. About half of all nonoil exports go to the United States and Colombia, mostly in the form of iron ore, aluminum, petrochemicals, and auto parts. Oil income tends to strengthen the Venezuelan currency relative to other Latin American currencies, making Venezuelan-produced goods very costly. Export items based on iron ore, steel, and aluminum are linked to traditional state-owned firms in those industries, although Venezuela privatized its steel industry at the end of the 1990s. Venezuela complained that its partners in the Andean Community enjoy preferential treatment for their exports to the United States, based on a 1991 law that granted benefits to Andean countries affected by drug trafficking and excluded Venezuela. Despite his many doubts about American hegemony in the region, President Chávez asked for Venezuelan inclusion in the Andean preference scheme in 2001, perhaps as a way of showing flexibility toward the United States and assuaging fears of his radicalism on the part of the recently installed administration of George W. Bush.

The Special Case of Oil

Since oil plays such a large role in the relationship of Venezuela with its trading partners and is also a key strategic product for the United States, it is worthwhile taking a closer look at the trends. In its drive for autonomy, Venezuela has long sought to reduce its dependence on oil, not so much by reducing the oil industry itself as by increasing the competitiveness of other sectors.[27] This policy was particularly marked in the 1970s and 1980s, during the heyday of the OPEC, when production was restricted. Eventually, pressures mounted for a change in policy, especially from the oil executives of PDVSA itself, who chafed at running a company that could not grow and who did not share the politicians' reservations about doing business with the large multinationals.

TABLE 2.1

Venezuela's Principal Trading Partners
1976–1999
(selected years and countries)

	SHARE OF EXPORTS (%)				SHARE OF IMPORTS (%)			
	1976	1986	1996	1999	1976	1986	1996	1999
United States	39.7	37.5	60.0	49.8	43.1	40.6	50.1	40.1
Colombia	0.2	1.0	5.8	4.0	1.8	0.8	8.2	5.8
Brazil	1.2	0.7	4.6	4.2	2.0	4.0	4.8	3.6
Canada	15.2	2.7	2.4	2.9	3.8	2.2	1.0	3.0
Peru	1.2	0.3	2.1	1.5	0.2	0.6	1.3	0.7
Germany	2.2	4.9	1.8	1.0	0.6	9.1	5.3	4.8
Japan	0.4	2.8	1.2	1.2	9.2	6.1	3.7	3.5
Netherland Antilles	20.0	2.3	1.1	n.a.	0.8	1.5	1.0	n.a.
United Kingdom	2.3	2.0	1.0	0.5	3.8	3.6	3.0	1.7
Spain	1.2	0.4	1.0	0.9	2.0	2.2	2.6	3.2
Mexico	0.2	0.05	1.0	0.9	0.8	0.7	4.5	3.9
Argentina	0.6	0.07	0.4	0.3	1.5	0.5	3.7	1.7
Total ($ billions)	8.7	10.0	20.8	19.7	3.8	8.6	9.5	12.7

Note: Statistics may vary according to source.

Source: 1976–1996: International Monetary Fund (IMF), *Direction of Trade Yearbook*, 1972–1997 (Washington, DC: IMF); 1999: Venezuela, Oficina Central de Estatdísticas (OCEI).

The new generation of Venezuelan oil executives aspired to become equal players in the world oil market through internationalization. First they looked to foreign expansion through investments in refineries and distribution, buying into refineries in Europe and the United States, particularly Germany's Veba Oil, and investing in a huge gasoline distributor, Citgo, in the United States. Oil industry leaders then worked to convince the government that production limits only served to open up markets for other producers and even stimulated investment in fields less competitive than Venezuela's. These arguments fell on willing ears during the liberalization phase initiated in 1989, so that thereafter production tended to increase.

Venezuela went further: in 1996 the "oil opening" was announced with great fanfare, and for the first time since the 1976 nationalization, foreign investment was to be welcomed, although under PDVSA's protective wing. Various schemes for associations and joint ventures were launched in 1997 and 1998, as Venezuela developed its plan to double oil production in ten years, increase foreign investments in the expansion, and fight for a greater share of world exports. Citizens were amazed at seeing the influx of foreign oil companies that had ceased operations in Venezuela over twenty years before. Gasoline stations bearing the names of Mobil and BP sprouted again.

What did this opening mean? In the first place, production plans for the next decade indicated that Venezuela would double oil activity, raising production to some six million barrels per day from its then level of three million. Secondly, fields for exploration and production would be auctioned off to oil companies. The initial results caught worldwide attention, and many U.S. companies such as Exxon, Chevron, Amoco, Conoco, Enron, Phillips, Texaco, Arco, and Mobil, excluded for twenty years from production activities, entered as contractors, as partners for special heavy oil projects, or under the new figure of "shared earnings."[28] It should be remembered that this change of strategy was carried out without a major reform of Venezuela's policy of reserving the oil industry to the state, so that foreign investors could not operate their own oil concessions but had to work as partners of PDVSA. Of course, the oil market had undergone a sea change in comparison with former years, when a few great oil majors dominated the scene. Now the American companies had to compete not only with Shell and British Petroleum but with a full field of companies from all over the world, from China to Argentina.

Even before the inception of the oil opening, PDVSA had received the green light to increase production. From an average production of some 1.8 million barrels per day during the 1980s, Venezuela's production reached 3.3 million barrels per day in 1997 and accounted for 78 per cent of all exports.[29] From the mid-1980s, the United States began to import more oil. The plan for expanding production in Venezuela had as its objective increasing the share in the growing American market. (See Table 2.2.)

While the oil opening contributed to excellent relations with the United States, the honeymoon ended early. Hopes for a buoyant export market fell on increasingly somber news from Asia after a financial crisis hit Thailand in mid-1997 and spread to all of East Asia, including important consumer countries such as Japan. At the same time, Russia confronted ever greater difficulties and turned to desperate efforts to sell its own exports at any price. From an average price of $18 per barrel for its oil in 1996, Venezuela saw its price more than halved by the end of 1998. World demand fell, not only for oil but for practically all natural resource–based products. A major crisis was under way, reversing optimistic projections for the Venezuelan economy in general. The United States was both a winner and a loser. Oil companies came under pressure from the lack of demand, but lower prices enabled consumers to return to buying larger vehicles, and the American economy showed itself to be immune from much of the chaos in the economies of Asia. The Clinton government benefited from a sustained boom, which helped it to weather even the impeachment process that resulted from the Lewinsky scandal in 1998. Only the oil companies seemed to be directly affected, leading to major mergers in which stronger companies absorbed the weaker.

TABLE 2.2

U.S. Petroleum Imports
1966–1999, various years
(thousands of barrels per day)

	Total petroleum imports	Petroleum imports from Venezuela	Venezuela as percent of total
1966	2,573	1,021	40
1976	7,295	699	10
1986	5,439	788	15
1996	9,478	1,676	18
1999	10,852	1,493	14
2000	11,093	1,519	14

Source: 1966–1976: American Petroleum Institute (API), *Basic Petroleum Data Book* (Washington, DC: API); 1986–1999: U.S. Energy Information Administration (EIA), *Petroleum Supply Annual, Petroleum Supply Monthly and International Petroleum Statistics Report* (Washington, DC: EIA, various).

This turn of events in the oil market between 1997 and 1998 occurred just at the end of the Caldera administration in Venezuela, contributing to dire predictions about the stability of the country as government income fell and threatened a major fiscal crisis. A drop of 50 percent in oil earnings directly affects government revenues, since oil constitutes close to half of all fiscal income. Hugo Chávez was building his presidential campaign at the time when oil prices began to slide. He attracted supporters who were known enemies of the country's expansive oil policy and he promised them that he would make big changes in the industry, replacing high executives and revising accords signed with foreign investors. This further concerned the U.S. government and American oil companies, who complained about the instability of government policy in Venezuela and feared the worst should Chávez be elected.

To end the glut of oil and restore profitable prices, OPEC and non-OPEC producers agreed to cut production, but prices continued low throughout 1998 and into the beginning of 1999, when Chávez would become president. He kept his promise to shake up the industry and continued to support production cuts, which finally restored higher prices in 1999, reaching near record levels by the end of the year. Prices went so high that U.S. concern now went in the other direction: oil prices of over $30 per barrel might stimulate world inflation and endanger the long economic boom enjoyed by the United States—and in an election year! Now the U.S. government went into high gear to try to convince OPEC that it should increase production quotas to lower prices, which it did at the end of March 2000, although not by a large amount, so prices remained high. In this period of stress, the Venezuelan government insisted on its independence from U.S. pressures, although Venezuela's oil minister took a leadership position in the OPEC meeting to promote a new system of price bands whose purpose would be to control excessive swings in the oil price, a policy that was more in line with the U.S. view. At the same time, Foreign Minister Rangel railed against a soon-to-be-forgotten proposal in the U.S. House of Representatives to cut off military aid to countries (like Venezuela) that participated in price-fixing actions.[30] Venezuela promoted the idea within OPEC that the group should hold firm because neither the United States nor Europe should complain so much about higher prices, since a large part of what consumers pay for gasoline, especially in Europe, takes the form of their own governments' taxes on petroleum imports.

Despite the changes in PDVSA to align it with the politics of the Chávez government, the long-term expansion plan was not tossed out but recalculated to project a somewhat more moderate rate of growth. During this period of OPEC production cuts and high international prices in 1999 and 2000, Venezuela faced a classic dilemma: when it reduces oil exports along with its OPEC partners, other countries often move into its markets, thus reducing its share of the world market. In 1999, Venezuela sank to second place in the ranking of oil suppliers to the United States, after Canada. Saudi Arabia would take second place in 2000, while Mexico was not far behind.

Should Venezuela truly wish to carry out its expansion plan, it will be hard-pressed to maintain its relationship with OPEC and respect the quotas set by the organization, which is one reason why the Chávez government feared going ahead with the big production increases planned by the former administration. There is every likelihood that the debate over oil strategy will continue to divide experts in Venezuela. The Caldera government had initiated its new expansion policy with the goal of increasing production and market share, even at the risk of falling prices; the Chávez government reverted to the traditional stance of OPEC loyalty and high prices at the expense of production. This is always a risky policy, because other oil exporters may try to take over Venezuelan market share, particularly in the United States. In addition, the United States could consider it preferable to depend less on Venezuelan oil, to the extent that it perceived the Chávez government to be less friendly than its predecessors. Perhaps concerned by such a possibility, President Chávez took measures to underline continuity in policy. Contrary to his campaign insinuations, he went forward with foreign investment projects and pressed for private participation in new ventures in the gas industry.

Oil policy in Venezuela means much more than economic policy, since oil is the lifeblood of economic well-being in the country. That the oil industry is under the control of the state also means that PDVSA may be an actor in international political relations. The company's traditional culture assumed an apolitical role both domestically and internationally, but its place in the world must undoubtedly be aligned with national policy. PDVSA's first links are with the United States, its chief market. This is both a source of strength for Venezuela and a vulnerability. But just as the Chávez government began to make explicit efforts at diversifying its global alliances, PDVSA did the same. Under Chávez, for instance, an old project to resuscitate the Cuban oil refinery at Cienfuegos was taken up again, although in the end the deal was scrapped and a special agreement was signed with Cuba to facilitate its access to Venezuelan supply. Following a state visit to China at the end of 1999, Venezuela announced a deal with that country in 2000 to produce Orimulsion, a patented product of PDVSA used as a coal substitute. The oil industry's strategy seemed to be adapting itself to the new foreign policy of Venezuela.

At the start of the George W. Bush administration in the United States, a change of energy policy was expected. After several years of violent swings in oil prices, the Clinton administration had evolved toward convergence with the Venezuelan line in OPEC that recommended joint efforts to stabilize prices on world markets. The Bush government, with its multiple connections with oil interests in the United States, would naturally share this perspective and want to ensure profitable levels of prices to protect American producers. This could be a double-edged sword for Venezuela, however, if such concerns lead the government to favor domestic production or regional sources of oil restricted to the United States, Canada, and Mexico. The Chávez government, like all Venezuelan governments since 1914, would have to make choices about just how independent it would like to be in its international policy, particularly when it came to oil. President Bush clarified his intentions in May 2001 with the publication of the "Report of the National Energy Policy Development Group" led by Vice President Cheney. That document stressed the special status of Canada and Mexico as energy partners within NAFTA and suggested the importance of signing a Bilateral Investment Treaty with Venezuela, presumably an implicit condition for recognizing Venezuela as an equal to its competitors in Mexico and Canada.

Foreign Investment

Despite the partial oil opening in Venezuela, no significant changes came about in terms of foreign direct investment by the United States in the country. Venezuela had not been a magnet for American investors for many years, and the liberalization process under way in Latin America created competition for investor dollars. Some countries, such as Argentina, Mexico, Brazil, and Chile, looked more attractive to American investors either because of the greater size of their markets or because of the greater stability and economic growth they offered. Along with its Andean partners, Venezuela put aside much of its discriminatory attitude against foreign investment—a vestige of the inward-looking policies of the 1970s—but so many countries were doing the same that the relative effect was not so strong.

In the brief period of 1991 to 1992, Venezuela managed to grow, but the nineties saw too much political and economic turmoil to stimulate a significant

TABLE 2.3
Venezuela's Share of U.S. Foreign Direct Investment
1975–1999, various years
(percentages)

	World	Latin America
1975	1.5	8.5
1985	0.7	5.6
1990	0.3	3.6
1995	0.5	4.4
1997	0.6	4.5
1999	0.7	5.0

Source: 1975–1997: U.S. Department of Commerce, *Survey of Current Business* (Washington, DC: August 1977–1992; October 1998. 1999: U.S. Department of Commerce, Bureau of Economic Analysis (www.bea.doc.gov).

renewal of American investment there. There were important exceptions to the rule. President Pérez managed to carry out the privatization of the local telephone company in 1991, in which the American firm GTE (later called Verizon) headed up the winning consortium. Telecommunications would prove to be one of the few sectors that would grow in the 1990s, and private operators, prominently Bell South, also began to exploit the opportunities of wireless telephone systems. This, along with stimulus from new investment in oil, allowed American foreign investment in Venezuela to increase slightly in the decade, recovering from the slump of the late 1980s. This is evidenced by the data presented in Table 2.3 showing the slow increase in the share of total U.S. foreign direct investment that went to Venezuela after 1990, in comparison with the relatively stable share that went to Latin America.

As in trade, the United States continues to represent a significant proportion of all foreign direct investment in Venezuela. Even in the 1970s, when restrictions tended to dissuade investment from abroad, American investors accounted for more than half of all foreign investment, and, as Table 2.4 shows, the relative weight of the United States continues to be dominant, at least in years in which investment is strong. The years of depressed investment from 1993 to 1997 correspond to the period of political crisis and banking failures that caused economic havoc until the stabilization associated with the new attempt at liberalization and oil opening renewed interest. The final years of the decade followed the pattern of a classic oil country that still had not devised good policies to even out the volatility of its economy in response to the ups and downs of the unpredictable oil market. Just as investment was poised to spurt with the oil opening in 1998, poor market conditions reversed many plans as the market plummeted.

With the approval of a new Constitution at the end of 1999, Venezuela promised a more stable environment by guaranteeing equal treatment for foreign and

TABLE 2.4

**Direct Foreign Investment in Venezuela
1979–2000
($ millions)**

	Total investment	U.S. investment	U.S. as % of total
1979–1991	4,096	2,041	50
1992	1,950	1,218	62
1993	417	47	11
1994	701	70	10
1995	333	89	27
1996	395	68	17
1997	665	245	37
1998	1,570	122	8
1999	528	74	14
2000	644	86	13
1979–2000*	11,299	4,060	36

* Yearly investment figures may be somewhat unreliable, since they depend on foreign investors registering their new investments with the Superintendency of Foreign Investments. Major revisions were made in the data going back to 1992, changing estimates significantly. By comparison, the U.S. data produced by the Department of Commerce indicate that total U.S. direct investment in Venezuela at the end of 1998 was valued at $5.7 billion, of which 23 percent was in the oil sector.

Source: Consejo Nacional de Promoción de Inversiones (Conapri).

domestic investors and committed itself to responsible fiscal and monetary policies with a mechanism for counterbalancing oil market volatility. A law for the protection of investments was approved as well, although it fell short of U.S. expectations for a bilateral investment treaty which would have gone even further as an incentive to new investments.[31] The opening of the gas industry to foreign investment and the reaffirmation of plans for expansion of oil production indicated that Venezuela sought to capture a greater share of international investment. In 2000, a major American electricity company, AES, bought the Caracas electric company, Electricidad de Caracas, and the Chávez government hailed the sale as a sign of investor confidence in the country. Even so, U.S. investors remained wary of Chávez. The Venezuelan president often criticized globalization and what he termed "savage capitalism," even as he welcomed foreign investors in recognition of their contribution to growth and employment. Despite the stumbles of the 1990s, Venezuela confirmed its interest in deepening its involvement with world industry.

Weltanshauung: Views of World Politics

During the 1990s, Venezuela experienced many stressful moments on the domestic front, while the United States recovered much of its self-confidence as its economy boomed and the world came increasingly to see it as the dominant world power. Asia´s economy faltered and Europe tended to consolidate its own integration. During the second government headed by Carlos Andrés Pérez between 1989 until his impeachment in 1993, Venezuela attempted to join the trend to liberalization and outward-looking growth, trying to open trade in non-petroleum products and increasing PDVSA's entry into the North American oil market.[32] In the second term of Rafael Caldera between 1994 and 1999, Venezuela received American support for Venezuelan initiatives in issues such as the fight against corruption and the promotion of regional democracy, despite the return of economic difficulties and financial crisis in Venezuela. Both countries signed an agreement to obtain the extradition of former bankers who had fled to the United States and an accord for mutual assistance in the administration of justice related to banking and financial institutions.

Such differences as did exist barely shook the base of good relations. The Venezuelan criticism of the Helms-Burton Act and the trade embargo imposed on Cuba would hardly be significant given the fact that even the closest allies of the United States (and even high government officials) shared the negative view of this policy, which threatened punishment to companies whose business in Cuba violated property rights of Americans. Other issues appeared but did not ruffle the fundamental relationship: difficulties in coming to an agreement to sign investment protection and double taxation treaties and a dispute over the sale of reformulated gasoline. One way or another, such conflicts usually get solved. President Chávez decided to give the green light to the double taxation treaty soon after taking office, which won him considerable goodwill at the time. The gasoline case led to a successful appeal by Venezuela together with Brazil before the World Trade Organization (WTO), alleging a violation of the free trade rules and discriminatory treatment by the U.S. government.

As this chapter has shown, generally friendly attitudes characterize Venezuelan-U.S. relations, even though specific problems inevitably arise. The nineties were no departure from the pattern of friendship that had always exist-ed, and not even President Chávez, despite his revolutionary rhetoric, questioned that the United States was and would continue to be a firm friend. He might decry the effects of globalization and equate "neoliberalism" with inhuman eco-nomic policy, but he could not roll back the greater integration of the world economy nor did he show much desire to do so. From a political point of view, it could be said that there exists a strategic coincidence favoring democracy and hemispheric security. On the economic front, oil continued to dominate exchanges in an atmosphere of mutual understanding that survives the natural conflicts of commercial relations.

The Venezuelan case is framed within what we have called "strategic coinci-dences and tactical differences." In other words, although there were no structural differences of a bilateral nature, considerable friction over specific problems could appear. Such friction, of course, was minor compared to bilateral problems that neighboring Colombia had when the United States decided to "decertify" that country because of its lack of control over the drug traffic and even denied a visa to its president; or to the distance that grew between the United States and Peru when President Fujimori dissolved Congress and assumed almost dictatorial powers.

In order to understand this friction one must bear in mind that since the restoration of democracy in the country in 1958, U.S.-Venezuelan relations were subject to the following perspectives firmly held in Venezuela:

1. Venezuelans believed that their case was unique, different from the rest of Latin America, in view of the economic weight of oil and the political system's stability and democracy that set Venezuela apart;

2. Venezuela did not fit the popular models proposed by the comparative politics analyses of Latin America positing tendencies toward instability;

3. "Nothing [important] happened" in the country such as a revolution or an attempted coup d'état;

4. Between Venezuela and the United States there was a close relationship, given Venezuela's traditional role as a safe and strategic oil supplier of the United States.

5. Relations were based on a stable control of the state by the alternating political parties, strongly centralized through the Venezuelan presidency, Venezuela's Foreign Ministry, and the Department of State.

6. As a sovereign state and member of the United Nations, Venezuela would oppose mightily any hint of foreign intervention, at home or in the rest of the world.

Venezuela might have felt comfortable with this vision of the world of relations with the United States until the 1990s, but at least a part of its worldview would be increasingly challenged. For the United States, for instance, Venezuela is just another Latin American country, even if it is an important supplier of oil and even if Venezuela were to continue to see itself as unique. Indeed, to some extent Venezuela lost its "exceptionalism"[33] as a stable country when the internal political crises of the 1990s broke out. Now, it seemed, things did "happen" there, and perhaps the Venezuelan model fit general schemes for analyzing the region more than had been formerly believed. The coups of the nineties and the disintegration of the traditional Venezuelan political system converted the country into an object of international concern.

In another sense, a changed perception on the part of the United States resulted from outside events, particularly the fact that democracy tended to stabilize in the rest of Latin America during the same period, making Venezuela just one of the many democracies of the region, and not necessarily the most stable. The breakdown of the strong two-party system in Venezuela also required an adjustment of perceptions about how things worked there. Even the world oil market tended to become much more diversified, thus reducing the prominence of Venezuela in the American view of its strategic position.

Venezuelan-U.S. relations had remained so essentially stable for so many years that perhaps the internal factors that were developing within Venezuela— and that would set the stage for a reassessment of the complacent view that "nothing happened" in Venezuela—failed to command sufficient attention. Many events indicated the discontent of the general population in Venezuela with the performance of the political and economic system during the 1990s and the probability that a profound change of leadership was likely.

With the government of Hugo Chávez, change did finally arrive in Venezuela, upsetting the traditional rhythm of relationships with the United States. With his particular rhetoric of strong—and sometimes undiplomatic—words, Chávez sought to show that he would be different in just about every area of domestic and foreign policy. The old perspectives would no longer serve as guides. It took some time for the United States to realize that it would be better to support the process of change than to assume the stability of traditional leaders in power. Certainly, many clues pointed to a more conflictual relationship with the United States and even the possibility of rupture should the rule of law be violated at any stage in the process. Yet the fundamental coincidences over the natural link between Venezuela and the United States did not disappear, nor would Venezuela's nationalistic instincts, which always counseled a wary view of its powerful northern neighbor.

Venezuela and the United States enjoyed a long period of excellent relations based on a real base of shared values, commercial links, and geographical proximity. Venezuela, as one of the main suppliers of oil to the United States, never failed as a reliable partner. Some would claim that the factors that underlay this positive relationship were weakening, and that the Chávez presidency would jeopardize stability. The following chapters will cast additional light on the forces of stability and change, showing that most of the elements that affect relations between the United States and Venezuela have to do more with global transformations and exogenous events than with the specificities of particular actors. What is more, the fact that the United States is less worried about Cold War issues would seem to allow it to tolerate more variety in the Latin American region and to be willing to support Venezuela as it experiments with new solutions to refresh its democracy and economy.

THREE

THE NEW ROLE
OF INTERNATIONAL
INSTITUTIONS

 THIS IS A BOOK ABOUT RELATIONS BETWEEN THE UNITED STATES and Venezuela in our times. If instead it were a history of those same relations before the twentieth century, it would certainly include many references to the other great powers of the era, England, Spain, and Germany, as well as the other emerging Latin American countries. There would be mentions of alliances among the great nations formed to achieve military or even economic goals, but there would be no place for international institutions, because these are mostly the invention of the twentieth century, particularly of the last fifty years. More and more, countries' bilateral relations tend to get mixed up with international rules and the institutions that draw them up and enforce them, especially contributing to the economic shifts analyzed in Chapter Two. Indeed, international organizations have come to play such an important part in mediating—and moderating—the relations between countries that it is well worthwhile to consider their effect as a way to understand better how two countries like Venezuela and the United States manage their relationship in the context of a world of supranational institutions.

The Age of Supranationality

Countries insist on their sovereignty, which means that there is no higher power than that of the state within national borders. The idea of sovereignty achieved the status of doctrine in the West as early as the Roman republic, fell into disuse for many centuries, and established itself formally in the sixteenth century, when Jean Bodin wrote of the unity and primacy of power.[1] States still insist on their absolute dominion, even though outside forces continue to limit their options. Excepting disputes over who represents the states, such as those that occur in civil wars and outright invasions, informal infringements on state power happen all the time. Some observers of the modern state claim that sovereignty faces its most important limit in the rules of the international system, particularly the rules set by international organizations, or "supranational" organizations, as they are sometimes called.[2] But countries can still argue that such organizations derive their power and influence only from the formal act by which a sovereign state agrees to the rules they set. In this sense, the state never gives up its sovereignty, since it always has the option to separate itself from those organizations that it chooses not to join. Strictly speaking, sovereignty is not ceded.

The reality of sovereignty is more complex than such a theoretical proposition might seem to suggest: the reach and importance of some international organizations render it practically impossible for all but the most powerful not to submit themselves to the rules; what is more, a myriad of organizations exist that do not even have formal membership but do impose sets of rules that require cooperation, even if such regimes are not even formalized. Woe to the country that attempts to set its own terms for international credit or thinks it can impose its own standards on the rest of the world. This reality of supranationality assumes ever greater importance in the modern relations among nations.[3]

While no country can liberate itself from the influence of international rules, be they formal or informal, small countries face special difficulties in protecting their own autonomy, both because they play lesser roles as designers of the rules and because they command few resources either to defy them or to alter them. Undoubtedly, the United States and other great powers possess just that influence and power that others lack and arouse suspicions that they make up the rules to suit themselves. Even during the Cold War, Latin American countries could opt out of the Western system only at great cost, as the Cuban alternative amply demonstrated. To the extent that the United States has the power to shape the world in which other countries operate, it exercises what Susan Strange has called "structural power," which is the ability to mold and determine the structure of the world political economy in which other countries, their political institutions, their firms, their scientists and other professionals must carry out their affairs.[4] Even so, the United States sometimes resists accepting international organizations' authority in ways that subject it to charges of inconsistency. Such were the cases of the Kyoto agreement to limit emissions of greenhouse gases and the treaty creating the International Criminal Court, the first rejected by the United States and the second delayed in the approval process.

The world today offers greater opportunities to small countries like Venezuela to protect themselves from random intervention by more powerful countries to the degree that international agreements and the organizations that implement them create higher levels of predictability and submit all members to the same rules of the game. Compare the situation of Venezuela in 1903, when European countries simply took over the customs house to ensure debt payments, with the harsh but civilized meetings of the "Paris Club," the group of developed creditor countries that comes together to work out solutions when debtors fall into arrears.

Venezuela and the International Organizations

Venezuela has gone through several phases in its approach to international organizations, often varying its tactics within the same strategy of seeking space for its own way of doing things with an acceptable level of autonomy. On the one hand, it has used some international forums to justify its positions and to ensure limits on the power of the United States in the Western Hemisphere. In particular, Venezuela fairly consistently resists unilateral intervention on the part of the United States or other external powers in Latin America, although such resistance generally takes the form of speeches and votes without teeth, such as when the United States invaded Panama at the end of 1989 to overthrow dictator Manuel Noriega. At the same time, Venezuela naturally benefits from its membership in multiple international organizations such as the United Nations (UN), the Organization of American States (OAS), the World Trade Organization (WTO), the World Bank, the International Monetary Fund (IMF), and the Interamerican Development Bank, although suspicions that some of these organizations, particularly those charged with economic functions, follow the line set by the United States never entirely disappear.

At times, international organizations awake opposition and even become symbols of external intervention or oppression. Are recommendations in favor of privatization of state-owned enterprises emitted by the World Bank or others the result of American preferences or are they truly welfare-enhancing for Venezuela? Many Venezuelans would argue that such pressures for "reform" do more harm than good. Practically all recent Venezuelan presidents have turned to "IMF bashing," based on the fact that IMF rules for financial aid require countries to accept recommendations for changing their economic policies.[5] Carlos Andrés Pérez at one time claimed that the IMF was a neutron bomb; one that kills only people and leaves the rest standing. When he later made an about-face and decided in 1989 to go ahead with the liberalizing economic reforms recommended by the international institutions, his opposition quickly took up the same issue in order to diminish his legitimacy before the populace. Much the same happened to his successor, Rafael Caldera, who took care to distance himself from the neoliberal position associated with the international institutions, although he too had to accept their help when economic crisis overtook his government in 1996. Perhaps recognizing the danger of having some day to eat his words, Hugo Chávez refrained from explicit references to these organizations, limiting himself during his presidential campaign in 1998 to vague references to the need to devise alternatives to the formulas of neoliberalism.

Various sorts of international organizations open up opportunities to a country like Venezuela to pursue its interests with greater independence from what it perceives as U.S. dominance. Large organizations such as the United Nations have more competing groups that desire to make the voice of less developed countries heard. The Organization of American States also serves as a forum for voicing differences within the region, and Venezuela has taken advantage of this arena to express its disagreement with certain U.S. initiatives. There are also organizations in which the United States is not a member and which provide a forum in which the United States is not even present.

In the days of the Cold War, Venezuela joined the movement to create a grouping of countries that sided neither with the United States nor with the Communist pole, calling themselves the "nonaligned nations" or the "Group of 77." During his first government (1974–1979), Carlos Andrés Pérez had promoted himself as a leader of the nonaligned movement and supported the concept of the New International Economic Order (NIEO) that would reverse the injustice of a system that favored the dominant Western economies led by the United States. He used the momentary strength of Venezuela's economy during the 1970s to bolster his position. But with the debt crisis that afflicted Venezuela and other developing countries in the 1980s, the wind went out of the sails of the NIEO, and little was heard of it thereafter. The fall of the Soviet Union in 1990 and the greater acceptance throughout the world of the market system suggested the necessity of devising other strategies.

Venezuela finds that international organizations provide the safest route to expressing differences with the United States, because it can join legitimately with other countries and thus avoid head-on clashes. In this way, for instance, Venezuela sided with Argentina in the Falklands/Malvinas War with Great Britain and, more recently in April 1999 and thereafter, voted against the U.S. position on human rights abuses contained in the UN Human Rights Commission Report condemning Cuba, Iran, and China. In another incident during the XXIX General Assembly of the OAS in June 1999, the Venezuelan delegation presented the "Participatory Democracy Declaration," an approach counter to the U.S. initiative for the creation of a support group for democratic nations in the region. The U.S. proposal failed to gain majority support, and although the debate was essentially rhetorical, it marked the first time in many years in which Venezuela could be found outside the U.S. camp in its positions on democracy. Under President Chávez, Venezuela would continue to press for a regional commitment to "participatory" democracy, at the Quebec Summit in 2001 and within the OAS. While in abstract terms it is difficult to argue against participation, there was some resistance to accepting definitions of democracy that originated with Chávez, due to some U. S. doubts about his democratic vocation. In 2000, Venezuela joined again with other countries to support China in a UN Human Rights Commission vote on a proposal to condemn China's human rights record in 2000, distancing itself from the traditional abstentionist position of other democratic countries of Latin America.[6]

International Organizations and the Search for Autonomy

There are no serious differences between the United States and Venezuela with regard to the desirability of democracy in the world, but in concrete situations there may be differences about whether some kind of international intervention is necessary or about how far global organizations should go in trying to define just what an acceptable democracy should look like. Sometimes, for Venezuela, international organizations represent a safe venue for joining with other countries to oppose the United States or pursue a variety of interests, but at times, the blade can cut in the other direction. One small incident illustrates this phenomenon: the international supervision of elections.

The OAS regularly sends missions to its member countries to observe their electoral processes and give an outside and objective view of the transparency of elections. The OAS visited Venezuela many times between 1998 and 2000, when multiple elections and referenda were held as part of the process of writing a new Constitution and electing new authorities. Most of these elections were carried out without a hitch, at least until the elections scheduled for May 28, 2000, when practically all public offices, including the presidency, were to be put to the vote. The election process was so complex, with thousands of candidates throughout the country, that the electoral commission, also filled with new and inexperienced members, failed to organize the process in time for the agreed date. Just days before the election, a suspension was mandated by the Supreme Tribunal, with all the foreign observers, including the OAS representatives, present. It was a great embarrassment for the government and even led to the threat of conflict with the United States.[7]

Soon thereafter, the Venezuelan foreign minister proposed at the OAS that rules be drawn up to control the role of international election observers, ostensibly to limit their political action. The Venezuelan government suggested that the organization's opinions be limited to communications with local governments and that they should refrain from public statements about the development of the process and about the functioning of electoral authorities. Of course, that would restrict them beyond recognition, in that the purpose of foreign observers is precisely to let the world know to what extent democracy is being respected.

Despite Venezuela's publicly expressed doubts about the role of international observers, the country once again invited the OAS and other groups to come for the rescheduled election of July 30, 2000, without mentioning any guidelines that might limit their freedom to speak out. Perhaps the trial balloon at the OAS had not floated well, or Venezuela understood that it would only generate doubts abroad if it were to take a position on the matter alone. In the same period, Peru had suffered severe international criticism over the lack of transparency in the reelection of Alberto Fujimori, whose inauguration was marred by street protests and by the absence of representatives from many other countries. Venezuela kept its own presence at Fujimori's ill-fated inauguration to a minimum and wished its own electoral process to be seen as democratic and honest abroad. On arriving in Caracas at the head of the delegation of the Carter Center, former U.S. president Jimmy Carter commented that his center worked only where it would have freedom to speak out: "We would not accept this. If the president of the country, or the National Electoral Council were to say that we cannot make declarations, then we would not come to Venezuela. This would take away our role as spokesmen. Why go to a country where one cannot speak out?"[8]

Just as the largest international organizations permit more room for maneuver for the less powerful countries, so too limited-purpose organizations open opportunities to countries like Venezuela to forward their positions in alliance with like-minded nations. Venezuela favors this option in a variety of circumstances. This was certainly the case when Venezuela sent its minister of mines, Juan Pablo Pérez Alfonzo, to Iran in 1960 to form OPEC, whose power came to be appreciated only a decade later. Less successful was the creation of SELA in the 1970s as a challenge to U.S.-led organizations for economic matters in the Americas and whose membership included Cuba, which did not belong to the other institutions of the inter-American system.

Similar goals for autonomy motivated the movement for regional economic integration in Latin America, where the European model served as a stimulus. Venezuela joined the Latin American Free Trade Association, the Andean Community,[9] and the Group of Three (Venezuela, Colombia, and Mexico), although sometimes domestic interest groups voiced their opposition on the grounds that they would confront unfair competition from their neighbors. In fact, the chief obstacle to widening Venezuela's integration with other Latin American countries has been the resistance of its own industrial and commercial groups to outside competition from lower-cost countries. In the meantime, other Latin American countries created additional organizations in favor of regional and subregional integration, among them the Central American Common Market, the Association of Caribbean Countries (CARICOM), and Mercosur.

The Resurgence of Organizations for Economic Integration in the Americas

As long as the regional groupings limited their aims to opening up trade within the area, they faced grave difficulties in widening their scope and influence. The Andean Pact practically died during the 1980s at a time when its members found themselves mired in local difficulties, unpayable debts, and stagnant economies. Venezuela was particularly inward-looking during the 1980s, having practically shut itself off from the free flow of trade and finance with exchange controls between 1983 and 1989, but soon interest in economic integration would spurt.

Two elements combined to give new life to Andean integration in the 1990s. On the one hand, the United States joined with Canada in a free trade agreement in 1989 that would be extended to Mexico with the creation of the North American Free Trade Agreement (NAFTA), signed by the newly elected President Bill Clinton in 1994 in the the wake of the Mexican financial crisis of 1992 to 1993. At the same time, important changes took place in Venezuela, as the government of Carlos Andrés Pérez decided to scrap the inward-looking approach followed by his predecessor Jaime Lusinchi, thus opening up the possibility of renewing efforts to resuscitate the Andean Pact.

As NAFTA quickly proved successful, the Clinton government in the United States began to push for its extension to the rest of Latin America. No Latin American government felt itself in a strong position to negotiate alone with the northern group, so the logic of strengthening the Andean Pact (which converted itself into the more ambitious "Andean Community" in 1996), Mercosur, and other regional associations indicated that it would be better to present a united front than to negotiate singly. In this sense, international organizations on a regional scale might serve the purpose of fortifying small countries in their attempt to play an effective role in the global context. But the unity of the regional groups was yet to be tested. At the third summit meeting of the Americas held in Quebec in April 2001, there were no specific positions taken by Mercosur or the Andean Community with respect to the common commitment to implement the Free Trade Area of the Americas in 2005. Only Venezuela, without support from other countries, expressed its reservations on the feasibility of the 2005 goal.

By the same logic, Venezuela and other Latin American countries make serious attempts to fortify their relations with other international groupings so as to establish a counterweight to traditional American influence in their region. Such an approach finds willing partners abroad, since other countries also seek to reduce what they perceive as American hegemony in the post–Cold War era. In particular, European countries, singly and through the European Union, court Latin America. Because of its historical and language ties, Spain stands out as an aggressive courtier, not least due to its own strategy of augmenting its weight within Europe as a country of global reach. For other European countries, however, the Latin option holds less attraction to the extent that the deepening of the relationship could weaken ties to former colonies and because of the relative unimportance of Latin America in their domestic systems. France certainly falls into this last category. When a grand summit took place in Rio de Janeiro in July 1999 to seal a general agreement between Latin America and the European Union, President Chirac of France expressed his conviction that France should not put its agricultural policy at risk by too ambitious an opening and that, in any case, specific negotiations should await the outcome of negotiations within the WTO to be initiated in the year 2000.[10] The European card serves a purpose from time to time.

When President-elect Hugo Chávez decided to initiate his entry into international politics before his inauguration, he first made a grand tour of Europe as a way of signaling to the United States that the cold shoulder offered by Washington could be replaced by a warm European handshake. Yet it is a card that tends to be more symbolic than real, more useful as a political signal than a serious alternative for Venezuela, given the small share that European countries actually have in trade and investment. In Chapter Two (Table 2.1, page 43), it can be seen that the United Kingdom and Germany have actually declined as trading partners with Venezuela; Spain accounts for only 3.2 percent of imports to Venezuela and only a minimal portion of its exports, while France and Italy cannot even be described as major partners at all. The Europeans concern themselves much more with their own task of integration and look to the East when they think about extending their economic ties. The United States is well aware of the weight it carries in the Venezuelan economy and the huge advantage it enjoys compared to European competitors, who are more removed geographically and culturally from much of Latin America. Miami merchants advertise their wares in local Venezuelan newspapers, while Europeans would not think of wasting their money in such a way.

The great question for Venezuela and its Latin American neighbors is not whether economic integration in the Americas makes sense, but rather how to go about making it possible. Subregional groups like Mercosur and the Andean Community play a central role in the first steps toward opening markets and may yet be the vehicles for permitting a more equal negotiating position for the region with the United States.

Economic Sovereignty and Foreign Relations

Since the late eighties, American attention has begun to focus on how to boost relations with Latin America and the Caribbean now that Cold War problems have receded. This new interest corresponds to a regional approach to globalization, incorporating both the promotion of democracy and economic integration as complementary goals.[11] In this way the United States proposes to exploit the congruence among the concepts of "good government," transparency, accountability, governability, free trade, economic and trade integration, and economic opening as tools of global cooperation with the region.

International Rules for Bilateral Relations

The United States, Latin America, and the Caribbean coincide in negotiating and assembling a common answer to globalization on these terms, understood as a process of political, economic, and technological transformation in international relations, based on the increasing homogenization of production and consumption.[12] Accordingly, as Elsa Cardozo claimed: "Integration, conceived in this way, is not then a mere succession of stages, it is a permanent negotiation process seeking to create the system (its principles, rules, agendas . . .) and to sustain it and adapt it to national, sub-regional, regional and global realities." [13]

The free circulation of goods and services, the elimination of tariff and non-tariff barriers, a common external tariff, a common trade policy, coordination of macroeconomic policies, and legislative harmonization are elements that condition the shaping of a new scheme of hemispheric negotiations permitting each country to conserve its negotiating power, to control the negative effects of globalization without negating its benefits, and to widen the possibility of obtaining a share of the North American market.[14]

Yet this common answer faced several hurdles from its inception. Jorge Castañeda, then a critical Mexican observer of the process of NAFTA, said: "On the one hand, as a matter of fact, the opening has given impulse to exports, has assisted in controlling inflation, has fostered the transfer of technology and has modernized the new production facilities. But it has also worsened unemployment, reversed a part of the previous industrialization process, and contributed to generating an important trade deficit, whose financing is increasingly difficult and expensive."[15] While other analysts would dispute Castañeda's judgment on the results of NAFTA for Mexico, his views reflected expectations in the rest of Latin America about the costs of integration with the NAFTA countries (including Mexico, which looks like an industrial powerhouse to some of its southern neighbors!). But Venezuela and its partners recognize another reality: the threat of international isolation, the obsolescence of their productive assets, the burden of foreign debt, and a regressive distribution of income that will be reversed only in the context of healthy economic growth.

When it comes to economic relations between the United States and Venezuela, the interplay of forces reflects the complexity that involves the countries themselves, the supranational rules of international organizations and NGOs, the interests of domestic actors, and the realities of markets for goods and services. While the United States pursues its own interests and seeks bilateral solutions on many questions of mutual interest, it increasingly looks to multilateral answers in areas where it does not make much sense to repeat the same treaty many times with many countries. This is particularly true in the economic arena, where the peak international organizations have gradually drawn up the rules of the game over many years.

The most important aspects of trade come under the WTO, after it took over the task from the General Agreements on Tariffs and Trade (GATT) in 1995; balance of payments and monetary issues are overseen by the IMF and the Bank for International Settlements; the UN organizations such as the United Nations Development Program (UNDP), the Food and Agriculture Organization, the United Nations Council on Trade and Development (UNCTAD), and others occupy themselves with a host of global issues. Other issues that are not explicitly economic carry economic consequences of importance, such as the agreement within the UN Environment Program to reduce the gases that cause global warning, signed in Rio de Janeiro in 1992. But bilateral relations hardly disappear even though international organizations have taken over many tasks. What is more, commitments to international agreements affect bilateral relations.

In some arenas, international organizations still do not exist to regulate global relations. This is the case, for instance, in the protection of international investments, where international standards conform to the general principle of international law that nations must compensate investors adequately and quickly for losses they may suffer as a result of nationalizations or expropriation of property. The United States aspires to a significantly higher standard of protection, however, and has signed over forty bilateral treaties for the mutual protection of investment; worldwide, over one thousand such treaties exist. Venezuela itself had signed ten treaties by 1998 and began negotiating one with the United States during the Caldera administration, without coming to an agreement.[16]

Negotiations on the Bilateral Investment Treaty with the United States illustrate well the common problems that come up in relations between the two countries. The United States, with so many treaties signed and with significant investment interests worldwide, judges that it cannot sign an agreement with one country that would affect its relations with the rest. Thus, when a country like Venezuela suggests a change in the text that would differentiate the treaty from others signed before, the United States protests that it cannot make exceptions. Venezuela objected that, as a sovereign nation, it could not simply be put in a category in such a way—its needs are different, its domestic rules require another formulation, and specific needs should be taken into consideration. It sent negotiators to Washington and received American officials in Caracas, only to find stone-faced bureaucrats who insisted they could not bend to Venezuela. All of this produced in the "negotiators" from Venezuela the sensation that there is no negotiation at all: either they accept the U.S. proposal or they must leave the game.

In the case of the investment treaty, the United States insisted on equal treatment for all companies, while Venezuela claimed that it was committed in the Andean Community to special rules for trans-Andean firms formed under a particular rule. The United States insisted that no special rules should be imposed on American investors in terms of how they should run their businesses; Venezuela answered that this prerogative was inherent in its own powers. The two countries haggled over these points for several years. Venezuela seemed to be ready to bend, particularly right before President Clinton's visit in October 1997, but did not sign at that time, nor before the termination of the Caldera administration at the beginning of 1999.

The government of President Hugo Chávez, whose overt nationalism would make him even more sensitive to issues of sovereignty and to slights by the United States before his electoral victory, initially showed itself equally resistant, without closing the door to future talks, however. In any case, unofficial criticism appeared frequently in the press, sometimes with strident claims about the dangerous effects of such a treaty, even in its aspects that simply repeat international norms for just and prompt compensation for nationalizations. But the consequences of not signing also count in Venezuela, where the need for foreign investment is widely recognized, and where business leaders stress the advantages of putting Venezuela on a level with other countries that welcome investors.

It was not initially clear whether Chávez would continue negotiations for the Bilateral Investment Treaty or not. It was, on the one hand, an opportunity for him to signal his good intentions at a time when confidence in his policy was low abroad, investment was falling, and the credit rating of the country was poor. But the same concern with possible limits on future economic policy had not disappeared. The most important government official critical of the treaty during the Caldera administration continued to wield influence under Chávez; indeed, his star had risen due to links with one of Chávez's closest collaborators. Facing the dilemma, Chávez chose a creative solution for the short term by getting the approval of a Venezuelan law for protecting investment that contained many of the points that the bilateral treaty would have included, with the exception of the issues over which Venezuela had balked.

The reality of asymmetrical power leads some to argue that the United States has the power to bend countries like Venezuela to its will in agreements that tend to favor the larger party. The United States responds that its requirements have a universal character. In fact, the general model it applies in its bilateral treaties for the protection of investment form the basis for a draft multilateral treaty called the Multilateral Agreement on Investment (MAI) under discussion in the Organization for Economic Cooperation and Development (OECD) that groups twenty-nine of the most wealthy developed countries. The MAI awakens fears in many countries that seek to maintain their own prerogatives in the treatment of foreign investors.[17] The United States, on the other hand, sees the MAI as a good way of reducing the need for difficult discussions on a country-by-country basis, thus avoiding pressures to differentiate its relations.

For Venezuela, treaties like the bilateral investment agreement run the risk of creating problems in the future, to the extent that they limit the options open to the country to revert to economic policies of a less liberal nature. Even for a government that has no immediate plans to implement such policies, it is daunting to declare, once and for all, that Venezuela will not impose restrictions on foreign investors of a type that were normal not so many years ago.[18] At the same time, Venezuela kept the door to negotiations open. For the United States, similar fears about the MAI in other countries make it less likely that it will be able to promote a multilateral solution, although it may have more success in convincing the developed countries to join it in such an effort.

With regard to trade, at first glance it would seem that the global rules belong exclusively to the supranational sphere, either in the WTO or the regional integration agreements. But even rules of international trade permit ample scope for bilateral relations. For instance, the rules of the WTO make exceptions for member countries when they are faced with difficulties from "dumping," that is to say, imports from countries that sell their goods at prices below cost. While it might not seem to make sense to sell at a loss, countries do so for various reasons: they may wish to use predatory pricing in order to bankrupt local competitors; they may wish to reduce excess inventories they have accumulated; or they may subsidize their own firms in order to maintain employment or satisfy political needs.

When Venezuela joined the GATT (later WTO) under the second government of Carlos Andrés Pérez, it agreed to these rules. Bilateral difficulties resulting from dumping have mainly come from United States actions against Venezuelan goods, resulting from the complaints by American firms before the Federal Trade Commission, the U.S. body charged with investigating dumping practices. Venezuela's economy, typical for oil countries, was long subsidized in a variety of ways through government efforts to diversify and strengthen industrialization. While economic reforms have removed many subsidies, particularly on energy, numerous complaints have been lodged against Venezuelan products such as steel and aluminum, which are energy-intensive. While the rules are universal, the effect on bilateral relations is direct, especially since the proximity of U.S. markets, as well as their depth, makes them natural for Venezuelan exporters.

Other problems have dogged Venezuela in trade relations with the United States, such as the tuna dispute and the conflict over Venezuelan exports of gasoline discussed in Chapter Five, resulting from environmental concerns. Globalization implies that all countries increasingly face the imposition of rules from outside their borders, be they the result of multilateral agreements or the national laws of partner countries. When the partner is a country as big and important for Venezuela as is the United States, there is a tendency to bitter feelings about the consequences. Dani Rodrik[19] sums up the sources of tension that come from the global market and that threaten social stability: 1) globalization affects different groups in an asymmetrical way such that some actors are free to move while others must absorb costs whether they like it or not; 2) globalization generates conflicts between domestic norms and the social institutions associated with them, when these differ from the external rule—that kind of conflict certainly exists in Venezuela, where many people feel that they are losing the right to have the kind of economic system they prefer; and 3) globalization imposes costs on governments that must provide social protection for groups that may have to adjust to the external market—and in Venezuela there are few social programs that truly cover the costs of unemployment or displacement that appear when market rules replace subsidies or expose formerly protected industries.

In sum, relations between the United States and Venezuela become ever more entwined by the spread of universal rules that would seem to restrict the sovereignty of smaller countries to a greater extent than they do for large nations. Venezuela seeks to participate in the world market—indeed, as an oil exporter, it has no choice but to do so—but it often chafes under the requisites of the complex of global institutions and rules. It pursues various strategies to diversify its relationships so as to counterbalance the natural dominance of the United States but recognizes that its chief trading partner, its chief investor, and largest neighbor will continue to play a large role in its international relations.

While government officials grudgingly accept the realities of the international system, voices on both sides of the Caribbean constantly remind citizens of the negative aspects of foreign relations, particularly in terms of their jobs and social institutions. A popular Uruguayan journalist, Eduardo Galeano, who publishes a column in the Venezuelan press, put it this way:

> Presidents no longer govern their countries: it is fear that is in charge. Countries tremble before the possibility that perhaps the money will not arrive, or that investors will flee. If they do not behave themselves, say the companies, we will leave for the Philippines or for Thailand or Indonesia or China or Mars. Bad behavior means collecting taxes from them, raising salaries in the country, organizing unions and protecting the natural environment, or what is left of it.

It is still to be seen if such opinions eventually move countries like Venezuela to reconsider their tepid enthusiasm for international rules that impose open markets and global agreements on their societies. In any case, tensions inevitably mark relations between two countries that have so much in common.

FOUR

THE DOMESTIC SOURCES OF FOREIGN POLICY

 N O ONE THEORY OF INTERNATIONAL RELATIONS PERMITS A full analysis of the myriad ways in which nations interact. Thus far, this book has adopted the "realist" approach to explaining the factors that have most influenced Venezuela and the United States in their relationship. Each country comes to the table with its history, its geographical forces, and its long-term interests and seeks to use its diplomatic, economic, and social connections with the rest of the world to benefit as much as possible its own national goals. The world balance of power may be taken as a starting position, and every country tries to act on it to tilt the results in its favor. Changes occur in the global scheme that impel reactions, and those nations with greater ability to influence outcomes enjoy an advantage over the others. Depending on their resources, both natural and man-made, the different states in the world system vie for benefits with greater and lesser success in different issue areas.

Now it is time to enrich our understanding of the relations between the United States and Venezuela by relaxing our assumptions and adding other elements. The realist approach serves to understand the broad sweep and direction of this relationship but faces some limitations when applied exclusively. The pluralist or "liberal" approach points to the need to look at the domestic factors that shape foreign policies. It suggests that a country is much more than just a unified state with a single vector of values that it seeks to maximize; competing interests, changing competencies within bureaucracies, economic dynamics, and internal power shifts imply that foreign policy results from an ever-changing constellation of forces. Not all governments share the same view of how best to pursue national interests, and at different times different interests may come to the fore. In this chapter, our lens will shift to the domestic factors that influence foreign policy in the United States and Venezuela in order to add a dimension that will extend our understanding of the forces that shape their relationship.

Institutions and Incentives: Who Moves Foreign Policy in Venezuela and the United States?

Any account of international relations would be incomplete without a view of the institutions that transmit the decisions made by those who carry out policy. We all know that no two institutions are alike, just as no two families are alike: each has its formal and informal ways of doing things that affect the behaviors of its members and the results of its actions. James Q. Wilson expresses this truth in his justly praised study, *Bureaucracy: What Government Agencies Do and Why They Do It*,[1] showing that "organization matters." Just a simple practice like letting lower-level officials make autonomous decisions and training them to do so can make or break an effort, as Wilson illustrates with the example of the success of the German army at the beginning of World War II, when it gained a clear advantage over what were, strictly speaking, superior forces. Douglass North insists on the vast influence of institutional factors not just on the quality of decision-making but on the long-run development of countries over time.[2]

Institutions for the making of foreign policy look rather similar on paper as we compare the United States and Venezuela. As in all countries, specific government departments or ministries take responsibility for international relations, and other parts of the government bureaucracy express sectoral interests that also form part of the country's international stance. The executive branch has special responsibility for representing the country abroad, and the legislative branch enjoys the power to approve international treaties and oversee the carrying out of its laws. Yet the forms and folkways of different governments can have important implications for the way foreign policy is carried out and sometimes can even contribute to misunderstandings between officials who fail to understand the perspectives of their counterparts. This is as true for Venezuela and the United States as it is for the rest of the world.

To understand why nations act as they do over long periods of time, the image of the state as a rational actor undoubtedly proves useful, but it may fall short when it comes to explaining the details and the vagaries of short-term events. We know that the United States seeks to promote a world in which it can do business in a certain way, in which democratic governments deal with each other with similar outlooks and in which the less developed areas of the globe have opportunities to grow and provide a decent life for their citizens. Venezuela shares these overall goals, with its special interest in ensuring markets for its chief export, oil, and in promoting the consolidation of a Latin American point of view with weight in the world.

Understanding the main purposes of nations helps predict their actions in general but often fails to provide full explanations for particular positions taken or for the specific ways that governments operate. Sometimes, policy even looks irrational in terms of overall objectives. Without a doubt, the perspectives of the individual actors that make up the state will color and shape policies on a day-to-day basis and even account for the changes that occur in time. The realities of bureaucracies, the people behind them, and the roles assumed by interest groups complete the picture of the process of policy-making in international relations.[3]

United States

The Constitution of the United States specifies simple rules for the making of foreign policy that belie the complexities of managing relationships with hundreds of countries and a host of international organizations in which the country participates as member. The president is commander in chief of the armed forces, signs treaties (as long as he has the support of two-thirds of the Senate), names ambassadors and consuls (again with the majority approval of the Senate), and manages the executive branch of government, including the State Department and other departments, bureaus, and offices that impinge on foreign policy. With so many tasks, both domestic and international, the president himself naturally delegates the great majority of foreign policy decisions to the relevant officials and generally devotes his attention only to the most important relationships and the crisis situations that threaten to affect U.S. interests significantly.

Asymmetries of Attention

Without a doubt, the challenge of foreign policy imposes a much greater responsibility on the president of the United States than it does on the presidents of most other countries, because of the great power status the United States attained in the twentieth century. For a great many countries, their single most important foreign relationship is with the United States. Their presidents focus attention on that relationship and give it top priority in their international strategies. Yet no one country merits such a status in American priorities, except when some crisis pushes it to the top of the agenda, not because its concerns are unimportant in themselves but because of the logic of the limited time and personal resources of the president. He must husband his time and energy, even at the cost of frustrating the many heads of state who seek his attention.

We have seen already the way in which multiple and simultaneous problems may divide a president's time, oftentimes forcing him to attend to foreign crisis while domestic crises divert his thoughts—(President Nixon faced the Watergate scandal at the same time that he had to handle war in the Middle East, attacks on the dollar, and the oil crisis of 1973 to 1974, not to speak of the normal tasks of government; President Clinton battled against his own personal scandals in the midst of serious problems in Russia and the Balkans. It should be no surprise that Latin America, where even the worst crises have little effect on the world balance of power, receives only passing attention from the president of the United States.

Necessarily, the great majority of exchanges within the Americas are carried out within the huge bureaucracy that is charged with the task. This is not to say that the presidency ignores Latin America entirely, and certainly the president keeps abreast of the important events that occur there, especially those that would affect democracy in the region or that relate to central U.S. economic interests. Most presidents plan a number of tours during their administrations in order to visit at least once the most important countries. Mexico receives more attention, of course, as a vital neighbor.

Personal contacts occur as Latin American presidents visit the United States, but perhaps the most frequent contact with the president comes about in the context of regional summit meetings or the yearly assemblies of the United Nations in New York, where short interviews are arranged with foreign leaders. With some effort, the president tries to establish a personal relationship with each, perhaps speaking by telephone to extend his congratulations on an electoral victory or to express his concern about events abroad. Presidents Kennedy, Carter, Bush, and Clinton visited Venezuela during their terms in office, although all of these visits were chiefly of symbolic value. Given these pressures, normal relationships with Venezuela tend to be managed by officials with specific responsibilities within the executive branch.

A president may play a greater role with respect to a given country should he have a personal reason to do so. One observation about American presidents is that few have ever shown a deep interest in Latin America. Most would hardly know much about Venezuela. President Kennedy had established a close relationship with Rómulo Betancourt when Venezuela struggled to institutionalize its democracy a the start of the 1960s and took the unprecedented action of extraditing former dictator Marcos Pérez Jiménez for judgment in Venezuela. President Nixon would surely remember his unfortunate moments in Caracas in 1958 as vice president under Eisenhower, when an angry mob stormed his car and threw rocks at him, luckily without doing him any physical harm. George W. Bush already knew something of Venezuela before his election in 2000 because of his visits there as a businessman.

On the whole, personal relationships between the presidents of Venezuela and the United States have been limited, mostly because of the low level of interest and knowledge on the American side and the press of larger strategic issues on an overcharged presidency. There is some sign, however, that the realignment of forces accompanying the end of the Cold War might lead to an assignment of more strategic importance for Latin America in general, as the United States perceives the convenience of consolidating its position in parallel to the strengthening and widening of the European Community as well as the reassertion of China in the Far East.

At the time of the presidential election campaign in 2000, candidates Albert Gore and George W. Bush both openly courted the growing Latino vote in the

United States and were pressed by journalists for their opinions on subjects such as more open relations with Cuba, free trade arrangements with Mexico, the drug and guerrilla war in Colombia, and the impartiality of presidential elections in Peru. While Venezuela was not a primary concern within the U.S. political scheme, certainly Latin America was coming more to the fore than was traditional. In the meantime, however, most Latin American issues remained in the sphere of the specialists.

The Foreign Affairs Bureaucracy

The Department of State, often called "Foggy Bottom" after the area of Washington, D.C., where its headquarters are located, is the executive department charged with the management of U.S. foreign policy. It is a vast organization with wide responsibilities, some 22,000 employees, and almost 250 offices in 162 countries. In such a huge bureaucracy, it might be difficult to locate just where policy toward Venezuela gets carried out. The secretary of state and his office, including the deputy secretary of state and associated staff, oversee several specialized agencies—Arms Control and Disarmament, the Agency for International Development (AID), and the United States Information Service (USIS)—multiple administrative staff, as well as five undersecretariats for political affairs, economic and agricultural affairs, management, and global affairs. This last undersecretariat is the newest, having been created by President Clinton at the start of his administration in response to the increasing load of the agenda for global issues such as human rights, drugs, environment, and migration.

While all of the offices of the Department of State may come into contact with Venezuela on a variety of issues, it is the undersecretary for political affairs who organizes country relations through a series of assistant secretaries charged with supervising relationships according to geographical area. Thus the assistant secretary of state for inter-American affairs oversees the Western Hemisphere (although Canada, for historical and cultural reasons, continues to fall under the eye of the assistant secretary for European and Canadian affairs). Within the inter-American secretariat, desk officers keep track of individual countries.

Of course, the ambassadors of the United States play a key role as heads of mission in the countries where the United States maintains embassies. The embassy is a small department of state, with offices that coordinate with other undersecretaries in economic affairs as well as with other executive departments of the government. The U.S. embassy in Caracas is an imposing structure in the south of the city, constructed, like most embassies, as a sort of safe fortress. In fact, some attacks on American embassies led during the 1990s to the rebuilding and relocation of older embassies, such as the original embassy in Caracas, which used to be located centrally in a busy commercial district.

Given the complexity of international relations today, the State Department exists in a kind of matrix, coordinating the diverse interests of other government executive departments, from Agriculture to the Pentagon. These departments may locate their own personnel abroad, within the structure of the U.S. missions in each country. Needless to say, such crosscutting interests require a great effort at coordination, and more than one ambassador will complain about the mixed signals that sometimes get sent from different parts of the U.S. government, which attempts to communicate a single line of policy that may get blurred when information flows in so many directions. Ambassadors are known to wince when visitors from other departments come to visit, since they may fear that carefully communicated policies could appear to clash with the declarations of their "guests," who may even feel that they represent more truly the position of the president or of the country.

Within the State Department, an important coordinating function falls under the responsibility of the Bureau of Economic Affairs, in charge of general issues of interest to the United States as they are managed in relation to different countries. Officials from this Bureau, for instance, would follow negotiations with Venezuela over the Bilateral Investment Treaty under consideration by both countries, keeping in close contact with the economic and commercial attachés based at the embassy in Caracas. Likewise, the United States Information Service coordinates with the cultural and press attachés, while the political officers maintain close contact and supply constant information to the Venezuela desk in Washington. While the flow of information assures that few details are missed, the work of Foreign Service officers and their ambassadors is not without its problems. Most personnel rotate every three years, so that a constant learning process must go on: new officers must absorb huge amounts of information, get to know the actors on the local stage, and quickly get to understand the dynamics of politics.

While ambassadors in former eras truly made foreign policy on the spot, modern diplomacy with instantaneous communications is a much more bureaucratic activity than it was in the past. No less important in this process is the trend toward the substitution of bilateral relations by multilateral rules, as discussed in Chapter Three. Strobe Talbott, former deputy assistant secretary of state, expressed the changes in this way:

> Meanwhile, our diplomats abroad, while still giving priority to U.S. relations with individual host governments, are nurturing regional and transregional relationships to a greater extent than before. Globalization has also increased the need for other departments and agencies of the U.S. government to play an active role in pursuit of American interests abroad—and for the State Department to cooperate more systematically with them."[4]

Surely the U.S. ambassadors who served in Venezuela during the 1990s, Michael Skol (1990–1993), Jeffrey Davidow (1993–1996), and John Maisto (1997–2000), would agree with Talbott's words, but they might differ about what this meant for them in their daily tasks. American ambassadors in Venezuela carry considerable weight; their every word is followed by the press; their movements are traced by the host government. Any misstep immediately gets a strong response, and any veiled threat is taken seriously. The weight of the United States in the hemisphere, and in Venezuela in particular, makes personal relationships matter.

The era of globalization does not quite mean the end of personal diplomacy nor negate the influence of the wide contacts that ambassadors and their reporting officers develop. No one would doubt the important role that Michael Skol played during the political crises in Venezuela in 1992 and 1993, when the United States wanted to send strong but friendly signals about the preservation of democracy. The imposing figure of Davidow during the harsh economic times of the mid-1990s was balanced by his warm personality and famous love of Venezuelan food. Likewise, his successor, John Maisto, faced delicate issues during the ascendance of Hugo Chávez to the presidency, when his calm demeanor and precise choice of words served to preserve diplomatic calm at stressful moments.

Ambassador Maisto's parting advice to his successor, Ambassador Donna Hrinak, was that above all that she "maintain a good sense of humor." Wise words for an ambassador in a country where things were changing at a rapid pace. In recent years, a posting to Venezuela became a good stepping stone to promotion for ambassadors to Venezuela, perhaps due to the higher profile of U.S.-Venezuelan relations. Ambassador Maisto would be named to President George W. Bush's National Security staff, and Otto Reich, an ambassador to Venezuela in the 1980s, was a candidate for assistant secretary of state for Latin American Affairs, although with opposition from the Democratic majority in the Senate.

Beyond the State Department

Despite its primary role in directing the foreign relations of the United States, the Department of State has increasingly found itself working in parallel—and not always in agreement—with other parts of the government. The State Department manages the overall relationship, but other bureaucracies make policy in concrete areas, often in the context of general objectives that go beyond bilateral issues. The Treasury Department, for instance, exercises broad oversight in international financial affairs with a view to ensuring systemic stability. Two areas are of particular importance: monetary policy and international debt. The Treasury does not tend to intervene directly in the monetary policies of countries like Venezuela, although it may bring its point of view to bear through the influence of the American director of the IMF should Venezuela enter into negotiations with that international institution. Thus the United States expresses its approval or disapproval of a country's policy, as when Venezuela imposed exchange controls from

1983 until the beginning of 1989, and in the period between 1994 and 1996. The United States opposes exchange controls that limit the free flow of capital or the repatriation of dividends by multinational corporations.

Treasury also concerns itself with the stability of the international financial system, monitoring events that might cause uncontrollable capital flows, devaluations that might result in chain reactions throughout the world, or banking crises that could lead to contagion. In these areas, it works together with the Federal Reserve Board, particularly the Federal Reserve Bank of New York, which is charged especially with responsibility for international financial relations. Both treasury secretaries James Baker and Nicholas Brady intervened directly in the 1980s and 1990s to avoid the deepening of the crisis suffered by many Latin American countries with respect to their foreign debt.

Venezuela was no exception during the period of crisis in Latin America, having run up a considerable liability with foreign commercial banks that had overlent in the region. To avoid massive defaults that would have endangered the solvency of many U.S. banks, first Baker and then Brady devised strategies that would permit a change in the terms of the debt and ensure the solvency of the countries and the banks. Under the Brady Plan, which was negotiated with Venezuela in 1989 to 1990, a restructuring of Venezuela's foreign official debt was achieved though guarantees provided by special U.S. government bonds, called "Brady Bonds," sold to the Venezuelan government. The important fact underlying this negotiation is that the Venezuelan plan was part of a larger operation that included other countries in similar situations during the period.

The Federal Reserve Board coordinates its management of monetary policy with the Department of the Treasury, recognizing that U.S. monetary policy generates monetary effects in the rest of the world. It is now widely recognized that higher interest rates in the United States contributed to the capital flight that would lead to the devaluation of the Mexican peso and to pressures on other currencies, including the Venezuelan bolivar, in 1994 to 1995. In 1994, President Caldera devalued the bolivar and sought relief from the pressures through the imposition of exchange controls, whereas Mexico addressed its problems with a huge loan from the Stabilization Fund managed by the Treasury and the Federal Reserve.[5]

The peculiar interdependence of international financial markets has led to recommendations that the United States adopt a less negative attitude toward some limits on very short-term or speculative capital movements precisely to limit the effects of large swings resulting from interest rate differentials, although such controls have been used in some countries, such as Chile, without generating much criticism. This issue once again opened discussions within the United States after the devaluation of Thailand's currency in 1997, which produced a domino effect in Asia and a threat to currencies in Latin America,[6] as well as a steep decline in oil prices in 1998 that would affect Venezuela profoundly. The secretary of the treasury must respond to all of these outbreaks of instability.

In 1998 at the annual meeting of the IMF, both Treasury Secretary Robert Rubin and IMF Director Michel Camdessus were besieged with questions about the effect of the Asian crisis on Latin America and on Venezuela in particular, due to its vulnerability in the oil market and the uncertainty surrounding its presidential election. The Federal Reserve, meanwhile, has to respond to banking and exchange policies made in Latin American countries, where what happens in one country, be it a run on the banks or a decision to adopt the dollar as the local currency, for instance, inevitably implies problems of joint policy coordination and supervision. The Federal Reserve Bank of Atlanta has specialized in the area of banking supervision in Latin America.

The role of American monetary authorities came into play during the serious banking crisis confronted by Venezuela in 1994, when one-quarter of the banks failed.[7] Some of these banks had offshore operations in the United States, and American authorities moved swiftly to avoid spillovers. The biggest problem turned out to involve the bankers themselves, many of whom fled to the United States to avoid prosecution at home. The Venezuelan government insisted on the need to reach an agreement between the two countries in order to extradite the so-called fugitive bankers living in the United States, but in the end Venezuela failed to mount successful appeals for extradition in the United States. The only banker successfully prosecuted was Orlando Castro, the former owner of the Latinoamericana-Progreso financial group, who was tried along with his son in a New York court for abuses at the Puerto Rico bank where his group owned a subsidiary bank. Castro later returned to Venezuela, where he could at least enjoy the benefit of at home detention until his release, which is the right of prisoners over sixty-five years of age in Venezuela.

At one time or another, many agencies of the U.S. government get involved with issues touching on U.S.-Venezuelan relations. The Department of Commerce manages international trade at the operational level, although the U.S. special trade representative (USTR), a cabinet-level post, is responsible for the negotiation of international trade agreements and for representing the United States in international organizations. The Commerce Department's International Trade Administration investigates violations of international trade law, an area that has involved Venezuela on various occasions with regard to charges that Venezuelan exporters have engaged in unfair trade practices.

The Department of Energy, its attention always focused on supply conditions and OPEC policies, naturally takes an interest in foreign policy issues involving Venezuela, given the importance of Venezuela as a source of imported oil to the United States. Politics and economics tend to merge, as was clear, for instance, when Energy Secretary Bill Richardson, a close collaborator of President Clinton, visited Venezuela in 1999 at a time of considerable political uncertainty when deliberations were in progress on a new Venezuelan Constitution that would determine how open the country would be in the future to private investment in the industry. Departmental interests also cross, as when Venezuela's (and other OPEC members') oil exports to the United States were threatened by a complaint made to the Commerce Department against OPEC suppliers and in favor of domestic sources of oil, in particular small operators in danger of bankruptcy during the period of low oil prices in 1998. The case inevitably interested Secretary Richardson, who applauded Commerce's decision against the complaint, saying: "The denial is a win-win for U.S. consumers and domestic oil producers. . . . It also protects our strategic relationships with Mexico, Saudi Arabia and Venezuela."

The bureaucracy executes foreign policy, but not in a vacuum. There are actors outside the government who are implicit partners in U.S. foreign policy. Oil is perhaps the best example of the interplay between government and nongovernment players. It is always assumed that a government defends "the national interest" and that this interest is somehow above the particular interests of pressure groups, corporations, or individuals. Yet the nation is also the sum of its groups, even if it might have been an exaggeration to say: "What's good for General Motors is good for the country." Certainly, the U.S. government identifies the health and international competitiveness of American firms as a crucial base for the strength of the American economy and thus uses government influence to ensure their position in international markets. It is a delicate task to promote the interests of U.S. business abroad without intervening in the affairs of other countries. Unhappy experience shows that in the past business and government have sometimes gone beyond the bounds of good behavior. In Latin America, memories are still fresh of the role of American companies and U.S. agencies in contributing to the failure and downfall of the government of Salvador Allende in Chile at the beginning of the 1970s. This experience led to calls for codes of good conduct for multinational enterprises.

Both government and corporations must act in concert but also avoid the risk of being seen as unduly involved in influencing the policy process abroad. In the case of oil, for instance, international oil companies certainly prefer policies in Venezuela that permit them to invest in the industry, and there is little doubt that they looked for ways to encourage Venezuela to reverse the prohibition against foreign investment that resulted from the nationalization of 1976. Much of the diplomatic action associated with this kind of initiative is slow and subtle and involves creating lines of communication among the private companies, PDVSA, and government actors on all sides. Common interests with firms from other countries also generate informal coordination among them. The terms of the oil opening of the 1990s were negotiated informally and in contact with foreign oil companies in Venezuela, who maintained a low-profile committee of firms from many countries whose main purpose was to share information and communicate opinions about the proposal to be made by the Venezuelan government. The U.S. government, along with other governments with similar interests, would keep informed of events through its own informal contacts with the companies.

No account of the involvement of American government departments and agencies would be complete without mention of security relations, which go beyond the Pentagon to include the National Security Council, the Office of National Drug Control Policy, and other institutions that advise the presidency on issues ranging from technology transfers to development policy. We have already seen how the collaboration among the armed forces of Latin America occurs within the framework of the OAS and the Rio Pact for training and coordination. Courses in the United States form a normal part of the education of higher Venezuelan officers. The U.S. armed forces are organized regionally, and it is the Southern Command, based in Miami, that deals with Latin America. The line between military and diplomatic relations sometimes blurs; no doubt visits to Venezuela by high-ranking officers are taken seriously. Similar to this, relations with the director of the Office of National Drug Control Policy, who reports to the president, also represent high politics between Venezuela and the United States. American antidrug policies imply many different ways in which the two countries carry out their foreign policies. Chapter Five reviews some aspects of the complex issues that derive from them.

The Legislators

The executive forms only one part of the government, and its power derives from the policies fixed by law. Since the U.S. Congress approves the laws, of course, the legislative branch plays a significant role in foreign policy. Its members are free to roam the world to observe how foreign policy is being carried out and to see for themselves what new policies are needed or what policies should be revised. Congress must approve ambassadorships and often holds up appointments, even for reasons that have nothing to do with the country to which an ambassador is to be named. Since Congress constitutes a varied group of individual representatives and senators who in turn represent the states of the Union with their diverse local interests, Congress may play an important role on very specific matters of policy. One congresswoman may devote herself to a personal crusade against the drug traffic, while a colleague concerns himself with helping out a constituent threatened by competing exports. It was said, for instance, that an influential company based in Maryland was able to apply pressure in Congress for rules that would have significantly reduced Venezuelan exports of gasoline to the United States.

Generally speaking, questions affecting Venezuela have not aroused a high level of interest in the U.S. Congress. Most mentions of Venezuela in congressional hearings fall within discussions of general hemispheric matters or refer to OPEC policies. An attempt was made by political and business representatives to create a special interest group or caucus on Venezuela within the U.S. Congress, and it finally became a reality in March of 2000 at a time of significant tensions between the two countries.

Legislative attention rises when possible instability threatens complacency. Such was the case when Venezuela underwent radical domestic political changes in the wake of the weakening and eventual impeachment of President Carlos Andrés Pérez in 1993, although even then it was the executive that managed the transition; several members of Congress visited Venezuela during the first year of the Chávez administration in 1999 to monitor the situation at first hand. One congressman who showed special interest was Representative Cass Ballenger, a personal friend of Ambassador John Maisto and member of the House Committee on International Relations. A Republican, he was accompanied by Democratic Representative Bill Delahunt of Massachusetts, who voiced a notably tolerant attitude toward the changes being carried out by President Chávez and who was known in general for his willingness to listen to even radical voices in Latin America, as evidenced by an interview to review the peace process in Colombia together with guerrilla leaders of the FARC[8] in June of 1999. These two members of Congress took the lead in finally forming the legislative group on Venezuela, which became the third such Latin American caucus after those on Mexico and Brazil. Ballenger would even invite President Chávez for a personal visit to his farm in North Carolina after the Quebec summit in April 2001 perhaps as a way of reducing the Venezuelan chief of state's distrust of the United States.

The Senate wields more power over relations with Venezuela than does the House of Representatives, since it must approve all treaties proposed with foreign countries. Senator Jesse Helms, veteran chairman of the Senate Foreign Relations Committee, long exercised extraordinary influence over the Senate decisions, based on his control of the agenda, although the Democrats would regain control of the Senate in 2001. Senator Helms, a conservative, made his weight felt on issues concerning Cuba and sponsored the Helms-Burton Law that aroused resistance in many countries, including Venezuela, on the grounds that this U.S. law infringed on acceptable international practices by imposing extraterritorial rules. Helms has never shown much interest in Venezuela, however, and when the treaty with Venezuela on double taxation came before his committee in 1999 it did not encounter problems, except with regard to technical issues that were quickly resolved. Helms did send staff members to Venezuela in 2001, however, to investigate press reports about threats to democracy under Chávez.

Many other American government bodies play a role in relations with Venezuela from time to time. State governments, city governments, the courts— there are examples of contacts at every level. While the president makes foreign policy, under the control of the Congress, no one doubts that in today's interconnected world, foreign policy can no longer be conceived as just high-level diplomatic activity. As we shall see in the next chapter, a decision by the governor of Florida can have as much importance as many decisions in Washington.

Chapter Six goes beyond government relationships to analyze how nongovernmental organizations (NGOs) create their own set of "foreign relations."

The rising importance of NGOs in recent years should not reduce our attention to the premier transnational organizations—multinational enterprises whose interests span the entire globe. This is not to say that Venezuela cannot touch the chords of any institution in the United States, including those of NGOs and firms, in its complex dealing with the United States. Without a doubt, foreign policy tends to be ever more decentralized in today's world. In the case of relations with Venezuela, however, the Department of State still plays a central role in coordinating the actions of the rest of the government, in part because of the relatively low level of interest throughout the rest of the bureaucracy.

Venezuela

Many of the same problems faced by the United States in trying to coordinate an ever more complex foreign policy also confront Venezuela, because no country can escape from the fact that traditional foreign ministries cannot deal with the diverse technical issues that belong properly to a wide range of ministries or government departments. But it is perhaps in institutional comparisons that the asymmetry of power comes most clearly to light. A small country of 23 million inhabitants, with a per capita income some one-tenth the level of that of the United States, simply does not have the resources at its command to carry out a foreign policy of the same level of technical competence or completeness. Where the U.S. government publishes multiple documents on the Internet and can train a large contingent of professionals for its foreign service and other government departments, Venezuela suffers the inevitable disadvantages of underdevelopment. This realization sometimes leads Venezuelans to adopt defensive attitudes in their contacts with American officials, on the grounds that they might be less informed, although perhaps the gap is exaggerated.

High Salience and Limited Resources

Given the importance of the relationship with the United States, Venezuelan officials can concentrate their attention and be sure of high-level support. It is the president who controls the relationship with the United States and determines the role of the diplomats. The Venezuelan ambassador in Washington will always have the ear of his president; such is not the case of the U.S. ambassador in Caracas, who must go through channels and who must sometimes feel somewhat ignored. Even so, personal relationships still determine the relative influence of different actors. Observers of the Washington scene noted in 1999, for instance, that the Venezuelan ambassador to Washington, Alfredo Toro Hardy, sometimes seemed to have less influence in Caracas than the ambassador to the OAS, Virginia Contreras, who had been a lawyer to President Chávez during his imprisonment and who initially enjoyed a more direct relationship with the president than Toro Hardy. On the other hand, Contreras's lack of experience would later lead to her removal,[9] thus giving support to the idea that professionalism has its merits in international relations. Toro Hardy would be transferred to London in 2001, and his replacement, Ambassador Ignacio Arcaya, was seen as someone closer to President Chávez.

The difference in bureaucratic capabilities between large and small countries may become more important at times of crisis or on questions of technical difficulty, when information must be mobilized quickly and efficiently by a well-functioning administration. Here countries like Venezuela will tend to find themselves less prepared. The Foreign Ministry must simply depend on others to do their work well and hope for the best. An example of this sort of problem occurred in a much-commented-upon trip by President Chávez to the United States in June of 1999. On that occasion, the president played his role well in a general speech before an audience of bankers and nonfinancial company representatives in New York. Yet when his economic ministers had to follow up with more specific presentations on the government's economic plans, the results were negative. Not only were the presentations poor, but the panel of government representatives chose to end the meeting early, something that the diplomats might not have done if they had had any power over the event. But they were stretched too thin and in any case did not have influence over that aspect of government policy. In an age when economic problems dominate in bilateral relations, the Foreign Ministry is not prepared to deal with technical issues.

Efforts have been made to improve the foreign ministry and increase its coordinating ability. Career diplomats in Venezuela traditionally graduated as experts in international relations from the Central University, while the Foreign Ministry runs its own diplomatic academy, the Pedro Gual Institute. In particular, training was increasingly being given in economic areas and also in negotiating skills, and the view that only a degree in international relations was suitable for the foreign service lost ground. In 2001, the law was changed to open career diplomatic jobs to qualified people of different professions, although the Central University professors would likely seek to restore their influence.

With good coordination, of course, experts from other parts of government are available to deal with specific issues. The smallness of Venezuelan government means that personal relationships allow the sort of cross-ministry communication that can make up for the lack of a full specialized staff at the Foreign Ministry. And where oil is the main issue, PDVSA often provides the expertise that is central, since it is a large and cosmopolitan company considered as an equal among the multinational oil firms. In fact, the oil industry gained so much influence from its powerful organization that, on assuming the presidency at the start of 1999, President Chávez moved to cut back its prominence and to restore the supposedly lost authority of the Energy Ministry in policy-making, both national and international.

At least since 1958, Venezuela's foreign policy has based itself on two main pillars: oil and democracy. Venezuelan diplomacy was characterized as an active policy with a high degree of political consensus under the control of the presidency and the Ministry of Foreign Affairs, and with a special role assigned in practice to the Ministry of Energy on oil matters and relations with OPEC.

Bureaucratic Complexity

Formally, the responsibility for foreign policy in Venezuela is much the same as that of the United States: the president directs foreign policy, and the legislature, or National Assembly, approves treaties. In Venezuela, the president plays a central role, determining the extent to which he delegates authority to other officials. As in most modern countries, foreign relations extend beyond the confines of the Casa Amarilla, the elegant yellow building that is the Foreign Ministry. This created no problems as long as the government team had one mind about the making of international policy. Indeed, during the 1970s, President Pérez named an extra "Minister of State" for International Economic Affairs, who served as a roving ambassador for promoting the New International Economic Order. Even in those days of relative consensus, the Foreign Ministry began to perceive that its functions were increasingly being carried out by different actors within the government and that it was more difficult to maintain a single line of policy. Conflicts of various types could break out. President Pérez took the undiplomatic step of replacing one foreign minister, Ramón Escovar Salóm, while he was on mission in Poland.[10]

The technical aspects of foreign policy have tended to disperse leadership even more as trade issues grew in importance, leading the Development Ministry (since 1999 called the Ministry of Production and Commerce) to assume greater responsibilities. Certainly, at the start of the 1990s, the political weight of the development ministers, Moisés Naím and his successor, Imelda Cisneros, as well as their expertise in trade matters, further shifted the locus of foreign economic policy execution away from the Foreign Ministry, which argued that such dispersion would tend to reduce the required coordination. Naím and Cisneros planned the reorganization of the Development Ministry, its transformation into a sleeker and more efficient organization, and the transfer of the Institute for Foreign Commerce from the Ministry of Foreign Affairs. The institute would be converted into the Bank for Foreign Trade.

The reorganization plan was finally carried out, after some resistance from the Foreign Affairs Ministry, in 1996, when President Caldera named an active businessman, Freddy Rojas Parra, to the Development Ministry (called the Ministry of Industry and Trade between 1996 and 1999, and later, Ministry of Production and Commerce) and decided, somewhat against his will, to renew the outward-looking policies that he had so criticized in his predecessor. The newly organized ministry began to take its role even more seriously than was expected under

Rojas Parra. To promote foreign trade, it developed plans to set up trade representative offices abroad, for instance. But such plans were put off in 1999 with the inception of the cost-conscious government of Hugo Chávez, whose strong foreign minister, José Vicente Rangel, worked toward the rationalization and greater centralization of foreign policy. The Development Ministry underwent another transformation when it was merged and converted into the new Ministry of Production and Commerce, without, however, losing its responsibility for foreign trade matters. When the economy improved somewhat, plans for international projection appeared again on the front burner. Chávez would expand the vision for trade relations with agreements with far-off countries such as China.

The armed forces exert influence over foreign policy, even though both the constitutions of 1961 and 1999 assigned them an apolitical role.[11] The minister of defense sits in the Cabinet, however, and was always a general or admiral during the democratic period, at least until President Chávez broke the mold by moving his foreign minister, José Vicente Rangel, over to the Defense Ministry in early 2001. The military's role traditionally meant that the leaders of the armed forces could at least impose a virtual veto over foreign policy decisions of which it disapproved, even if its opposition would take the discreet form of private warnings.[12] No president dared to open up the negotiations with neighboring Colombia or Guyana over long-standing border disputes, because the military (and others) would never consider ceding an inch. Even less possible was the option of taking the disputes to international tribunals or arbitration, since it is the firm conviction that Venezuela could lose and that international courts have never favored its causes.

The official role of the military tended always to be subordinate, respecting civilian supremacy according to the law. On the other hand, as we have seen in Chapter Two, the widening of the concept of national security would contribute to the armed forces' belief that, as guardians of security, they should play a more important part in both domestic and international politics.

The Widening Role of the Armed Forces

President Chávez explicitly promoted greater integration between military and other national objectives. High military officials could increasingly be found in key posts in his government, and many observers noted, for instance, the influence of military personnel in the Venezuelan embassy in Washington. Later ministerial changes would bring a retired colonel to the top position in the Foreign Ministry in 2001, along with other military personnel who would displace (and irritate) the career diplomats.

The military point of view might be expected to privilege more rigid positions on a wide range of issues and be highly sensitive to any appearance of U.S. meddling in Venezuela according to stereotypes. In response to a request by the United States to allow U.S. overflights of Venezuela from nearby bases in the Caribbean to monitor possible drug trafficking, the Chávez government (like that of Caldera before) insisted that the Venezuelan armed forces were quite capable of monitoring the skies without outside assistance. Venezuela viewed with distrust the fact that the United States was setting up facilities in nearby Aruba and Curaçao to replace the bases it was closing after the return of the Panama Canal Zone. Foreign Minister José Vicente Rangel—the very minister who would later find himself in the chair of the minister of defense—repeatedly gave the same negative answer to successive envoys from the United States, and, ostensibly, the then-minister of defense shared this position.

Rumors emerged after a visit by the State Department official Thomas Pickering to Caracas in February 2000 that Venezuela was softening its stance and would permit overflights with the accompaniment of Venezuelan planes. Rangel, in Spain at the time, denied that this was the case and was annoyed that an issue that they had agreed not to publicize had surfaced again. It seemed that different agencies within the Venezuelan government were negotiating among themselves as much as with the United States: the Defense Ministry, the various armed forces, the Anti-Drug Commission, the Foreign Ministry, and the president himself, just to name the frontline players.

In the same vein of looking for alternatives to U.S. leadership, President Chávez even suggested the idea of a coordinated military command in Latin American during a June 1999 summit in Rio de Janeiro, independent of the existing arrangements for hemispheric military coordination under the Rio Pact. It should not be assumed, however, that the impulse for such seemingly anti-U.S. initiatives necessarily comes from the armed forces. Professional contacts with military colleagues in the United States also engender confidence. When then–Defense Minister Raúl Salazar solicited the help of the U.S. Army Corps of Engineers in cleaning up after the torrential rains that destroyed much of the infrastructure of the north central coast of Venezuela at the end of 1999, it was Foreign Minister Rangel who announced that such aid would not be needed, even though troops were already on the way and were forced to turn back despite the planning and expenditure involved (just as it was the foreign minister who took a hard line on the overflight issue). Increasingly, it appeared that it was the Foreign Ministry, perhaps more than the Defense Ministry, that looked for ways to distance Venezuela from the United States. Minister Salazar soon left the government after the dispute over American military aid. In 2001, Rangel would himself be named minister of defense, to the apparent dismay of at least some high military officers.

Defense Minister Salazar accepted an ambassadorial post in Spain after his falling out with the president. In Venezuela (and elsewhere), it is not unusual that troublesome politicians or out-of-work generals be awarded comfortable ambassadorships. This time, however, it looked as if the armed forces might be more divided than it appeared over Chávez's foreign policy toward the United States.

Just weeks after General Salazar's exit from the Cabinet, another conflict between military and civilian elements within the government came to the fore, in which additional resignations of high officials with military backgrounds were announced. This group, called the "comandantes" since they had formed the original group that carried out the coup attempt together with Chávez in 1992, expressed its opposition to the powerful "civilians" in the government, explicitly questioning the influence of Foreign Minister Rangel. The most prominent among them, Governor Francisco Arias Cárdenas, a partner in the coup attempt of 1992 with Chávez, criticized the policy of confrontation with the United States associated with Rangel and soon declared that he would run for president against his former comrade.[13]

Like any institution, the armed forces in Venezuela include people with varied perspectives; some might share the American desire to defeat Colombian guerrilla forces by military means or to attack drug traffic in a combined effort, while others distrust such operations on the grounds that they would compromise national autonomy. By the end of 1999, it appeared that relations between the United States and Venezuela had also come to generate differences of opinion within the Venezuelan armed forces, which historically had never suffered divisions on this score. Other rumored divergences emerged later on, although the public stance of the military remained firmly loyal to the government. Thus when Rangel was installed as defense minister in 2001, the move was interpreted as something more than just a symbolic message that civilians were in control. Ironically, however, Rangel was replaced at the Ministry of Foreign Affairs by an active general who would increase the weight of the military in that ministry. Without a doubt, the influences on the making of foreign policy can be contradictory, even within the same branch of government.

Other Actors

Despite the influence of the military on certain foreign policy issues and the trend toward the sharing of foreign policy with the Energy Ministry and the economics ministries, other executive agencies of the Venezuelan government and even the legislature have had only a small role in influencing the international relations of Venezuela. There is no powerful Foreign Relations Committee or influential member of the legislature to block the executive, although a president without a sure majority there will have to hammer out compromises to get the majorities he needs to approve treaties or name ambassadors. On one issue, border delimitation, the executive traditionally suffers from a lack of independence. Disputed borders with Colombia and Guyana simply remain in dispute. A combination of legislative and military opposition to any cession of territory has led every president to back off from prospective settlements. The legislature can use its investigative powers to expose scandals or question initiatives, but excessive intervention in the delicate task of making foreign policy would probably boomerang. On matters of a less sensitive nature, such as authorizations for foreign debt operations, the National Assembly (the unicameral body that replaced the Congress under the Constitution of 1999) may make its influence felt, but even here, the government gets its way. The president is in charge, and it is up to him to keep his ministers in line. The National Assembly must ratify international treaties, of course, but recognizes the primacy of the executive.

In the economic sphere, the technical nature of relations favors the greater role of the Energy Ministry in oil policy. In exchange rate policy and international financial relations, the Central Bank and the Finance Ministry, and sometimes the Planning Ministry, also play an important part for the same reason. In oil policy, tension tends to arise naturally between the Energy Ministry and PDVSA. PDVSA reports to the ministry but has the advantage of greater knowledge of the industry, more detailed information, and greater financial and human resources inherent in the size of the company. Energy ministers repeatedly find themselves at loggerheads with the president of PDVSA, a company that prides itself on operating like a multinational enterprise as opposed to a state-owned company.

PDVSA was designed at its creation to be politically neutral, but over time it gained considerable influence in setting national policy within OPEC. Conflict inevitably arose as the character of the company seemed to become more political to the extent that it would battle to push its own views, sometimes against the position favored by the ministry. The fact that PDVSA came to own a large number of companies outside Venezuela gave it a different perspective; turning itself into a large, integrated company with worldwide connections made business sense but also augmented the possibility of independent action. Who would make policy became a function of the coalitions within the government and, most importantly, of whether the president favored the minister or the company president. Under President Caldera, PDVSA seemed to call the shots; the design of the long-term plan for expanding domestic production was drawn up in the company, not in the ministry. One of President Chávez's announced aims was to bring oil policy back into the government and reduce the autonomy of the firm's executives, but the concentration of resources in PDVSA would continue to be a fact of life.

In international monetary and financial matters, the relative influence of different actors depends again on the particular power of different ministries and the trust that the president gives to each. The Finance Ministry is the natural leader and, despite the nominal independence of the Central Bank,[14] important matters such as the exchange rate system or debt negotiations are led by the finance minister, with the Central Bank generally playing a supporting role on technical matters. The Central Bank does concentrate more technical expertise, because it is one of the few institutions in the Venezuelan system that has developed a permanent staff of well-trained experts. From time to time, the planning minister assumes greater responsibility, a situation that depends on the authority or influence granted to him by the president. Thus, in the end, the president's power determines who makes policy, although the president himself generally does not intervene in the detailed process of policy. Neustadt[15] defined presidential power as the power to persuade. In this case, his power derives from being persuaded by his competing ministers, although in the end it is the president who determines the result.

Different groups within Venezuelan society represent the conflicting government views of the external world and, in particular, of the proper relationship with the United States. Most political parties, including the formerly dominant AD and COPEI parties, have traditionally adopted the standard view that good relations with the United States were of high importance but that Venezuela should always insist on its own sovereignty in order to maintain its negotiating position before such a powerful country. Both presidents Pérez (AD) and Caldera (COPEI) in their first governments sought to emphasize their independence from any U. S.-led bloc. Farther to the left, smaller parties like the Movement Toward Socialism (MAS) would stress even more the need for distance. The Movement for the Fifth Republic (MVR), formed by Hugo Chávez to support his drive for the presidency, and whose allies included the small leftist parties of the past, adopted a more U.S.-friendly stance than was expected, especially given sensibilities over the refusal to grant Chávez a U.S. visa during his campaign. But the party's personalistic character indicated that its positions would simply follow those of its dominant leader, whose change of pace and tone has tended to keep both friend and foe slightly off balance. Chavez's campaign for a "multipolar" world could be taken as anti-American or not, according to different interpretations.

Business interests have long tended to lobby for a more pro-U.S. view, in line with their close ties to the United States, and continue to do so. The peak business association, Fedecámaras, which represents the wide variety of industries, many of which are local companies without international links, supports private industry in principle but tends to adapt to government policy in a somewhat defensive way, looking always to ensure links to whatever government is in power and recognizing that survival is at stake in a country where the government is so powerful, receiving the bulk of all income from exports and dispensing benefits according to its own lights. Yet there are member organizations of Fedecámaras that take stronger positions. The Caracas Chamber of Commerce, Consecomercio (the federation of chambers of commerce), and at times Conindustria (the federation of larger industrial companies) have all taken positions against excessive government intervention in the economy. This general stance hardly requires consistency, however, and, not surprisingly, specific industries also look to government to intervene to protect their position.

No single group dominates the press in Venezuela, which offers a wide range of outlets for different opinions. Even newspapers generally associated with business interests, such as *El Universal*, the prestigious Caracas daily, invite columnists from diverse ideological positions to contribute. Readers can choose among the many competitors in the lively national and local print media. Radio multiplies options even more and offers a two-way communication that reveals the vitality of free speech in Venezuela. Three privately owned national channels dominate commercial television, with a weak fourth, the government-owned channel, which has never found great favor with listeners. There are also some regional and UHF stations, of which Globovisión, an all-news station, gained prominence especially in providing lively political discussion. As in the United States, governments routinely accuse the media of bias against them, which may be taken as a sign that they enjoy enough independence to make a bother of themselves.

The television stations must maintain a certain impartiality given their dependence on government concessions and regulations (which prohibit foreign ownership of all Spanish-language media), but their international links inevitably bias their attitudes toward favoring the free flow of foreign investment and open trade, since a large proportion of their programming is purchased abroad, especially from the United States. Cable and satellite stations increasingly provide options for more wealthy viewers, with full access to international sources of news.

The Venezuelan-American Chamber of Industry and Commerce, Venamcham, represents a more internationalist (but no less self-interested) approach, given its mission in favor of promoting business between the United States and Venezuela. While Venamcham's original members tended to represent the large multinational companies, it has grown to include more than one thousand company members comprising many Venezuelan companies as well, such that it has become a general lobbyist in favor of open economic policies and unencumbered bilateral business relations. Venezuelan businesspeople can thus have it both ways, belonging both to Fedecámaras and Venamcham and supporting one or the other according to the issue at hand.[16] Venamcham often backs U.S. government positions, such as the treaties for protection of investors and on double taxation, but it also takes stands independently. Venamcham (not unlike the American Association of binational chambers in Latin America, AACLA) criticized the Helms-Burton Act for its extraterritorial pretensions and also supported the Venezuelan national oil company, PDVSA, when it confronted difficulties over environmental rules in the United States. Venamcham played an important role in supporting the creation of the Venezuelan caucus group formed among members of Congress in 2000 and retains a representative in Washington to keep it informed of relevant issues in that capital. Another small organization, the U.S.-Venezuela Business Council (CEVEU), seeks much the same goals as Venamcham, although with a more discrete and personalized approach. It is organized differ-ently, with a Venezuelan membership that is interested in maintaining a good relationship between the two countries.

Other Venezuelan organizations, weighing in with views less consistent with United States positions on trade and investment, can be influential at times. The mildly protectionist Pro-Venezuela Association supported the government's import substitution policy that lasted until 1989; its place was taken over for a time by Fundapatria, a small but noisy group that defended national sovereignty with great energy and whose leading spirit, the businessman Luis Vallenilla, expressed a high level of coincidence with the positions taken by the Chávez administration. Fundapatria opposed all mention of privatization in the oil indus-try, and spent large sums of money taking out newspaper ads denouncing the supposed vices of the proposed U.S.-Venezuelan treaty on double taxation in 1999. Prominent members of Fundapatria supported the ascension of Hugo Chávez to the presidency in 1998, seeing him as the incarnation of their nation-alist orientation, but the organization tended to disintegrate as its members lost influence over the president, especially after a major financial scandal that dis-credited Vallenilla, leaving the nationalist flank open again for Pro-Venezuela or another organization to fill.

In the purely economic sphere, there are also some organizations that lobby for free market policies in line with American positions, although their orienta-tion is apolitical. One such group in Venezuela is the Center for the Diffusion of Economic Culture (Cedice). This small group maintains communication with American think tanks such as the Heritage Foundation, the Liberty Fund, and the Atlas Foundation, often bringing in speakers from abroad whose object it is to develop ideas in favor of market economies. Cedice was a strong supporter in the 1990s for the adoption of a currency board in Venezuela, which would imply a tying of the Venezuelan bolivar to the dollar, following the Argentinean model.

In contrast to Venezuela, the United States does not have many groups inter-ested particularly in promoting relations with Venezuela. Much as American foreign policy approaches its problems according to global issues, so U.S. interest groups enter into contact with Venezuela according to questions of overall inter-est. These interest groups tend to become international themselves, with chapters that unite similarly minded people across borders, be they environmentalists, human rights activists, or feminists. When it comes to business, issues are more specific and sporadic, and chiefly related to competition, be it from oil, steel, or other imports from Venezuela. Equally, U.S. business lets its interests be known to its government, which is expected to support business when it looks for mar-kets abroad or when it wishes to invest. The U.S. government provides information on many trade and investment issues to help American business keep informed of opportunities. Much of the interplay of these forces will be seen in the cases reviewed in the following chapter.

Personal Diplomacy: A Tale of Two Visits

Bilateral relations take on fresh urgency when leaders come face to face. Between presidents, all issues look like high politics, at least for the few hours of direct contact they share on these occasions. Because presidents have power to make foreign policy, the moments in which they meet reveal an important aspect of international relations. Agreements signed during presidential visits usually reflect what the normal channels of communication would have achieved in any case, although the imminence of a high-level visit usually makes officials speed up their work to get results in time for the event. Two presidential visits illustrate the dynamics of these intense moments.

Venezuela was excluded from President Clinton's 1997 tour of Latin America, scheduled for the month of May, during which the president visited Mexico, Costa Rica, and Barbados. Both private and official reactions indicated that Venezuela would feel slighted if it were excluded (as was rumored) from a second trip to the major South American countries, Brazil and Argentina. The Venezuelan ambassador in Washington, Pedro Luis Echeverría, moved to get Venezuela on the agenda, and success was deemed to be a Venezuelan diplomatic victory. Foreign Minister Burelli said—in a gesture of unusual arrogance—that Clinton's visit would be "more beneficial to the United States," reminding anyone listening that " . . . both in war and in peace, Venezuela has been the safest and most trustworthy of all of North America's oil suppliers."[17]

Clinton's visit was postponed until October 12 and 13, when cooperation agreements in certain areas would be signed. Foreign Minister Burelli visited Washington early in July 1997 in order to establish with U.S. officials the agenda for the visit, contemplating the signing of six pending agreements. Expectations rose that it might even be possible to sign the Bilateral Investment Treaty and the Bilateral Tax Treaty, although hopes soon died as positions hardened.

President Clinton arrived in Caracas on October 12, 1997, for a visit lasting almost 24 hours. Air Force One landed at the Simón Bolívar airport at 2:45 in the afternoon, with a tight agenda including on the same day a state welcome, an interview with President Caldera in the presidential residence, and a state dinner (where the veteran Caldera offered warm advice to the presidential couple on their wedding anniversary, based on his own long and successful marriage). On the morning of the 13th, President Clinton spoke to American and Venezuelan businessmen and executives at a breakfast sponsored by Venamcham. He then went to the National Pantheon, where he placed a wreath at Simón Bolívar's tomb and won over an informal crowd with his open style (somewhat to the chagrin of his security personnel). At a formal meeting with President Caldera, the two presidents signed several bilateral agreements and a joint statement, with a salute to local notables and the diplomatic corps. Finally, the presidential caravan went to the airport, where Clinton boarded Air Force

One, leaving for Brazil in the afternoon. Nothing of much importance had transpired.

Bill Clinton was the fourth U.S. president to visit Venezuela. Before him had come Presidents Kennedy in 1963, Carter in 1978, and Bush in 1990. Clinton was accompanied by, among others, Madeleine Albright, secretary of state, Federico Peña, secretary of energy, and William Daley, secretary of commerce, indicating U.S. interest in oil, drugs, and trade in its bilateral relation. During President Clinton's visit the following legal instruments were signed in a effort to foster the relations between both countries: 1) Agreement on Mutual Legal Assistance in Criminal Matters; 2) Agreement on Scientific and Technological Cooperation; 3) Agreement on Mutual Assistance between Customs Services; 4) Memorandum of Understanding between the National Institute of Parks and the U.S. National Parks Service; 5) a document on the Strategic Alliance Against Drugs; 6) Agreement on Energy Cooperation between the Ministry of Energy and Mines and the U.S. Department of Energy.

While the Clinton visit pleased both sides from a symbolic point of view, perhaps all were aware that the Caldera government, close to its conclusion, would mark the end of a period in Venezuela, and that new winds were blowing. None of the agreements signed could be considered of great importance since they were all matters on which no great differences existed. Those who had hoped for the signing of bilateral treaties on investment and on double taxation were certainly disappointed that the Caldera government had balked during negotiations. By 1998, Caldera would be a lame duck in a democratic system undergoing deep transformation. The comfortable arrangement between the two democracies would surely undergo some changes to the degree that many of the old structures of politics in Venezuela—the political parties, the oil-dependent state, the delicate equilibrium among local elites—were coming under question. Perhaps for this very reason, Venezuela had been omitted from the original Clinton agenda, since it would be a new generation that would be leading Venezuela in the future. Yet Venezuelans were glad to have captured the U.S. president's attention, if only for a day. He would be more alert to events in Venezuela after having seen the country, met its people, and developed a warm memory of a pleasant, if uneventful, visit.

President Chávez visited the United States for the first time as president of Venezuela on June 9 and 10, 1999. He had passed through Washington earlier in Jaunary as president-elect, but on that occasion, President Clinton arranged only a short and casual greeting off the formal agenda. Venezuela had hoped for an official presidential visit in June but this time, Clinton could not receive him at all. Chávez visited New York and Houston, showing his recognition that Venezuela needed to stress its openness to foreign investors at a time when grave doubts existed about the economic orientation of the new government. In New York, Chávez visited the Council on Foreign Relations and spoke at a luncheon arranged by the

Council of the Americas and the Venezuela-American Chamber of Commerce, in which he addressed more than six hundred people. He talked privately with the heads of American banks and firms with interests in Venezuela, and he visited the New York Stock Exchange. As a baseball fanatic who dreamed of playing in the big leagues, Chávez had the honor of tossing out the "first ball" at a Shea Stadium game between the Mets and the Blue Jays. In Houston, President Chávez made another round of business contacts and met former U.S president George Bush's family, including Governor of Texas George W. Bush, then a top-seeded presidential candidate for the year 2000 elections in the United States.

Since the Chávez visit to the United States was not a state visit, no agreements were signed. Most important, Chávez referred to his plans to open the gas industry to foreign investment and to restructure Venezuela's foreign debt within the rules of the game. He met his objective of showing his goodwill toward the United States (with no hard feelings shown over the earlier denial of a visa), his understanding of the preferences of foreign investors, and his recognition of the importance of oil (hence the inclusion of Houston on the itinerary) and of demonstrating his democratic intentions (counterbalancing an image of defiance of existing institutions). The trip was marred by an impression that his economic team still lacked cohesion and a clear view of its strategy, but overall it looked as if Venezuelan-American relations would continue on an even keel, despite the harsh rhetoric used elsewhere by Chávez with regard to capitalism, globalization, and American hegemony.

Later on in the year, in September, Chávez would have the opportunity for another short visit with Clinton when he went to New York to give a speech at the United Nations. The U.S. president takes advantage of the yearly UN meetings to greet the many foreign heads of state who attend. Chávez also visited Washington again, limiting himself to meetings at international organizations and with some members of Congress. It seemed to Venezuela that the United States government had decided not to accord President Chávez prolonged or high-level contact with President Clinton, even though Chávez undoubtedly wanted it. A presidential visit in Washington could signal the moment when the Chávez government would receive the full support and trust of the United States.

Many observers commented privately that President Chávez wanted to establish a personal contact with President Clinton, and later with President Bush, more than he would admit. They asked themselves whether his frequent statements praising Cuban society were meant to show that he did not want to be seen in the American camp or were aimed at provoking the Americans to take him more into account. Ambassador Maisto received hints and even pleas from Venezuelans saying that he should do everything possible to get Chávez an invitation to the White House as a way to better relations. As the Clinton presidency advanced through its last year, attention turned to the intentions of his possible successors.

Do bilateral relations depend on the personalization of politics, or, in the end, do the underlying issues depend on broader forces that reflect interests, bureaucratic decisions, and structural aspects underlying the relationship? While presidential visits appear superficial, it may nevertheless be important that leaders know each other personally, feel comfortable speaking together at times of stress, and be available to unblock stalled negotiations at times. Presidents do not generally get involved in low politics, but any issue may transform itself into high politics without warning. Presidents, meanwhile, set the tone, transmit global messages, and play a symbolic role that mirrors the true state of relations between nations. If anything, modern diplomacy has seen an increase in personal contacts among world leaders, who seem to agree that their direct involvement in the international relationships of their countries will contribute to more understanding and better prospects for negotiation should conflict break out in the future.

Dilemmas of Foreign Policy in an Asymmetical World

Since the early sixties, Venezuela has favored an active foreign policy. The promotion of democratic regimes in the hemisphere, the launching of economic initiatives based on cooperation and integration among Venezuela and her peers, and a high profile in the diplomatic community contributed to its complex and important role within the framework of the political system.

Having an active foreign policy, Venezuelan governments formulated and implemented a diplomatic style which was defined on two levels. On the one hand, the main political goals gave priority to relations with the United States, the promotion and defense of democratic relations with her neighbor nations, pacifism, and the defense of sovereignty. In the economic sphere, the main goals were the defense of oil prices, support of OPEC, industrial diversification, and Latin American integration. All of these goals were widely shared within Venezuelan society, despite some inner contradictions among them.

In order to maintain an active foreign policy based on its goals, Venezuela had to build a diplomatic and financial base consonant with its ambitions: a big foreign policy for a middle-level nation. The Cold War helped Venezuelan objectives to the extent that its insistence on democracy and self-determination tended to support the U.S. position. Even then, however, dissident voices were heard in Venezuela: Was not self-determination the right of any country to do as it liked internally? Venezuela felt attracted to the goals of the nonaligned movement in the 1970s; however, since the early eighties, the world had changed rapidly. The Cold War was over, the Soviet Union had collapsed, and the international agenda had filled with economic rather than geopolitical issues, such as environment, human rights, migration, and trade. At the same time, nonstate actors began to act as international actors: multilateral, multinational, and nongovernmental organizations. At the same time, the Venezuelan political system began to change, the internal economy had several problems, and foreign policy began to be in the public eye.

It was not easy for Venezuelan decision-makers and analysts to understand the global and internal changes. Since the early eighties, the consensus over foreign policy had begun to have problems. In the wake of the exchange crisis of 1983, Venezuelan generosity to poorer countries came under question. The model of development looked increasingly out of date, and new actors demanded changes.

One of the most striking factors in U.S.-Venezuelan relations is the increasing impact of the U.S hemispheric and world agenda and the decreasing weight of purely bilateral issues. Yet Venezuelan decision-makers find it politically difficult to justify international or global criteria for a given stance, because they seem to relegate Venezuelan concerns to second place. Thus it is easy to understand why Venezuelan decision-makers and analysts perceive U.S. interests in Venezuela as part of a worldwide and hemispheric strategy little adapted to the issues that used to link the two countries: democracy and oil. What used to be a special relationship, from the point of view of Venezuela, seemed increasingly to come out of a cookie cutter.

The tendency toward homogenization has been more visible in recent years. The launch of a "Hemispheric Policy" that posits open economies, good government, and antidrug policies constitutes a general agenda for the United States. Venezuelans believe, however, that their country is a special one that requires greater specificity and understanding. That is to say, the United States should show its appreciation for the long years of stable oil supply and democracy by making allowances and not treating Venezuela just like all the others. The United States should even show tolerance for "deviant" positions assumed by Venezuela from time to time—voting against American positions in the United Nations, for instance—just as a longtime friend forgives occasional lapses. The Venezuelan press gives close attention to reactions in the United States to such actions; even slight mentions of Venezuela in the foreign press receive front-page coverage; U.S. government representatives visiting Venezuela will listen time and again to the same question: How do they see us up there?

Seen from another perspective, such concerns show how hemispheric issues play an important role in the general impact that external factors have in the Venezuelan economy and politics. Not only does the Venezuelan government consider itself important in the worldview of the United States; its citizens think their country should be seen as important, although, for instance, most reviews of comparative politics in Latin American fail even to include Venezuela, perhaps because its history over the last decades does not fit in well with many theories of political development. What is more, Venezuelans do not want to see themselves as just an example of some broader trends in the region or the world and resist such characterizations. Comparisons with other oil countries can be taken almost as insults. Uniqueness even requires the primacy of internal forces over external forces. Globalization, then, may be perceived with even warier attitudes in Venezuela than in other countries more comfortable with their status in the world. For all of these reasons, Venezuelan political culture often generates negative reactions to Washington's hemispheric initiatives in political, economic, and security matters.

In the end, while global issues and international rules sound like the answer to problems of unequal power in the form of a new and fairer world order, it should be remembered that a country like Venezuela cannot really escape from the asymmetry of national strength that characterizes its relationship with the United States. Power politics are rarely expressed openly, but neither country can be unaware of the differences in wealth and military might that separate them.

FIVE
GETTING ALONG: ISSUES IN U.S.-VENEZUELAN RELATIONS

T HE 1990S WERE DIFFICULT YEARS FOR RELATIONS BETWEEN THE United States and Venezuela, despite the long period of tranquility that had preceded them. At the same time that the United States turned to the standardization of its foreign policy, Venezuela began to suffer profound changes in its domestic system that would also tend to alter its view of its international position. As a result of the political instability of the nineties, everything came under question, including foreign policy in its widest sense. Venezuela repeatedly questioned the validity of what it perceived as the American model of the global economy. By the time of the election of President Hugo Chávez at the end of 1998, it seemed that the population was ready to authorize Chávez to turn policy on its head in every area, from social policy to foreign policy. Inevitably, tensions would arise, particularly on the political front, as Venezuela made efforts to carve out a fresh position and prove that things would indeed be different.

This chapter tells the story of some of the specific incidents of Venezuelan-U.S. relations in the areas of politics, security, and economics, illustrating the general arguments about how the two countries get along. What emerges is an account of how the structure of common interests, the realities of relative power, and the international rules of the game tend to impose themselves on both countries. Venezuela might bridle under the restrictions of globalization but nevertheless finds that its best defense is a good offense in the form of playing a more effective game in international organizations and trade negotiations. Somewhat to its surprise, it can win when its arguments are compelling. The United States sometimes tries to put pressures on Venezuela to do things its way, but recognizes that the rules of nonintervention require it to respect even a smaller country's determination to maintain its own position. Foreign policy, as a result, shows much more continuity than change.

The context of the 1990s reveals a sharp contrast between the situations of the United States and Venezuela. In the United States, economic growth and global leadership raised national confidence, while in Venezuela, decline seemed to be the order of the day. The distress in Venezuelan politics arose from a number of sources, but the chief reason centered on the failure of its democracy to deliver on its promises of prosperity and equality. The lost decade of the 1980s, when most of Latin America suffered economic problems and undertook severe adjustment programs, was particularly shocking for a country like Venezuela that had grown at a fast clip for most of the postwar period, enlarging the opportunities for its citizens in health, education, and income. In the 1980s, the economy destabilized, inflation skyrocketed, and government controls failed to solve the problem. Efforts to liberalize between 1989 and 1992 only shook the political system more, feeding doubts about the "neoliberal" economic reforms that were seen as being inspired by the United States. A second wave of reform initiated in 1996 was quickly snuffed out by political uncertainty and a falling oil price in 1998. The economic balance of the 1990s was no better than that of the 1980s.

In three areas, events during the 1990s reflect the tensions arising out of the different views of the world that characterized the Venezuelan and United States governments during the period. For the first time in almost forty years, the United States began to pay close attention to the weakening of the political system in Venezuela, making its opinion known in a way that would create an uncommon breach between the two countries. Political differences would also spill over into the area of security, as Venezuela defined its own security in terms further away from the traditional acceptance of the American protectorate in Latin America. Equally, economic relations would be influenced by distrust of global recipes in Venezuela, matched by the perception that the United States did not always practice what it preached in terms of open trade and nondiscrimination. The litany of complaints, coupled with radical political changes in Venezuela that encouraged questioning of all traditional policies, would transform Venezuelan-U.S. relations by the end of the decade, raising doubts about the continuation of a long period of comfort with "business as usual." Yet it should be remembered that while political posturing raised the discomfort level, the broad fabric of the bilateral relation remained intact, a product of common interests that neither country could deny.

Democratic Forms and Democratic Substance

Human rights, citizen diplomacy, and the promotion of civic society, transparency, governability, democracy, free elections—all of these form a "freedom package" to be implemented, according to American thought, in each nation of the world. The "freedom package," consistent with Venezuela's approach to world politics, paradoxically arrived just as concern about Venezuelan democracy was at its most intense. This concern dominated political relations throughout the 1990s and led to a series of incidents in which the United States felt called upon to exert pressure in favor of the preservation of the democratic system in Venezuela, while Venezuela, for its part, expressed its irritation that the United States should doubt its democratic vocation and meddle in its internal affairs.

The Crisis of Democracy in Venezuela: Coups and Renewed Attention

"There is room for growth in the space between the United States and Venezuela." These were the words of the then–foreign minister of Venezuela, Fernando Ochoa Antich, when he delivered a speech on the relations between the two countries, sponsored by the Venezuelan-American Chamber of Commerce and Industry, Venamcham, on July 29, 1992. During those months, Venezuela had gone through democracy's worst crisis: the failed coup d'état against President Pérez on February 4 of that year. From the official point of view, Michael Skol, then U.S. ambassador in Venezuela, had warned that "any action against the Constitution in Venezuela would be unacceptable to the United States."[1] It was clear to opinion leaders, intellectuals, and the business sector that for the United States it was preferable to "negotiate with a democracy and not with an illegitimate government."[2]

At the same time as the strategic commitment of the United States was reaffirmed, some problems were appearing, already evidenced since 1990, as the result of a new tactical link between Venezuela and the United States. This relationship rested on two new realities. On the one hand, Petróleos de Venezuela (PDVSA), the government-owned oil corporation, was preparing itself for the opening of its business to private capital; it was already participating as a partner and main shareholder in American companies of the oil sector—Citgo, Champlin, and Unoven—investments made in the United States as part of an overall strategy of converting PDVSA into a major oil company with access to its own final markets.[3] At about the same time, signature was pending on a series of agreements[4] deriving from President Bush's proposal called the "Initiative for the Americas," as was the implementation of the framework agreement for creating the United States–Venezuelan Council, signed by both governments in Washington in April 1991. Apart from the issue of Venezuelan political stability, the rest of the problems were of the normal sort of day-to-day relations, although it was already evident that American positions obeyed the general principles that increasingly informed U.S. foreign relations.

Bill Clinton and the Democrats won the 1992 presidential elections, and as is usually the case with a change of administration, questions arose as to the future of hemispheric relations with the new government.[5] This time, however, most analysts and decision-makers were right in believing that in the era of global changes Clinton would respect Bush's hemispheric initiatives. In the specific case of Venezuela, and with President Pérez's open sympathy with the Democratic victory, most experts predicted only small differences between both leaders and a continuation of excellent relations between the two countries, especially given the Pérez government's adoption of market-oriented reforms.[6]

Things would not quite turn out the way the experts thought they would. Shortly after Clinton's election in November 1992, a second coup attempt occurred in Venezuela. Quickly squelched, it seemed at the time to have few practical consequences, although Washington showed concern about the fractured stability of a country where, finally, "things were happening." Political attacks against Pérez were intense, calls for his resignation frequent, and talk of yet another coup was in the air. In March 1993, Albert Coll, deputy undersecretary of defense for special affairs and low intensity conflicts, visited Caracas. He used his visit to let it be clearly known that " . . . the United States would not support at all a Venezuelan government imposed or created by the military against the constitutional authorities."[7]

Pérez was forced out of office in May according to the procedure set by the Venezuelan Constitution, even though his ouster raised some doubts about the legal process itself. The same line about respecting the Constitution was reaffirmed by spokesmen from the Department of State when President Pérez left office and was duly replaced by Ramón J. Velázquez,[8] who had to conclude the remainder of the presidential term; it was frankly expressed again by Clinton's new secretary of state, Warren Christopher.[9]

Shortly before the December 1993 presidential elections in Venezuela, and in the presence of a new U.S. ambassador in Venezuela (Jeffrey Davidow, who replaced Michael Skol), Caracas was visited by Assistant Secretary of State for Inter-American Affairs Alexander Watson. Watson met President Velázquez, to whom he delivered a personal letter from President Clinton. Meeting with Foreign Minister Ochoa Antich and with several presidential candidates, Watson reiterated American support for Venezuelan democracy. Unrest and rumors were still common in Venezuela at the time, despite the fact that the system seemed to be returning to the normal rules of the game. Watson's visit was considered as having great symbolic power, since it indicated that Washington would not support a coup d'etat.[10] During the same visit, Watson, at a Venamcham conference, said that " . . . the maintenance of Venezuela's brilliant democratic tradition is an indispensable prerequisite for normal relations between the United States and Venezuela."[11] Many of the businessmen present realized the gravity of the moment only when Watson, pressed to expand on the possible consequences of a de facto government in Caracas, mentioned sanctions that could even include the freezing of Venezuelan private accounts in U.S. banks. Perhaps for the first time since political instability had broken out in 1989, Venezuelans realized that a political break with the United States could affect them where it would hurt most.

Despite fears of coups or other irregularities, Rafael Caldera, who had been president from 1969 to 1974, won the Venezuelan presidential elections of

December 1993. The victory of Caldera, who had maintained cordial but rather stiff relations with the United States during his first administration, was seen by the U.S. government as a possible cooling off of a political system that had been so severely convulsed during recent years, although the octogenarian was hardly seen as either a reformer or an advocate of free markets. His political campaign stressed his differences with the Pérez reforms, which had been in line with American preferences. Caldera himself referred to this issue when he gave a lecture sponsored by Venamcham, where he said that he was "conscious of the importance of the U.S. for Venezuela, since anything happening in the north has repercussions in our country, especially in matters relating to oil."[12] Successive visits by U.S. officials were deemed as repetitions of Washington's support of Caldera.[13]

Planning for the 1994 Hemispheric Summit provided several opportunities for visits by high U.S. officials, such as ambassador Charles Gillespie and Deputy Secretary of State Strobe Talbott. With regard to the summit, Venezuelan authorities underlined their intention of promoting the issues of a compensatory program to contribute to the solution of the social problems resulting from the opening of the economies—implicitly criticizing liberalization as promoted by the United States—and a hemispheric energy integration plan; they also proposed a hemispheric action plan against corruption, which provided a noncontroversial issue for President Caldera to champion.[14] Venezuela's support for the goal of free trade in the Americas would not be forthcoming except in the vaguest terms, and the United States would also fail Venezuela's expectations. At the end of 1994, the United States openly supported the election of former Colombian president César Gaviria as secretary general of the OAS. This contributed to the defeat of the Venezuelan candidate to the secretariat, Foreign Minister Burelli Rivas, putting a small and temporary dent in the relations between Washington and Caracas.[15]

During the year 1995, the most important political issues on the agenda of both countries' relations touched on the problems of the growing drug traffic that spilled over from neighboring Colombia, and the alleged violation of human rights by Venezuelan police and prison authorities, which had already been denounced by spokesmen for American NGOs. The government was further ruffled by indirect criticisms of its economic policy, which was still under a regimen of iron controls in the wake of the banking crisis of early 1994. These temporary measures were looking increasingly permanent and made any opening of the economy, much less the oil sector, difficult, although in 1996 Caldera did finally carry out a turnaround that produced positive results immediately.

It took a long time for the Clinton administration to announce Jeffrey Davidow's successor as the U.S. ambassador to Venezuela after Davidow was appointed assistant secretary of state for inter-American affairs in May of 1996, mainly due to delays in the Senate that affected many ambassadorial appointments at that time. The chargé d'affaires, John Keane, took charge of the embassy in the interim, leading Venezuelans to feel somewhat slighted at the idea that they should be left without high-level attention for over a year. The new ambassador, John Maisto, whose former post had been ambassador to Nicaragua, presented his credentials to President Caldera in March 1997, a year after he was appointed by the White House. Maisto had experience with political instability and was seen as a hard-liner, both on drugs and on democracy. Indeed, the Caldera government would later post a protest against Maisto's language on the need to increase anticorruption measures, not because the government disagreed in principle—Caldera promoted regional efforts to combat corruption—but because it objected to the implication that the Venezuelan government was not doing enough about it; the succeeding government of Hugo Chávez would also criticize Maisto's implicit support for decentralization, a controversial issue of domestic politics considered outside the purview of international relations.

In time, Maisto would come to be perceived as the main voice in favor of a tolerant attitude toward the changes occurring in Venezuela, ostensibly arguing that the concrete actions of the Chávez government were much less radical than his rhetoric, which was mainly aimed at popular audiences within the country. Maisto would later be named as chief adviser on Latin America in the National Security Council under George W. Bush, signaling continuity in American policy toward Venezuela, despite the change of government in the United States in 2001.

Most of the time, Venezuela's traditional positions have been consistent with U.S. foreign policy. On a state visit to Paraguay, President Caldera gave a speech before that country's Congress where he said that " . . . those who want to commit themselves to the adventure of a coup d'état or similar actions may no longer count on the support they might have thought to receive from the United States," registering agreement with Washington's frequent declarations.[16] Nevertheless, the United States would lose the support of Venezuela (and of many other countries as well) for its controversial policy toward Fidel Castro's Cuba. In November 1996, Venezuela condemned the U.S. blockade of Cuba and opposed at the United Nations the promulgation of the Helms-Burton Act, in a clear demonstration of the use of world forums to differentiate itself on some occasions from the U.S. international policies, although always in the company of other like-minded countries.[17] Similarly, Venezuela voted with the majority in the Organization of American States in condemning the Helms-Burton Act in 1996. Domestic pressures, especially from the Cuban community in south Florida, made it difficult for any American president to propose ending the embargo against Cuba or softening its terms, but the almost universal rejection of U.S. policy toward Cuba contributed to new efforts to reconsider its effectiveness.

Human rights issues would generate more substantial differences. At the end of 1996, the White House announced that it would release the State Department report to the U.S. Congress on human rights (published in January 1997), which would include references to certain violations in Venezuela, especially in its prisons. On that occasion President Clinton said that " . . . the defense of human rights shall be an essential component of [my] second term."[18] In February 1997, the Venezuelan government sent a document with an official response, denying the truth of some allegations.

In contrast, when Venezuela was sued in international courts for human rights violations that occurred under the Carlos Andrés Pérez government, the government of Hugo Chávez would admit to the accusation, laying responsibility at the feet of his predecessor. This is not to say that the Chávez government would absorb foreign criticism of itself lightly; later reports would provoke the response that outsiders should not intervene in the domestic affairs of Venezuela or of other countries. Chávez would even go so far as to suggest that important U.S. newspapers were engaged in a conspiracy to discredit him, an accusation that might be taken very seriously if the president were not also disposed to visit the offices of the *New York Times* personally to talk over his gripes.

The United States and the Coming of the Chávez Government

As testy as relations with other governments sometimes were, U.S.-Venezuelan relations would see their most difficult moments with the election of Hugo Chávez, whose democratic credentials were not trusted in the United States until he had fully shown by his actions that he would respect democracy. Even then, Chávez's unusually combative language left vestiges of persisting doubts. During the 1998 Venezuelan elections, the U.S. government firmly stated that Washington would support the electoral process in Venezuela, implying that it would have no problem with Chávez as president as long as he gained power by the ballot. Secretary of the Navy John Dalton, in a visit to Caracas seen by some as not so casual, mentioned that U.S. soldiers would be ready to resolve any problem in the Western Hemisphere. This was a clear sign that Washington would not allow any political turbulence in the country during the electoral processes of 1998.

On a visit to Caracas U.S. Secretary of Energy Bill Richardson reiterated the same themes. Some analysts interpreted this visit by a close collaborator of President Clinton and representative of oil interests as another show of concern that the likely victory of Hugo Chávez might disturb smooth relations and even endanger the successful opening of the oil industry in Venezuela to foreign investors, which Chávez said he would want to "review."[19] Days before the Venezuelan presidential election, with a Chávez victory practically assured, U.S. Secretary of Defense William Cohen, while visiting Cartagena, Colombia, during the second meeting of Ministers of Defense of the Americas, made a final repetition of the U.S. position.

In spite of some warnings coming from political analysts and political leaders—both from Washington and Caracas—that a Chávez victory would worsen

Venezuela-U.S. relations in the future, U.S. policy was just to "wait and see." It was clear to everybody in the United States and Venezuela that Chávez was going to win the election and that Clinton's government was ready to recognize his victory and to resume standing bilateral relations without any change.[20]

The U.S. government did not hesitate to congratulate Chávez hours after the first official results were announced on December 8, 1998. On the following day, Ambassador Maisto visited the newly elected president of Venezuela and delivered a personal message from President Clinton. In this message President Clinton said: "On behalf of the American people and on my own please accept my congratulations for your election as President of Venezuela. The high percentage and your incredible margin of victory is a clear testimony of the enduring and strong democratic conviction and the wishes of positive change that Venezuela wants." Days after the election, the government of the United States issued a diplomatic visa to Chávez, and Ambassador Maisto visited him a second time and stressed that Venezuelan-U.S. relations "are excellent, and I am sure that this will continue forever because both countries have the disposition to work together on an agenda that we share not only in the bilateral arena but also in the hemispheric one."[21]

On December 19, 1998, the president-elect of Venezuela was the keynote speaker at the annual meeting of Venamcham. On that occasion, Chávez assured the audience again of his wishes for good relations between Venezuela and the United States and his hope that American investments would increase the U.S. presence in the country. On December 30, Assistant Secretary of State for Inter-American Affairs Peter Romero visited President-elect Chávez in Caracas in another sign of acceptance of the new government.[22] On January 25, the United States and the outgoing government of Venezuela finally signed in Caracas the Treaty on Double Taxation in the expectation that the Venezuelan Congress would ratify it in its next session with the support of President Chávez.[23]

By the eve of the start of the Chávez government, U.S-Venezuelan relations were in a more promising stage, despite wariness on both sides. Between 1994 and 1998 the two governments had signed eleven treaties and memoranda related to drug trafficking, justice, defense, customs, energy, technology, environment, and double taxation, and in Washington there were hopes for a good relationship with the new government, despite fears that President Chávez might hold a grudge over the denial of his visa before his election. Cautious optimism in the United States reflected the fact that despite the political noise, the two countries would continue to share common interests, and the arrival of Chávez should not contradict this basic fact.

The United States was now paying close attention to events in Venezuela, although maintaining a certain distance, and making it clear that its willingness to maintain amicable relations was contingent on the preservation of democracy in Venezuela. Given Chávez's repeated claims that all Venezuelan institutions had been corrupted and should be replaced by others through a Constituent Assembly, the Clinton administration continued to pursue a policy of "wait and see."

How would relations develop once President Chávez began to govern? During 1999, Chávez quickly consolidated his political power through the process of writing a new Constitution for the country. He used the opportunity to virtually replace the Congress with an all-powerful Constituent Assembly, and although he often stretched the meaning of the law to do so, he made clear efforts to maintain the democratic process. The United States continued to observe events in Venezuela with care but also expressed its satisfaction that the new Constitution, approved by referendum in December 1999, would initiate a fresh attempt to consolidate democracy.

The chief concern was that Chávez's very political strength tended to reduce the normal give-and-take of the democratic process. His popularity led to the total demoralization of opposition political parties and to their exclusion from government bodies that normally acted as counterweights to the concentration of power. Some of Chávez's actions seemed designed precisely to bother the United States, such as his intense relationship with Fidel Castro or his defiant trip to Baghdad in August 2000, despite Iraq's status as practically an international pariah under United Nations sanctions. U.S. State Department spokesman Richard Boucher admitted that the visit with Saddam Hussein was "particularly irritating,"[24] but the barbs did not go beyond a brief exchange of sarcasms.

Full trust would require the reestablishment of political equilibrium in Venezuela. "Wait and see" also meant paying more attention to the concrete actions of the Chávez government than to the sometimes incendiary rhetoric of the Venezuelan president, which often just repeated fragments of popular criticisms of the United States abroad. This kept conflict to a minimum, reducing the probability that peripheral differences might escalate and permitting a clear distinction between matters of national interest and problems of lesser importance.

Issues in Security

Since the revolt of dissatisfied Venezuelan military groups against the political system in 1992, and especially since the Chávez electoral victory of 1998, security issues had gained importance, both within Venezuela and among those in the United States attentive to the turn of events in an important oil supplier and democratic ally. The election of a military figure as president brought with it the increased presence of military personnel in civilian posts, an enlarged role for the military in traditionally civilian activities, and conflicts between the government and its opposition over new constitutional arrangements defining military prerogatives. Once again, rumblings troubled the atmosphere, with opposition forces chafing under the perceived threat of militarization and government forces irritated by the constant sniping against their policies. The United States became less sure that Venezuela would continue to be a firm ally across a wide range of security problems.

Drugs and Andean Instability: A Challenge to Good Relations

The incident that best characterizes the spiny problems that developed between the United States and Venezuela with the Chávez government is the skirmishing over how to monitor possible movements of drugs coming up from the south and from the west, principally from Colombia, and even perhaps passing through Venezuelan territory or airspace. The reversion of the Panama Canal Zone to Panamanian administration required that the United States rearrange the disposition of its military forces in the Caribbean. Apart from its main bases on American territory, the United States looked for some forward stations in the north of the continent. It achieved successful terms from Holland to use Aruba and Curaçao and also from Ecuador and Costa Rica, but, as mentioned above, Venezuela made it clear that it was not interested in opening its airspace to the overflights proposed by the United States, since it would be equivalent to a cession of sovereignty.

The government always phrased the Venezuelan "no" in polite and friendly language designed especially for the local press, recognizing the common goals of the countries in stopping the drug trade but reminding the United States that Venezuela would take responsibility for its own backyard—as if to say, "good fences make good neighbors." For its part, the United States let it be known that Venezuelan territory was being repeatedly violated despite the supposed effectiveness of Venezuelan surveillance, making public its view that Venezuelan sovereignty was hardly being protected by such a policy. Backing off for the time, United States decided not to insist on its request for overflights of Venezuelan territory but tried in the meantime to work closely with Venezuela on training and in a common effort. Venezuelan officials claimed that the goals of the two countries coincided completely, although they continued to insist that they could take care of their own surveillance over Venezuelan territory.[25]

If it were only a case of a resistance to lending its support to the U.S. overflights, there would not be much significance to the Venezuelan position. Indeed, the Caldera government had been equally negative about American radar stations, without much being made of it. But given American doubts about the stability of democracy and the preservation of its institutions arising out of the uncertainty surrounding the intentions of the Chávez government, every declaration by the two countries provoked a good deal of speculation about its larger meaning. The Venezuelan government seemed to be looking skeptically for small signs that perhaps the United States wanted to improve its readiness for any "emergency" intervention should events take an undesirable turn either in

Venezuela or indeed in Colombia, where guerrilla and paramilitary groups were threatening the stability of that country.

Chávez was accused by Carlos Castaño, the leader of the violent antiguerrilla paramilitary group United Self-Defense of Colombia, of siding with the guerrillas against the Colombian government, but Chávez responded by saying that he would look for support in the United Nations, the OAS, and even with the Pope to avoid military intervention by the United States, revealing his distrust of U.S. actions in that country.[26] Even some Venezuelans suspected that the rejection of cooperation on overflights perhaps had a darker motive in avoiding any possible scandals should trafficking activities of Venezuelan citizens be discovered, not least of all, activities of Venezuelan military personnel. Others speculated that tensions within the armed forces might be at the root of the country's unwillingness to cooperate.[27]

The United States protested its pure intentions in the face of fears that a large package of aid for antidrug operations in Colombia (approved by the U.S. Congress in 2000) might imply military presence with political ends: "It is inconceivable to think of a U.S. invasion of Colombia or any other country," said Assistant Secretary for Inter-American Affairs Peter Romero, on a visit to Venezuela in July 1999. Yet even if the United States had no interest in such a political objective, the reinforcement of Colombian military capacity resulting from U.S. aid through "Plan Colombia" would contribute to an alteration of the balance of power in the Andean region to the detriment of Venezuela and could even create the risk of worsening the situation, with the United States again involved in a civil war from which it would be hard to withdraw.

Many feared that local success in suppressing drugs and rebellion in Colombia would spread negative effects to Venezuela as well as other bordering countries, should hard-pressed guerrillas try to move their operations across the border in order to evade repression in their own country. Kidnappings and protection schemes ostensibly directed by rebels across the border were already becoming a common affair in the west of Venezuela. The Colombian government, while accepting U.S. aid, also insisted on pursuing a negotiating strategy with the rebels in the hopes of some day achieving domestic peace. All parties acknowledged that a more regional and collaborative approach to the Colombian problem might help reduce the worst consequences of the conflict.

Venezuela's security, as it sees it, requires that the United States never involve itself in internal affairs, much less intervene directly. United States security requires stability in Venezuela and sure supplies of oil. Doubtless, neither side was quite as sure of the other in 1999 as former governments might have been; at such moments, diplomatic moves, subtle comments, and high-level visits can mean much.

Sparring over the best strategy to control drugs in the region could get mixed up with political differences and also spill over into economic relations. Chávez alternated positive and negative messages in his comments. President Chávez visited New York and Houston in mid-June 1999, spreading words of fellowship and conventional views of economics and politics. The United States sent messages as well. An unusually high-level group visited Caracas soon after, on July 8—the top officials in charge of Latin America at the State Department, the National Security Council, and the Office for the National Policy on Drug Control and representatives from the Southern Command and the Departments of Justice, Health, and Defense. Even if the ostensible reason for the visit was to talk about coordinating antidrug activities, the implicit communication said: we are highly concerned with events in Venezuela and wish to maintain close and continuous contact.

Official visits to Venezuela are often complemented by the arrival of other personalities from nongovernmental organizations that tend to reinforce the same message. While no obvious coordination links these different visits to Venezuela, a sort of invisible hand would seem to lead different interests to try to maximize communication between Venezuela and the United States at moments of high stress, as occurred during the days preceding the elections for the Constituent Assembly in July 1999 in Venezuela. Perhaps the instinct to preserve good relations in this way serves as the best indicator that the security concerns of Venezuela and the United States are congruent and that neither side wishes to rock the boat excessively.

Another example of how the different perspectives of the countries could lead to mutual discomfort is the annual review carried out by the United States on foreign governments' efforts to control drugs in their countries. The United States Congress has required this annual report since 1986 because it is unwilling to grant aid and trade privileges to countries that fail to contribute to international efforts to control trafficking. While this makes sense in terms of not aiding those nations that may even be complicit with drug barons, it creates in effect a system of unilateral certification when seen from the perspective of third countries. Throughout the 1990s, tensions arose between the United States and Venezuela over certification, and the prospect of joint operations against illegal drugs declined.

In September 1993, the director of the U.S. government's Drug Enforcement Agency (DEA) had offered Washington's support in the fight against drug traffic. The DEA officer said that he expected to "cooperate with Venezuela in order to cope with problems resulting from the rise in drug transit operations and money laundering in the country."[28] In March 1994, the State Department presented its annual report on drug traffic in the world, pointing out that there was drug corruption and drug traffic in Venezuela. The Venezuelan Foreign Ministry responded, acknowledging that: "Venezuela is not a drug producer, but it is suffering from the consequence of illegal traffic of narcotic and psychotropic substances, and especially from the laundering of drug related money," and

recalling that a memorandum of understanding had been signed in order to cooperate in the fight against drug traffic.[29]

The Clinton administration insisted that in Venezuela there was no firm policy against drug traffic, given police and judicial corruption, and denounced the
participation of officers of the National Guard in the diversion of a controlled
drug delivery (not all the detected cargo was delivered). The presidential pardon
of the Colombian drug trafficker Larry Tovar Acuña in 1994 (a pardon which
interim president Velázquez apparently signed by mistake, having been tricked
by a subordinate), the participation of Venezuelan judges in pardons of alleged
suspects, together with evidence of tainted trials, provoked a hostile reaction in
Washington. In February 1995, Venezuela was included in the list of countries
where efforts against drugs were considered only partial, although in the annual
report sent to Congress by the executive for the year 1994, Venezuela had been
deemed as being one of the countries supposedly willing to cooperate with the
antidrug policy with the installation of radar units on the island of Margarita
with U.S. support.[30] The go-it-alone attitude of Venezuela continued under
President Chávez, and resistance to undertaking joint action with the U.S. military against the drug traffic heightened, although a certain level of coordination
of specific actions continued without problems.

In February 1996, President Clinton, in his State of the Union Address to the
U.S. Congress, included a reference to drug policy. In this speech, Venezuela once
more appeared among a group of thirty-one countries where antidrug action was
considered insufficient. In March 1996, U.S. Secretary of Defense William Perry
visited Caracas. Perry talked with the Venezuelan authorities on the Clinton
administration's hemispheric security policy centered on the fight against drug
traffic. In his meeting with Venezuelan Minister of Defense Moisés Orozco
Graterol, the secretary of defense referred to the issue of the possible installation
of radar units in Venezuelan territory and to the possibility that Venezuela would
allow flights and patrolling by U.S. military aircraft in its airspace. The occasion
allowed the Venezuelan minister of defense to ask for military assistance in the
form of the donation of twenty helicopters and the eventual purchase by
Venezuela of two F-16 fighter jets and eleven amphibious vehicles. In September
of that year, General Lawson McGruber, the chief of the U.S. Army's Southern
Command, then based in Panama, visited Caracas to promote joint investigation,
cooperation, and training plans in order to fight the drug traffic and to participate
in joint operations.[31]

In March 1997, the Venezuelan Navy had some differences with the U.S. Navy
over the matter of boarding of vessels in the Caribbean. According to the
Venezuelan Navy, the 1991 agreement on maritime operations allowing for monitoring and control of air and sea navigation by the U.S. in international waters
did not extend to the participation of third-country ships nor to operations by the
U.S. Navy in Venezuelan waters. In July 1997, both governments signed a proto-

col to the 1991 agreement, known as the "Agreement on Cooperation against Illegal Traffic of Narcotic and Psychotropic Substances by Sea," in order that ships with third-country flags (the U.K., Holland, and France) might also participate in joint operations.[32] But Venezuela stood firm on the inviolability of its territorial seas and airspace, in contrast to neighboring Caribbean countries such as Trinidad and Tobago and the Dominican Republic. The U.S. evaluation of Venezuelan efforts hardened in 1997: " . . . Venezuela did not show during 1996 sufficient willingness to maintain strong opposition against drug traffic, to encourage military and police forces to cooperate, nor to develop effective coordination."[33] Venezuela did pursue an antidrug war at home, however (President Caldera named his own drug "czar" and gave him ministerial rank), and remained "certified" for the purposes of the U.S. Congress.

The Chávez government, with strong influence from the military, which had traditionally supported antidrug policy (as well as being its chief executor), followed the same line as its predecessors in limiting direct American action over Venezuelan territory. While the military abhors drugs, it also tends to share the view that there is no reason to allow American military forces any use of Venezuelan airspace. During the Twenty-Ninth General Assembly of the OAS in June 1999, the new minister of foreign affairs of Venezuela, José Vicente Rangel, criticized U.S drug policy and stressed with some irony that while the U.S government might worry about drug trafficking in Latin America and the Caribbean, Venezuela also worried about drug consumption in the United States. The drug problem, in the Venezuelan view, is a complex social phenomenon that will not be solved with interdiction, although control of trafficking is necessary for all countries. During a high-level visit by U.S. officials to Venezuela in July 1999, the two countries agreed to consolidate the dispersed collection of existing agreements on collaboration signed over the decade into a coherent joint policy, and the United States offered once again technical assistance, training, and equipment for fighting various aspects of the drug problem, including corruption, money laundering, and traffic in chemicals used in the manufacture of narcotics.[34] Yet U.S. officials insisted that Venezuela's approach fell below the effort required. Was this a friendly hint or a veiled threat?

Given President Chávez's sensitivity to American power, it is not surprising that he declared his rejection of the U.S. certification process. When the annual report was released at the beginning of March, 2000, Chávez immediately expressed his disapproval and noted that, in his view, it was the United States itself that was ineffectual in controlling the drug phenomenon.[35] For its part, the United States also recognizes the advantage of substituting its unilateral policy for multilateral cooperation (President Clinton's drug czar, Barry McCaffrey, admitted this), but Congress resisted accepting the faith in multilateral organizations that the executive sometimes favors. Venezuela has always passed the certification test with American recognition of its national efforts and cooperation, although the report consistently classified it between 1996 and 2000 as an important transit route for cocaine. Venezuelan refusal to allow overflights seemed not to be an issue that affected relations seriously, at least. In any case, Venezuela's policy tended to diverge from that of Colombia, which increasingly looked to the United States for help in controlling both its drug lords and its guerrillas after the election of President Andrés Pastrana, who projected himself as entirely different from his predecessor, Ernesto Samper, whose financial relations with drug lords had led to the decertification of Colombia as well as to the denial of an American visa to the president.[36]

Collaboration between Colombia and the United States under Pastrana grew to such an extent that when the U.S. Congress moved to grant the large aid package of $1.3 billion to Colombia,[37] Pastrana's government even hinted that it might seek a free trade arrangement within NAFTA. In Venezuela, the assistance to Colombia, largely in the form of aid to help control the production of drugs, was viewed as dangerous; it would increase Colombia's relative military power and might act as an incentive to guerrilla forces and drug traffickers to shift operations to Venezuela. Some even saw the danger of a new Vietnam. Thus drugs, guerrillas, and trade all combine to affect relationships. As Colombia moved closer to the United States, Venezuela seemed by default to be moving farther away from its two closest friends. There were even occasional rumors, said to be confirmed by U.S. intelligence, that Chávez harbored sympathies for the Colombian rebels and that he helped them (and dissident groups in Bolivia and Ecuador as well) with financing and protection. Enough was made of such rumors that both Chávez and his foreign minister, Rangel, were often forced to declare that Venezuela acted only in concert with the legally constituted governments in those countries. Chávez further fueled doubts when he said that guerrilla forces in Colombia were not the enemies of Venezuela; his minister of internal relations "clarified" the country's position by saying that the guerrillas were indeed enemies. Who was to be believed?

Recognizing the objections of Colombia's neighbors, the United States would propose extending the scope of "Plan Colombia." Despite his earlier doubts, President Chávez announced in 2001 Venezuela's interest in cooperating in the regional plan against the drug industry. The Venezuelan government's contradictory signals thus continued to confound both its immediate neighbors and the United States.

Further Complexities

Students of international politics understand the difficulty of abstracting bilateral relations from the network of the overlapping and interconnected associations on the larger world stage. We have seen how the Cold War, a conflict over issues that often seemed far from Venezuela's concerns, colored many aspects of foreign policy before the 1990s. The end of the Cold War hardly brought the end of the links among apparently unrelated events. The example of the war against drugs is one of many that illustrate how U.S.-Venezuelan relations get drawn into the relationship between the United States and Colombia. Often, diplomats are even taken by surprise when seemingly isolated events far from their agendas turn into bilateral issues. There are so many international actors, governmental and nongovernmental, that it can be hard to keep track of all of them.

American Ambassador John Maisto must have sensed the complexity he faced as the representative of the United States in Venezuela when he was alerted that a problem was brewing between Venezuela and its eastern neighbor, Guyana, just as Maisto was preparing his suitcase for a return to Washington after the elections of 2000. His departure from Venezuela was already overdue, since his replacement by the newly designated American ambassador, Donna Hrinak, was put off for two months as a result of the rescheduling of the Venezuelan elections, after serious administrative failures on the part of the National Electoral Council. Just as the election campaign was finally coming to an end, the Venezuelan foreign minister involved the United States government in a complaint against Guyana.

The Venezuelan-Guyana border is a major focus of security concerns for Venezuela, since the country has claimed that an arbitration settlement of 1899 unjustly assigned a large swath of territory, called the Essequibo, to then British Guiana.[38] The issue rose to the surface repeatedly over one hundred years, continuing after the Guyana achieved independence from Great Britain. At that time, in 1966, the dispute was recognized by the Geneva Accord, providing for a system of negotiation with the good offices of a neutral party to aid in reaching an agreement between the two parties. Under this agreement, Venezuela consistently requires that Guyana not grant concessions in the disputed area without Venezuela's acceptance, although Guyana, for its part, tended to ignore this requirement.

Such was the situation when Foreign Minister Rangel protested against a concession given by Guyana to the American company, Beal Aerospace Technologies, for the building of a base for launching satellites in the Essequibo region, close to the Venezuelan border. The U.S. government was immediately drawn into the dispute when Rangel described the deal as part of official U.S. policy. Ambassador Maisto claimed that the American government had nothing to do with the concession, since it was the result of a commercial agreement between the government of Guyana and a private firm. He did admit that Beal Aerospace would have to apply to the U.S. for a license for the export of sensitive technology but said that this did not involve the American government at all in the situation. The Venezuelan press speculated that the satellite launch base would be protected by U.S. troops, which the ambassador denied. Foreign Minister Rangel and President Chávez referred to the base as a missile launch base and not a satellite launch base, suggesting implicitly that the operation might have military uses. In fact, Guyana had previously granted concessions in the area, but none so close to the Venezuelan border.

The plot thickened somewhat as Venezuela considered its possible responses. In the heat of the electoral campaign then in process in Venezuela, some claimed that the case was evidence of typical saber rattling of the sort that leaders use to show their strength and patriotism, especially in political campaigns. Others saw it as another example of the way in which the Chávez government looked for ways to show its objections to U.S. presence in Latin America. Yet the complaint was consistent with the traditional Venezuelan policy of maintaining a firm claim to the disputed territory. What was new, perhaps, was the involvement of the U.S. government in the situation. It was clear, however, that the Venezuelan government had no wish to see the issue overblown. Foreign Minister Rangel quickly made appearances on television to explain the problem and to clarify that while many alternatives were being considered, any military response was excluded. Having sheathed the sword, he suggested that Venezuela might offer tit for a tat, awarding its own concessions for oil and gas exploration offshore in areas that were also under negotiation between Guyana and Venezuela and where Guyana had also offered concessions to American energy companies. Such an act, if carried out, would bring even more international companies, as well as the state-owned oil company, PDVSA, into an already complex relationship. In the end, Beal withdrew from the project in Guyana, and the issue receded from public attention.

The Guyana border problem, hardly noticed by any other than the parties directly affected, shows the intricacies of international diplomacy, which get played out in all of their complexity in even the smallest incidents. What seems to be a simple bilateral problem soon involves other countries; what seems to be a matter of government-to-government negotiation draws multinational firms into security politics. Small crises arise when least expected, and no ambassador can ever be sure that a minor incident will not convert itself into a major problem. Economic issues become security issues.

In the meantime, other ambassadors in Venezuela might have been resting peacefully, relieved that the Guyana problem belonged to Ambassador Maisto and not to them. Such luck would not be granted to the Chinese representative in Caracas, Liu Boming, when a similar protest was made by Venezuela just a few days before the elections of July 30, 2000, against another concession granted by Guyana, this time to a company from China. The surprised Chinese ambassador admitted that he had no information on the matter and that his government would, of course, look into it.[39] The Venezuelan government had found a creative way to send a message to the United States that its complaint against the Beal Aerospace concession reflected the global position of Venezuela with respect to its dispute with Guyana. Minister Rangel would manage to silence those who claimed that Venezuelan foreign policy was biased against the United States or in favor of countries like China that are perceived as powerful counterweights to the United States in international relations. The Guyana case summarizes well the way in which security issues can only rarely be reduced to purely military questions. It also reminds us that bilateral relationships can hardly ever be separated from the many crosscutting issues of international politics.

Economic Consensus and Economic Conflict

Those who denounce American foreign policy as imperialistic usually claim that its basis is economic. By its overweening power, the United States forces the rest of the world to accept economic arrangements favorable to the center and harmful to the periphery. A close study of economic relations between Venezuela and the United States would hardly support the imperialist charge: the United States has not intervened, at least directly, even at important moments when Venezuela abandoned free market policies; most economic disputes have been of a technical nature and have been resolved at the technical level; and some of the more delicate conflicts have pitted Venezuela not against the American executive power but against Congress and even governments at the state level. In the long dance of negotiations over the possible format for hemispheric economic integration, it is clear that agreements will be reached only if the major Latin American countries agree, because integration is like the tango: it takes two to do it, and even a great power like the United States cannot force anyone to take to the floor against its will.

Choice of Economic Models

Economic issues usually fall into the category of "low" politics, that is to say, the area of relations where no strategic issues are at stake. Contrary to what many would think, the United States maintains friendly relations with countries with very different kinds of economic systems, from Communist China to free market New Zealand, as long as certain basic rules are respected: just compensation for nationalization of properties, security of contract for investors, and the carrying out of international agreements. Brusque changes that complicate business decision-making are also frowned upon, but as long as a country manages its economy responsibly, it does not make much difference today what balance that country chooses when it comes to the role of the state in the economy.

Sometimes the fine line between tolerance for different economic systems and intolerance of poor economic policies tends to blur. When Venezuelan Ambassador Pedro Luis Echeverría presented his credentials to President Clinton in 1994, during the worst period of economic controls and upheaval resulting from the banking crash of that year in Venezuela, Clinton went so far as to administer advice, saying: "We accept your government's position that the controls are temporary, but we believe also that history has demonstrated that such policies are not the best means for achieving growth and economic stability."[40] The Caldera government reacted defensively, expressing its view that there were those interested in discrediting Venezuela in the United States, as Treasury Minister Julio Sosa Rodríguez claimed. This was probably true to the extent that both national and international firms chafed under the controls, and the economy was sinking ever lower.[41] In circumstances of this sort, the U.S. government need hardly take an open stand; the facts were there for all to read for themselves. President Caldera read those facts as well. As the economy sank and investment fell, so did his popularity. By late 1995, his government was preparing to return to liberalization, and when the moment arrived to remove exchange controls in 1996 and announce an opening to private investment in the oil industry, he found a quick, positive response on the part of both the U.S. government and investors.

According to market principles, investors can freely decide where to place their money and countries will simply face the consequences to the extent that they fail to provide a good place to do business to potential foreign investors. The standard rules of the game agreed upon in international organizations like the World Trade Organization or through regional or bilateral treaties are not obligatory, but neither is it easy to get along without them.

In the globalized world of economics, information plays a leading part in guaranteeing respect for the rules of the game. Governments hardly need to intervene. In international bond markets, the price of a country's financial paper—and the risk premium associated with it[42]—reflects what the markets judge to be the solidity of the country's economic policies. Thus exchange controls, price controls, slack attitudes toward the protection of trademarks and copyrights, reversals of contractual agreements, and a whole range of actions considered negative for foreign investment simply get publicized, as do positive moves toward modernization and reform. The results may be bad or good according to the circumstances, ranging from severe capital outflows and attacks on currencies to waves of confidence beyond what reality might justify. Venezuela has passed through wildly different phases, from the exchange crises of 1989 and 1994 to the heavy interventionism of the period 1994 to 1996, to the ebullient markets of 1992 and 1997 when Venezuela briefly fell into the category of "darling" among emerging market economies, and again to deep depression in 1998 and 1999, when the international oil price fell to historically low levels.

While the United States welcomed the market-oriented policies to which President Caldera finally returned in March 1996, its interest seemed as much political as economic, perhaps due to fears that continued economic decline in Venezuela would endanger political stability. President Clinton himself praised the measures adopted (currency devaluation, elimination of the exchange control system, and the search for an agreement with the IMF), referring to the fact that the United States was "deeply interested in the welfare and economic stability of Venezuela for which we compliment and applaud the economic reforms announced by President Rafael Caldera." President Clinton also reiterated that "Venezuela is a bastion of Latin American democracy. It is also our main oil supplier and one of our main economic partners in the Hemisphere."[43] U.S. Deputy Secretary of State Strobe Talbott visited Caracas a second time in the month of May of 1996. Talbott voiced Washington's support for the economic measures adopted by the Caldera administration, saying "the United States will avail itself of its position in multinational forums, in the International Monetary Fund, the World Bank and the IDB to give its support to Venezuela and ensure success for its economic plan."[44]

While the United States and Venezuela appeared to have achieved a common view about the direction of the Venezuelan economy between 1996 and 1998, storm clouds were forming on the horizon in the form of a collapse in the world price of oil in 1998 following the economic crisis in Asia. Caldera's market policies and partial opening of the Venezuelan oil industry to foreign investment came under attack in the presidential election campaign of 1998. On taking power in early 1999, the Chávez government sought to distance itself from its liberalizing predecessors and made frequent criticisms of what the president called "savage capitalism" and neoliberalism. The United States chose to view much of the rhetoric as political and refrained from commenting, although American investors worried that Venezuela might return again to heavy government intervention in the economy. Every time that President Chávez made reference to what he called the "sea of happiness" made possible by the social gains of the Cuban revolution in education and health, for instance, investors felt a chill. Many saw such statements as explicit attempts to define the Venezuelan economic system as essentially different from the capitalist one espoused by the United States. But, they reasoned, no Venezuelan government could ignore reality: Chávez would need foreign investment and would probably just have to play according to the rules of the international economy.

Management of Economic Crises in Venezuela

Despite the ups and downs, the swings between controls and free markets, economic conflict with the United States has always been kept at the level of "low politics." Venezuelan decision-makers, politicians, and sometimes entrepreneurs and journalists might still claim or believe that American policy somehow contributed to the nation's ills, often because of a lack of understanding of the real difficulties faced by developing countries, especially in paying off their foreign debts. The United States tends to leave such problems to the markets and to the supervision of its own financial institutions.

The sequence of economic events within Venezuela from the 1980s to the present suggests a high level of tolerance for poor economic policies on the part of the United States. In the 1980s, during the government of President Jaime Lusinchi, Venezuela faced severe pressures resulting from excessive debt that had been run up on the expectation that oil money would never run out. When it did, no long-term strategies were developed to solve the problem. Lusinchi maintained exchange controls throughout his five years in power, finally reducing Venezuela's international reserves to unsustainable levels. The United States hardly took notice, although it did welcome the change of model adopted by the following government headed by Carlos Andrés Pérez.

Pérez assumed the presidency in 1989 with few alternatives but to accept the advice of the IMF and negotiate new terms for the country's foreign debt. Venezuela was not the only developing country with such problems, and the United States recognized that impending bankruptcies in Mexico, Brazil, and Argentina could affect the international financial system and decided to take direct action. The motive was the perceived threat to the stability of the system itself and particularly the threat to those banks with heavy exposure in Latin America. Citibank took heavy losses in 1988, for instance. The solution took the form of the Brady Bond program, designed for a large group of countries in similar straits,[45] which permitted Venezuela to restructure its foreign debt in the early 1990s along the same lines already negotiated with other countries.

Brady Bonds, named for the U.S. Secretary of the Treasury Nicholas Brady, allowed countries to restructure their debt by replacing it with these specially issued U.S. government–guaranteed bonds available to those creditors that agreed to the terms. Restructuring meant longer periods for paying off the debt, lower interest rates, and even some debt forgiveness, depending on the different options available. The operation was carried out almost exclusively by the Department of the Treasury and the Federal Reserve Bank, with little input from the State Department.[46] The positive experience with this negotiated bailout led to further efforts to supervise the international financial system and provide solutions to countries with structural imbalances, although critics would also claim that the existence of such aid would act as an incentive to irresponsibility.

In Venezuela, the adjustment policies of the Pérez government turned out to be short-lived as a result of domestic political opposition to Pérez, which produced his downfall and eventual replacement by President Rafael Caldera, whose platform promised an end to Perez's supposedly shortsighted "neoliberal" policies. Once again, the United States refrained from direct comment, although undoubtedly it viewed the possibility of a return to inward-looking and protectionist policies with chagrin. President Caldera faced his own crisis between 1994 and 1996, when he was also forced to negotiate with the multilateral lending organizations. Like Pérez before him, he encountered opposition from his soon-to-be successor, Hugo Chávez, whose campaign in 1998 for the presidency echoed Caldera's own platform of 1993. Despite attempts to achieve a sound base for its economy, Venezuela ended the decade of the 1990s with a record of failed efforts that left many of its underlying problems unresolved.

Of course, low politics can turn into high politics when small problems explode into big ones. Economics and politics run together. The failure of Venezuela to resolve its economic difficulties in the 1990s, the pressures from domestic interests to return to protectionist solutions, and the political disintegration that followed from economic decay would paradoxically generate political forces that many analysts saw as unfriendly to the United States' vision of democracy ("the freedom package") and of economics (the "neoliberal package"). Yet much of the supposed conflict over economic solutions owed as much to language as to reality. Both Caldera and Chávez appealed to voters with their criticisms of liberal policies at the same time that leaders in developed countries were doing the same. Britain's Prime Minister Tony Blair adopted the idea of the "Third Way" as his version of capitalism with a human face, a concept that appealed to both President Clinton and President Chávez.

Regardless of the ideological debate, the need to maintain positive economic relations with the United States could never be far from Venezuelan leaders' concerns. The brief, steep fall in the oil price that hit Venezuela in 1998 meant that Chávez would take office at a time of severe shortfalls in government income and deep recession at the start of 1999. The new president could hardly afford to take risks by adopting unorthodox or populist policies, especially since so many doubts surrounded his likely economic program. It was no secret that Chávez used his influence to make sure that the new Venezuelan Constitution was well received by foreign investors in its economic clauses protecting private property, recognizing equal rights for foreign investors, and respecting economic rights.

This is not to say that there was no cause for concern. The Venezuelan president never lost an opportunity to decry the defects of "savage capitalism" and often expressed his sympathy for the plight of desperate groups that invaded private lands for squatter settlements. While he defended private property, he was also quick to add that it was not "sacred" but subject to limits and responsibilities. There was just enough ambiguity in his words to put foreign investors on alert, and the new Constitution, approved at the end of 1999, contained some clauses that also gave rise to doubts about the kind of economy Chávez had in mind. The United States once again showed tolerance and refrained from associating itself with opponents of Chávez who claimed that the Constitution violated principles of the free market, even if officials entertained some private doubts about the climate for investment in the country.

Venezuela and the Free Trade Area of the Americas

In 1994, the new U.S. president, Bill Clinton, the president of Mexico, and the Canadian prime minister signed the North American Free Trade Agreement (NAFTA). With the signature of this treaty, the ground was set for the development of a free trade area, which its signers hoped would one day extend itself to the rest of the hemisphere. In December 1994, a summit was held in Miami, where thirty-four heads of state and government began to discuss the possibility of adopting a joint hemispheric opening and free trade program known as the FTAA (Free Trade Association of the Americas).

Touching on the varied issues of trade, regional integration, democracy, government reform, sustainable development, the fight against corruption and drug traffic, the eradication of poverty, and other matters, the leaders at the summit approved an ambitious Statement of Principles. The accord, to which Venezuela also agreed, set the goal of creating by the year 2005 a free trade area in the Americas and adopted an action plan for the elimination of barriers to the trade in goods and services and the signing of agreements on nontariff barriers. Three meetings were held at the presidential level, in Miami in 1994, Santiago de Chile in 1998, and Quebec in 2001. Fifteen working groups were created to deal with the issues of investments, services, government purchases, technical standards, sanitary and phytosanitary measures, customs procedures and copyrights, subsidies, antidumping and compensatory rights, safeguards, competitiveness, and dispute resolution.[47] Special meetings occurred regularly among trade ministers, finance ministers, and the like.

To permit a gradual approach, the countries decided that each could negotiate entry into the FTAA individually or as a bloc. Chile started to negotiate individually, while most others—the Andean Community, Mercosur, and CARICOM—looked for allies before going it alone with such a powerful group as the NAFTA countries. Paradoxically, and to Chile's disgust, the U.S. Congress showed little enthusiasm for the scheme and balked at giving President Clinton "fast-track" authority to facilitate negotiations. Thus progress tended to slow on the creation of the FTAA, a fact that seemed clear at the second Summit of Santiago in 1998. Only when newly elected George W. Bush reaffirmed his intention to renew the effort did some hopes rise for a second wind. At Quebec, all countries agreed again on advancing toward the FTAA by 2005; only Venezuela expressed its formal reservation with regard to the feasibility of the date.

The project for an FTAA raised questions on a wide range of issues for many countries. 1) What would be the effect of the FTAA on trade between Latin America and the Caribbean and the other countries of the European Union and Asia? Would it increase American hegemony in the hemisphere? 2) Would there truly be possibilities to penetrate the North American market for the developing countries, or would the benefits run in only one direction? 3) Would great investment in the region require acceptance of changes in domestic legislation in the field of labor, standards of origin, intellectual property, environment, and competition that might be difficult in terms of internal politics? 4) Would the U.S. Congress and public support the president even if it were possible to reach agreements? Such questions only became more urgent after the failure of trade negotiations within the WTO meeting held in Seattle at the end of 1999, where the most vociferous protesters were American groups with powerful backing. The protests in Quebec in 2001 were no less disturbing for advocates of the FTAA.

The idea of a free trade area in the Americas raised these and additional doubts. Although there is in the region full awareness of the political, economic, and social implications of a project of this kind, the preparatory work of the involved governments and organizations tended to concentrate on technical economic questions, leaving aside more sensitive political and cultural aspects.[48] From the Venezuelan point of view, opening up the American market might look less attractive than it would to other Latin American countries, since its main export, oil, would not benefit from liberalization. Venezuela's oil economy makes it a large importer and only a small exporter of nonpetroleum goods. Other Latin American countries might benefit more, as did Mexico from NAFTA. Equally, domestic manufacturers in Venezuela, already pressured by imports, never showed great enthusiasm for trade liberalization, which threatens their domestic advantage. For many, it was an article of faith that the lowering of tariffs in the 1990s had led to the deindustrialization of the country and that local producers would be wiped out if they lost the protection of tariffs and nontariff barriers to trade. Venezuela was not likely to be a booster for the FTAA, whatever the government in power.

In the midst of these circumstances, the member countries of the Andean Community, Venezuela among them, began to debate over whether to promote a restricted approach to the FTAA or a wide vision of it. Both the Caldera and the Chávez governments sought to create ties with other countries before choosing their own strategy. Thus Venezuela began to look for a link to Mercosur, even threatening to do so without the company of its Andean partners. And when this approach met resistance, Venezuela and Brazil met to explore bilateral alternatives, such as improving transportation links, integrating electrical systems, and creating a joint venture in oil between PDVSA and Petrobras (the Brazilian oil company), announced in June 1999. In 2001, Venezuela did ask for associate status in Mercosur, although at that time, Mercosur was itself under intense pressure resulting from an economic crisis in Argentina. Latin American and Caribbean countries at the same time organized a high-level summit with European countries whose purpose it was to create a "strategic alliance" between the two regions. This alliance served at least as a symbolic answer to American influence in the hemisphere, although its practical implications appeared limited in the face of European barriers to agricultural exports.

Overall, Venezuela consistently tended to avoid giving clear signals on the FTAA. The multiplicity of international identities, the importance of oil, and the reiterated position on the need for mechanisms that would give protection against U.S. dominance explain why Venezuela has not played a feature role in FTAA negotiations. At the same time, Venezuela could hardly let itself be left behind if others were to go ahead with the FTAA. One fear was that its neighbors might abandon their commitment to a joint approach. Chile had initiated such a strategy, and Colombia began to discuss the advantage of entering FTAA on its own, which could only irritate Venezuela.

At the same time, Venezuela was not showing sustained interest in deepening integration within the Andean Community. We have already seen how the Chávez government terminated the free transit of trucks from Colombia in 1999. Other disputes emerged as well, mostly with respect to Venezuelan limits on imports of agricultural goods from its Andean neighbors, including vegetable oil, garlic, eggs, coffee, sugar cane, and milk. The Andean Court of Justice ruled against Venezuelan restrictions on coffee and garlic and allowed that extra duties could be charged on a limited number of goods by other countries in the community as a sanction.[49] Chávez's vice-minister of trade announced that Venezuela would suggest that the Andean Community do away with the Court of Justice— whose decisions are binding and without redress—in favor of a much less binding system of conciliation to resolve conflicts.[50] At the same time, Venezuela instituted a system of licensing for some agricultural imports, a clear reversal of its former commitment to reduce quantitative restrictions on trade. Venezuela's commitment to integration seemed to be fraying at the edge, even though its rhetoric hailed the necessity of regional solidarity, especially with Latin countries that shared Bolívar's vision of a united continent. If the Andean Community were to be weakened by Venezuela, why would its partners not look for alternatives?

Even if Venezuela's interest in promoting free trade were weak, its need for foreign investment would require it to go along with any real prospect for a free trade regime in the hemisphere should a regional consensus emerge. In the meantime, Venezuela could count on resistance to the FTAA, and to trade liberalization in general, among important groups within U.S. domestic politics. President Clinton failed to win congressional approval for fast-track negotiations to lower trade barriers and chose not to push hard on a controversial issue as a lame-duck president. Opponents of free trade in the United States showed their force in protests during the Seattle meeting that would supposedly launch a new round of negotiations within the WTO at the end of 1999. President George W. Bush seemed determined to take up the banner of the FTAA after his election, but no one could doubt that he would face opposition within the United States. Venezuela, in no hurry, could not complain.

Low Politics: From Tuna to Trademarks

Everyday relations between two countries that have a high level of contact are full of small problems that only rarely have long-term implications, although they can rattle nerves from time to time. Over the course of the decade of the nineties, Venezuela and the United States found themselves with numerous difficulties that caused irritations but that usually got resolved through normal bureaucratic channels. As long as these problems result from general rules applied without discrimination, technical treatment tends to suffice; when evidence mounts that a policy in one or the other country affects one industry in particular, however, questions arise about motivations and protests rise to the political or diplomatic level.

Environmental and trade conflicts usually result from the application of general rules without distinction by country. Venezuelan tuna fish exports to the United States ran into an embargo when fishing technologies designed to protect dolphins were required for imported products. As a member of the Interamerican Commission on Tropical Tuna, Venezuela signed an international agreement in 1995 to reduce the killing of dolphins, a step toward the suspension of the embargo. Similar environmental strictures threatened shrimp imports to the United States from Venezuela, where methods were said to endanger tortoises. A joint inspection was carried out by American and Venezuelan officials to study the situation, and in April 1995, Venezuelan shrimp was certified for export.

The tuna and shrimp cases clearly fell under general rules with particular significance for Venezuela. This contrasts with other cases of environmental rules that led to the conclusion that particular interests in the United States took advantage of the popular support for a clean environment in order to gain competitive advantages against Venezuelan exports. In another case, in the mid-1990s, the Environmental Protection Agency (EPA) published a set of complicated regulations on the level of contaminating elements permissible in gasoline sold in the country under the Clean Air Act. Among the requirements were rules for calculation that differentiated between American companies and foreign companies, apparently due to assumptions about the greater reliability of domestic figures. The regulation also referred to different contaminants in such a way as to disfavor Venezuelan reformulated gasoline, which was already subject to an investment program aimed at reducing the contaminants sulphur and benzene. While an agreement seemed imminent with the EPA, the U.S. Congress intervened to prohibit the change in the regulation. According to the industry, a competitor in the United States had lobbied to achieve this result.

Undaunted, PDVSA put its lawyers to work on the issue in Washington, and Venamcham lent extra support with its own petition favoring the Venezuelan position. President Caldera made counterthreats that Venezuela could stop buying U.S. wheat, although such a move would probably have cost him more in domestic support than he could afford. In the end, Venezuela (together with Brazil) made a complaint in September 1994 to the GATT (the General Agreements on Tariffs and Trade, transformed into the World Trade Organization in 1995) and won its case in 1996 on the grounds that the U.S. treatment was discriminatory, although in the longer run, PDVSA will have to adapt its products to EPA rules that require, for instance, a 90 percent reduction in sulphur emissions by the year 2006.[51] The victory gave a shot of confidence to Venezuela and strengthened the idea that the international organizations could truly achieve neutrality.

PDVSA confronted another competitive block in its efforts to sell its coal substitute, called Orimulsion (a mixture of water and heavy hydrocarbons), for use in the generating plants of the Florida Power and Light Company. Orimulsion contaminates less than coal but more than fuel oil, yet environmental interests began to lobby against the Orimulsion contract. In fact, American coal companies felt threatened, and Venezuela argued that the environmentalists were being used for other purposes. The governor of the state of Florida, when pressured to favor the Orimulsion contract, showed himself unwilling to take a position that seemed to go against the strong environmental lobby. The contract did not get signed.[52] Interestingly, when international trade issues take place at the state and municipal level, outside the purview of international rules for nondiscrimination, fewer options exist to defend a small country's interests.

For a country whose contacts with the United States are as strong as Venezuela's, American regulation of civil aviation becomes almost extraterritorial. The United States requires that flights arriving in the country from abroad comply with a series of safety rules considered indispensable by the International Civil Aviation Organization. The rules themselves have a global character, but their implementation depends on each member country. The United States applies them strictly, classifying the places of origin according to their adherence to the rules. During the 1990s, Venezuela fell from Category 1 (full compliance) to Category 2 (incomplete compliance, with time for correction), under which no new airlines can receive approval to fly to the United States. Successive ministers in the Venezuelan Ministry of Transport and Communications (now called Infrastructure) insisted that they would soon resolve the difficulty, but each left without having achieved anything. In 1999, a bill on civil aviation was drafted in Venezuela and, illustrating the great influence of the United States, was under study by the Federal Aviation Administration to check for its compliance with the requirements for Category 1.[53] Despite the delay in dealing with this problem— which could even threaten all Venezuelan airlines should the classification drop to Category 3—no Venezuelan official made the least complaint about foreign imposition or violation of sovereignty, given the multilateral nature of the system of rules. By 2000, major construction was under way at Maiquetía Airport in order to restore Venezuela to Category 1.

Intellectual property rights, including the protection of trademarks, copyrights, and patents, frequently pit U.S. (and non-U.S.) companies against the weak institutions that enforce these rights in Venezuela. As member of the WTO, Venezuela committed itself to complying with the full implementation by the year 2000 of the global rules for the protection of intellectual property, called TRIPS, which refers to "Trade Related Aspects of Intellectual Property" and, as signatory to the Paris Convention, must also comply with the international rules on intellectual property in general. In the meantime, full compliance with the TRIPS required reform of the Venezuelan Industrial Property Law by 2000,[54] viewed as unlikely during the legal uncertainty associated with the writing of a new Constitution during 1999 and even thereafter.[55] Heavy lobbying by local domestic pharmaceutical manufacturers contributed to the consistent efforts by the Venezuelan government to put off compliance as long as possible.

Venezuelan firms have often violated intellectual property rights with great impunity, and some government rules even encourage such practices, as is the case in the production of medicines by local laboratories. Despite the creation of a new office for property rights, the Autonomous Service for Intellectual Property (SAPI, by its Spanish initials), the courts accorded only weak protection to well-known trademarks, leading to constant complaints by companies and their governments with respect to the lack of "judicial security" in the country. The American government put Venezuela on its "Watch List" in 1989 under the Trade Act of 1988, which requires the monitoring of trade practices in other countries. A report of the United States Trade Representative stated in 1998: "There is still widespread piracy of well-known trademarks, videos, satellite signals, and other protected works. Moreover, the Venezuelan court system has proven to be an unreliable means for pursuing IPR claims."[56]

The improvement of Venezuelan standards for the protection of intellectual property also formed part of the conditions required for the signing of a bilateral investment treaty with the United States. The Caldera government recognized that such a treaty would advance the compliance date already specified within the WTO for the year 2000, but this and other problems led Caldera to put off negotiations and leave this thorny issue for his successor. Somewhat surprisingly for those who predicted a more nationalistic position on its part, the Chávez government showed its willingness to support the international rules by giving the green light to a clause in the new Constitution that would clearly give precedence to the rules set by organizations for economic integration. Thus when the Andean Community approved Decision 485 in 2000, putting the community in line with WTO rules, Venezuela automatically committed itself to respect the global rules on intellectual property.

Despite the doubts it might have about judicial security in Venezuela, the United States has only a relatively short list of complaints about protectionist trade policies there. When the Pérez government liberalized trade in the early nineties, reducing tariffs to low average levels, eliminating most quantitative restrictions, and creating the Anti-Dumping Commission to administer complaints on a technocratic basis, the United States itself became vulnerable to charges that its own protection tended to discriminate, particularly against imports from poorer countries. In fact, like most countries, both Venezuela and the United States have devised a series of remedies to protect their own agricultural production. Here, sanitary requirements often do the job that tariffs cannot.

The United States objected, for instance, to a ban on poultry imports based on the risk of avian influenza, which, according to USTR, is not scientifically sustainable.

Such skirmishing is normal, but the threat of approval of a bill on food security in Venezuela supported there by the Agriculture Federation (Fedeagro) generated the opposition of American multinational food companies that feared that the inclusion of the concept of food security would signal a regression to a policy of minimizing dependence on foreign sources. More radical adherents of protectionism in Venezuela argued that the country should try to shift consumption away from wheat products, which are largely imported from the United States, toward local staples like rice and corn. Some supported the idea that this principle should be included in the new Constitution and partially won their point. Yet the final text referred to food security only in somewhat ambiguous terms whose meaning would depend on how later governments would interpret them.

Under the rules of the WTO, member countries can impose compensatory tariffs to counteract the "dumping" of goods from abroad, that is, goods with prices below costs in the exporting country. Dumping violates the rules of fair trade by destabilizing markets. Various Venezuelan products, including ferrosilicates, rebars, nails, welded pipe, and steel wire, have faced dumping charges made to the Federal Trade Commission, usually based on the alleged existence of government subsidies (through low energy prices or state-owned enterprises) that permit below-cost pricing. The U.S. Commerce Department also threatened sanctions against Venezuelan and Caribbean banana producers who had signed an agreement with the European Community in 1994, and initiated an investigation of possible subsidies on Venezuelan cement. The mid-nineties saw a profusion of conflicts of this type, although most were resolved in favor of Venezuela. In 1995, the United States included Venezuela in its General System of Preferences (GSP) for a five-year period. Exports to the United States in 1999, however, were at about the same level they had reached in 1995, so it cannot be said that inclusion in the GSP served as a great incentive to increase trade. The same would probably be true should Venezuela be included in the U.S. system of preferences for Andean countries that combat the illegal drug industry.

These experiences taught Venezuela that technical preparation and solidly built arguments go a long way in bolstering its position in trade conflicts, since the international rules provide a relatively even playing field. Yet technical arguments require a high degree of professionalism, a fact that puts poorer countries at a disadvantage at times. There is considerable pressure in Venezuela in favor of training government officials in the ways of global rules as well as preparing them as negotiators. It is notable that when, in 1999, a group of small oil producers from Texas charged PDVSA with dumping its oil in the United States, the Venezuelan response had matured: both PDVSA and the government asserted that the technical basis for the complaint was wanting (Venezuela is one of the world's lowest-cost producers) and quietly began preparing to meet the challenge.

As a country learns how to defend itself in international trade disputes, it also learns more sophisticated methods for getting around the rules in a legal way. Venezuela's Anti-Dumping Commission was originally designed as a truly independent authority charged with investigating possible violations by trading partners. As time went on, it seemed that the government feared that an excess of independence might harm the country's interests. Taking full advantage of the rules of the WTO, the Chávez government approved a Commercial Safeguards Act in 2000 that would permit temporary trade restrictions on destabilizing imports and reform the rules of the Anti-Dumping Commission, reducing its independent power of decision.

Apart from trade and intellectual property issues, judicial security comprises a wide range of problems that concern foreign investors and that come to the attention of U.S. authorities. Venezuela usually finds itself close to the bottom of the rankings in competitiveness published by the World Economic Forum of Davos, Switzerland, and one of the most negative factors noted by the annual reports is the lack of confidence in the judicial system. The honesty of local courts also concerned Venezuelans, and reform was first initiated in the Caldera government with the support of the World Bank; this program was overtaken by a sweeping decision by the Constituent Assembly to overhaul the court system entirely. The outcome of the venture was difficult to predict, and some observers thought that the country ran the danger of replacing one group of politicized judges by another. One real improvement from the point of view of foreign investors was the greater acceptance of international arbitration incorporated in the 1999 Constitution, which at least opened up the possibility of resolving disputes in neutral courts.

Several other cases illustrate the nature of the complexities of government rule-making. When President Chávez named as his energy minister Alí Rodríguez, oil companies that had won contracts to explore for new oil in Venezuela feared that their plans might come to naught, since Rodríguez had challenged the contracts as illegal when he was a congressman, taking the case to the Supreme Court. By 1999, two years after the suit was brought, the Court had not given its opinion. Rodríguez himself softened his position and, on assuming his ministerial position, recognized that insistence on the contracts' illegality would contribute to the view that contracts in Venezuela could not be trusted; he promised that future contracts would be framed in such a way as to conform to the letter and spirit of the law and supported the new text in the 1999 Venezuelan Constitution that would give legitimacy to the contracts. Despite a challenge in the Supreme Tribunal (the new name for the highest court under the 1999 Constitution), the contracts were upheld, and stability seemed to have been guaranteed in Venezuela.

GTE, owner of the telephone company since its privatization in 1992, suffered some doubts similarly in 1999, when the new authorities at the

Telecommunications Commission (Conatel) expressed the opinion that despite the fact that the temporary monopoly granted the company had not run out, the company had already had enough time to prepare for competition; additionally, the formula for rate increases would not be applied because the quality of service was deficient, even though the company responded that such a charge should be backed up by facts and that, in any case, telephone rates were not subject to quality indicators. In the end, a satisfactory compromise reduced the tensions between the government and the telephone company, and the programmed transition to competition went ahead without serious snags at the start of 2001.

Another case involved private oil companies interested in the opening of the market for domestic distribution of gasoline. The Caldera government approved new regulations to allow foreign companies to operate gasoline stations. They were encouraged to invest even though the final arrangements had not been approved, on the understanding that they would be able to compete on pump prices (although they would all be subject to a single wholesale price from the industry). As it turned out, the law on commercialization of gasoline products did not allow price competition at the pump and companies that had gone ahead with investments, including Mobil Oil, complained that they had been led on by the authorities. Needless to say, the imminence of discussions on a new Constitution awoke fears that restrictions might further limit the principle of nondiscrimination or create new insecurities. The Chávez government argued that the opposite would be true: the new constitution would provide for just that basis of judicial security that the investors had lacked under the former regime.[57] Minister of Industry and Trade Gustavo Márquez (who had been one of the most unyielding opponents of the privatization of the telephone company in 1992) sought to calm the nerves of the investors by proposing a new bill for the protection of foreign investment, which many simply saw as a weak substitute for the stalled Bilateral Investment Treaty with the United States when it was finally approved in 1999.

Trade and investment issues provide a constant diet of small conflicts between countries. Technical rules usually exist to determine the outcomes, but in many circumstances, disputes arise over the meaning of the rules. Increasingly, transparency plays an important role in reducing the temptations countries may have to interpret the rules according to their interests. To the extent that this is true, smaller countries like Venezuela find themselves on a more level playing field. For this reason, in the low politics of commercial relations, explicit rules and agreed-upon procedures for settling disputes tend to permit a symmetry of relations that lowers the impact of power inequalities and gives smaller countries like Venezuela greater confidence in their place in the world.

Global Negotiations

Since the rules set by international organizations increasingly provide the context in which differences among countries are be negotiated, how these rules are set becomes an important part of the story. A country with a gripe now has the option of looking for redress in global institutions, widening the range of possibilities. We have assumed until now that the international rules are a sort of given, affecting countries without their having any control over the game itself. But international rules for trade or investment or other values such as human rights are not brought down from the mountain by Moses—they are hammered out in international forums by the countries themselves. Not surprisingly, the United States enjoys an advantage in drawing up the rules based on its bargaining resources of all types: skilled personnel, financial strength, range of logrolling issues, and global interest.

To strengthen their position in such international negotiations, countries like Venezuela look to allies to represent shared interests. Sometimes it is a question of joining with regional partners to counteract the arguments of more developed countries, although at other times, the national interest leads to teaming up with the United States itself. Such was the case when Central American banana producers looked to the United States to stand up to European barriers to their product. On international trade and investment questions, the alliances shift with the issues. For Venezuela, the Andean Community, despite its frequent internal conflicts, constitutes an important mechanism for taking stands within the WTO, for instance, which was especially evident in the preparations leading up to the Millennium Round that was to be kicked off in Seattle at the end of 1999. In 1997, at the Council of Andean Presidents meeting held in Bolivia, a mandate was given to the group's foreign ministers to strengthen the joint negotiating position of member countries. This was reiterated the following year in Guayaquil, Ecuador.

Venezuelan Secretary General of the Andean Community Sebastián Alegrett supported the objective on the basis of the view that "globalization and the serious consequences of its excesses require adequate international regulation, especially for developing countries."[58] His view was seconded by Acting President of the Andean Community Néstor Osorio Londoño of Colombia, in a meeting of the General Council of the WTO in December of 1998, representing the five Andean nations together. The intention was clearly to present a common front in the WTO negotiations; to identify those issues where the Andean Community already had a common policy to be defended in the global organization; and to decide on the new issues that would require developing a position, such as electronic commerce, transparency in government purchasing, and rules for regulating competition and investment. It would also be necessary to coordinate on problems of tariff setting, textile trade limits, and conflict resolution, as well as dealing with the sensitive questions of workplace issues and the environment.

Venezuela simultaneously worked to refine its own positions and capabilities for the negotiating round. It was especially interested in future discussions on intellectual property as related to the particular problems of development and the need for a longer period before the full application of the rules on biodiversity and access to genetic materials, and on trade in services, especially as they related to energy. Its ambassador to the WTO in Geneva maintained close contact with Caracas and promoted training for officials in negotiating techniques as well as study of the global rules applying to the limits on industrial policies aimed at giving incentives to local firms.

The issue of industrial policy—specific policies to give incentives to the development of particular industries—was especially close to the heart of both the Caldera and the Chávez governments, both of which wished to preserve national prerogatives in development policy, somewhat to the concern of the United States, which tended to oppose any state intervention that might put its own foreign investors at a disadvantage vis-à-vis local firms. Venezuela considered it to be especially positive, at least from the symbolic point of view, when a Venezuelan, Miguel Mendoza Rodríguez, was named deputy director in the WTO. The episodes surrounding the opening of the new round of negotiations within the WTO in Seattle, complex from every point of view, are only one example of how bilateral relationships become intertwined with multilateral and regional ones in the interdependent world of today. Both Venezuela and the United States operate at various levels to shape their international relations in such a way that purely bilateral issues fill less of the common agenda.

To sum up the issues that make up the substance of relations between Venezuela and the United States, it could be said that the two countries play out their differences in a bilateral framework increasingly subsumed in a set of rules agreed to in international institutions ranging from global organizations to regional associations to special purpose agreements. This fact tends to smooth the edges of bilateral conflicts to the extent that solutions can be found at a higher level, even recognizing the greater resources of the United States in gaining influence in multilateral institutions. Some problems inevitably remain strictly bilateral, of course, but the change that marks world politics in general surely transformed Venezuelan-U.S. relations in the nineties.[59]

SIX
TRANSNATIONAL POLITICS AND BILATERAL RELATIONS

FOREIGN POLICY IN A DEMOCRACY INEVITABLY GOES BEYOND THE confines of government itself. Increasingly intertwined with official policy are the multiple contacts among individuals and groups across societies. This is not to say that such contacts occur without relation to government policy; after all, even tourists must accept rules about visas and passports, currency exchange and customs. At the same time, pressures from organized groups lead to changes in foreign policy in response to public opinion, and, in this sense, many see that a new actor has assumed a place in international relations in the form of nongovernmental organizations (NGOs) that have interests of a regional or global scope. Many of these organizations defend human rights, the environment, and other supranational interests, but it should not be assumed that all are saintly altruists. Money launderers and exploitative sects also roam the international scene, often clothing themselves in the same heavenly robes as their more legitimate opponents. In this chapter, we will look at some of the ways this new factor in world politics, a part of the general phenomenon of globalization, influences relations between the United States and Venezuela.

Foreign policy in a democracy involves the participation of all sorts of groups, from special interests to defenders of general values. High politics get mixed with low politics. For example, Venezuelan oil exports to the United States, formerly seen as strategic, now involve environmental issues in individual states, as the Orimulsion case reviewed in the last chapter showed. Venezuelan democracy is monitored by many NGOs[1] and the mass media; meanwhile, competitors keep track of Venezuelan economic policy as well. Even as a high U.S. official praises Venezuelan democracy, an independent report criticizing human rights violations in Venezuelan prisons might be in the news. Bilateral relations certainly go beyond governments. This chapter will look at some of the ways in which people make foreign policy, even the common citizen who thinks he is minding his own business.

Drug Cartels as Transnational Actors

One of the most important issues in international commerce never gets to the negotiating table at the World Trade Organization because of its illegal nature: the trade in prohibited drugs. Drug trafficking, which represents a huge business today (estimates of illegal drug sales in the United States range from $40 billion by official estimates to $150 billion according to some academic sources[2]), comprises an underworld of relations that exists in spite of vigorous government efforts to squash it. Some would go so far as to argue that it flourishes precisely because governments repress it.[3] Because of the harm done to its society by the spread of drug use, the United States has pursued an active antidrug policy for many years. The Reagan administration stepped up spending on antidrug policy, approving Anti-Drug Acts in 1986 and 1988, a policy continued through the Bush and Clinton administrations.

Even as drug "czars" came and went, large amounts of narcotics were seized on the seas and at the border, and Latin American countries received aid to reduce cultivation and break up cartels, consumption continued in the United States. U.S. administrations paid more attention to the Latin American argument that as long as American society demanded drugs, the fight to suppress supply would have little effect. The largest source of drug supply in Latin America was traditionally Colombia, where guerrilla warfare against the regime weakened state capabilities and even produced the phenomenon called "narcoguerrillas," as the drug traffic turned into a source of revenue for guerrilla forces. Inevitably, effects from narcotrafficking and guerrilla activities spread to neighboring Venezuela, whose long and lightly defended border with Colombia would permit incursions by guerrillas, kidnappings, and eventually the use of Venezuela as an indirect route for transporting drugs. Chapter Five reviewed the difficulties that developed between the United States and Venezuela with respect to their different visions of how to deal with the problem.

The economic significance of the international drug market has turned drug criminals into major actors in an underworld with its own rules of the game, both defying governments' efforts to restrain them and even infiltrating them in order to buy independence and freedom of action. Venezuela has been reluctant to admit that such infiltration may have occurred in its own bureaucracy or in its armed forces. Of course, corruption can occur in any system, and all governments shoulc be alert to the insidious methods of drug criminals.

In Venezuela, doubts persist about the effectiveness of antidrug policies, despite active efforts to pursue traffickers, the creation of the Anti-Drug Commission, and increased surveillance of possible money laundering by the superintendent of banks. No one could ever explain how it was that a pardon of a known drug trafficker was slipped among the papers to be signed by interim president Ramón Velázquez in 1993. Others saw it as ominous that a clause forbidding extradition of Venezuelan citizens was approved virtually without debate in the Constituent Assembly preparing the new Constitution of 1999 when, in neighboring Colombia, the controversial extradition law is seen as a prime tool in deterring drug lords, who fear the U.S. courts more than they do their own.

It is well known that the illegal drug industry establishes links with financial institutions to facilitate the "laundering" of its income, which is another name for transforming unexplained cash and other income into what appear to be legitimate assets. Money laundering is only one aspect of the bilateral problems that arise out of banking operations. Money is notoriously more difficult to control than goods, reduced often to a mere entry on a computer in any part of the world. In a controversial case, U.S. drug agents mounted a sting operation called Casablanca that implicated several Venezuelans. The bulk of the accusations in the Casablanca operation affected Mexicans, and an outcry was heard against the United States for using undercover agents in Mexico. But the Venezuelans muted their protest, since the operation affecting their citizens was apparently carried out on U.S. territory.[4] In any case, a higher court would eventually overturn the ruling against an important Venezuelan banking official, giving support to the claim that American agents had gone beyond ethical principles in their pursuit of potential criminals.

The United States exerts pressure on banking authorities in Venezuela to require effective procedures against money laundering similar to those applied in the United States. Both the banks and the monetary authorities cooperate with these efforts, not least of all because the banks themselves want to comply with the rules, since a clean bill of health is necessary for their own private business relations in the United States. This quiet cooperation is similar to the attitude of Venezuelan airlines, which hardly want their government to make an issue of sovereignty over matters, such as airport safety, where common interests predominate. In any case, the autonomous functioning of international finance presents special problems for governments. In combination with the huge economic power of the drug mafias, a large network of illegal transactions is possible, creating transnational actors on the margin of the law.

People on the Move

The United States prides itself on being a melting pot, a country of immigrants that has absorbed successive waves of people looking for a better future and willing to contribute to building a unique culture. Nevertheless, the integration of new groups has often caused conflict in American history, particularly when a local population feels threatened by the influx of cheap labor or when it is felt that foreigners might achieve such influence that they could displace existing groups in some way, entering politics, speaking another language, or even changing a neighborhood. Certainly, the most notable group of immigrants in recent years comes from Latin America—Cubans who fled their island after the revolution led by Fidel Castro in 1958, Mexicans who crossed the border, Caribbean groups and other Latin Americans who looked for a better economic prospect, and others who fled from political repression. Venezuelans were rarely found among the huge numbers of Latin Americans arriving in the United States, but their numbers are growing. As this occurs, governments increasingly confront certain difficulties.

During the years of economic abundance up until 1980, Venezuelans rarely wanted to emigrate; the brain drain might have been a problem for the rest of Latin America, but not for them.[5] Emigration from Venezuela started to rise in the 1980s and intensify in the 1990s in response to poor economic prospects and to political uncertainty. Since the United States applies strict limits to the number of foreign residents it will accept every year, illegal entry became the only option for those willing to take the risk. According to one estimate, some 150,000 Venezuelans live in the United States, of whom some 70,000 are illegals.[6] In 1998, the Venezuelan Foreign Ministry reported that 48,657 Venezuelans were registered at its consulates in the United States (of a total of 113,000 persons registered at consulates worldwide). Most, some 40,000, registered in Miami. The growing numbers and the apparent increase in illegal residents forced the U.S. government to limit the granting of visas and to apply rigorous control on the entry of Venezuelans to the United States.[7] The rules made it particularly difficult for a young, unmarried, and unemployed person to get even a tourist visa to the United States.

In March 1997, Venezuela's consul general in Miami, Gustavo Rodríguez Amengual, responded to a revelation by the U.S. commercial attaché in Venezuela, Renato David, that 55,000 Venezuelans resided illegally in the United States. According to the consul: " . . . Venezuelans living in the United States constitute a very small minority, one not being reflected in immigration studies carried out at North American universities, nor deemed to be a problem for that country's immigration authorities."[8] Despite the growing number of Venezuelans seeking economic stability and personal security in the United States, then, their numbers are scant compared to the huge Hispanic population from other Latin countries.

The very lack of a significant Venezuelan population in the United States implies that there is no strong lobby for Venezuelan concerns, although the rise of emigration from Venezuela creates pressures for joint action. Sometimes a salient event mobilizes such latent forces. After the destructive rains and flooding that struck Venezuela at the end of 1999, leaving thousands dead under mudslides and destroying the homes of some 50,000 people, Venezuelans in the United States organized themselves for the first time. Following the example of refugees from Hurricane Mitch in Central America, Venezuelans met to petition the United States for special status that would allow them to receive work permits in the United States on the grounds that they would have few options in Venezuela and that such a solution would constitute aid to the country. The Venezuelan government supported the movement, despite the fact that expatriates in the United States were often described as people who had abandoned their country instead of devoting themselves to its development. As the crisis waned at home, however, the claim for special status lost force.

While the Venezuelan population resident in the United States hardly constitutes a major factor in international relations, it is increasingly a group with a distinct voice. Venezuelans in Miami were seen, for instance, as opponents of the Chávez government, voting against the president in far greater numbers than was the case at home. Some seemed to see themselves as economic or even political refugees, perhaps influenced by the Cubans with whom they entered into contact in the Miami region. Anti-Castro Cubans were quick to criticize the friendly relationship that President Chávez established with Fidel Castro, and Miami newspapers such as the *Herald* (and its Spanish version, *El Nuevo Herald*) adopted a negative editorial line against the Chávez government. The *Herald* columnist, Andrés Oppenheimer, caught the wrath of the Venezuelan president for his articles. Venezuelan immigration to the United States is unlikely to play a significant role in American politics, and it is a minor factor in Venezuela as well, yet the small concentration of individuals is slowly converting itself into a recognizable group.

Cultural Waves in the Age of the World Wide Web

Americans and Venezuelans engage in foreign relations all the time, and their governments sometimes do not even take notice. Tourists go back and forth frequently,[9] adolescents go abroad daily through the Internet, students from Venezuela flock to U.S. colleges and universities, businesspeople move about indifferent to the nationality of their coworkers, slum dwellers watch *Ally McBeal*, and the Audubon Society signs up affiliates throughout the globe to monitor the protection of flora and fauna. Venezuela is particularly prone to looking to the United States for cultural symbols, standards of modernity, and goals for the good life.

Business serves as the channel for much of the back-and-forth, but not exclusively. The American government encourages the widening of knowledge about the United States in a variety of ways. University students covet the scholarships of the Fulbright Commission as a direct ticket to acceptance at U.S. colleges and graduate schools, and the United States Information Service (USIS) works within the State Department to organize study groups that wish to learn about U.S. ways of doing things, from running the court system to managing cities. USIS also runs a speakers service that brings American academics to other countries, including Venezuela.

From the Venezuelan side, the Ayacucho Foundation grants educational credits for foreign study, sending thousands abroad for advanced education. In 1999, almost 50 percent of the 1,118 students sent abroad by the foundation went to the United States, more than four times the number going to other popular countries such as England, France, or Spain.[10] Some 63,000 students have been sent abroad since the start of the program. The Ayacucho Foundation has been operating since 1976, and many consider that the influence of the generation that has had the opportunity to study abroad has already been great and is likely to provide the human resources for the Venezuelan leadership of the future. Of course, the possibility of contributing to Venezuela's development requires that returning graduates find opportunities in their own country, which some claim to be limited.

The movement of so many students through the Ayacucho program inevitably involves the governments of the two countries. The United States must grant visas to the visiting students and decide the terms of their stay. For many years, no significant problems emerged, although the increased interest in emigration to the United States noted above began to affect the program, as graduating students showed less inclination to return to Venezuela. Financial difficulties at the Ayacucho Foundation also caused some headaches, since delayed payments to the students could often leave them without money for their needs, creating problems in their academic performance and pressures for the universities where they were enrolled. At one point, the U.S. consulate in Caracas suspended the granting of student visas in order to put pressure on the foundation to meet its commitments. The president of the Ayacucho Foundation assured the press that the problem was resolved, although the crisis even came to be discussed by members of the U.S. Congress.[11]

As economic and political difficulties in Venezuela dampened the enthusiasm of students abroad to return to their country after completing their studies, it was also revealed that the foundation was tightening its requirement that students return after graduation, pressing for the payment of large debts by the families of those who refused to return to Venezuela. In any case, the cultural influence of students who have studied in the United States and elsewhere is considerable in Venezuela. Improved economic results would tend to reduce the problems that have emerged in recent years, so that this army of educated graduates will fulfill the promise of the Ayacucho program.

We have already noted the intense involvement of business interests in promoting U.S.-Venezuelan relations, but the influence of business is more pervasive than any other transnational factor. American companies dot the landscape in Venezuela, side by side with investors from Europe, Japan, and Latin America. Given the close contact of the job environment, companies provide a locus for cultural interchange perhaps more powerful than all the government programs combined. In her study of human relations in the setting of multinational firms,

Elena Granell found distinct characteristics of Venezuelan workers and managers that indicate a particular cultural outlook.[12] Granell's purpose was to provide understanding among cultures, so that foreign investors should know how to extract the best from their partners and workers, and also to identify those cultural traits that might be transformed into more productive channels in the future. Granell is careful to respect the characteristics of all nationalities, although she implicitly recognizes the pressure for Venezuelans to adapt to standards of objective achievement, universality of rules, and individual initiative.

The dual nature of Venezuelan society, marked by a gaping difference between the small, educated, "middle" class and the dominant population relegated to informal jobs and economic precariousness, is perhaps reinforced by the workplace, where jobs in multinational companies tend to inculcate the values of the employer firms. Despite the visibility of the cosmopolitan groups that slide comfortably between cultures, only some 3 percent of Venezuelans speak English, which means that globalization may be a much thinner phenomenon than is popularly claimed. A study of poverty carried out by the Catholic University in Caracas found that modern values predominated among workers at large companies, while small local firms tended to reproduce traditional values.[13]

It is common today to claim that globalization erodes national values and cultures. Some would recommend greater efforts to limit international contacts in order to preserve local autonomy. But little is really known about the effects of globalization, and it is difficult to draw a line between fostering ignorance and protecting cultural purity. For instance, CNN supplies global news in Spanish to the public in all of Latin America. Does this network slant information to favor the perspectives of the United States or of the developed countries more generally? Or does access to a greater number of sources of information widen the horizons of people all over the world, making them more aware citizens better able to judge their own societies?

Whatever the nature of the contact, the multiple points of interchange between Americans and Venezuelans, from medical conferences to vacations at Disney World, generate a transfer of cultural values. Such transfer, in the case of Venezuela, tends to be unidirectional, apart from the small contributions of Venezuelans to the American cultural scene. While Americans should be proud of the force of their culture, they should also be aware that the asymmetry of these flows produces grave doubts among Venezuelans.[14] Children and families in Venezuela spend many hours in front of a television screen watching American shows. In particular, intellectual circles disdain much of what they perceive as the detritus of American society: McDonald's, violence and sex in movies, consumerism, drugs, and crude individualism. Writers rail against the thoughtless acceptance of U.S. standards for everything from what to have for breakfast to how to bring up children, yearning to preserve, rightly, the best of their own society. Even those who embrace American values absorbed during study abroad often harbor resentments about perceived racial discrimination or arrogant attitudes on the part of Americans, who often assume unthinkingly the superiority of their own way of doing things. Venezuelans will listen to American officials preaching about the need for honesty in government and respect for human rights in police forces, all the while thinking of the hypocrisy of a country in the throes of the Monica Lewinsky affair or the scandals over police brutality in Los Angeles or New York.

The New International Actors

Apart from the many individual contacts among countries, a new force is gaining space in international relations in the form of nongovernmental organizations. The definition of NGO is broad and includes just about any kind of group imaginable, from neighborhood associations to bowling leagues to churches. Most are local, and few have any influence on international politics. Yet a growing number of such groups are global in their reach and increasingly act as independent and powerful forces beyond government control. Their influence can be seen in many fields.

International NGOs may originate in any country. If we include organized religions with international scope, we can see, for instance, how the Catholic Church or other religious organizations may come to exercise great influence within countries or in international affairs more broadly. Certainly, the Catholic Church played a role in the fall of communism in Poland, and Moslem and Jewish groups constantly affect the ebb and flow of conflict in the Middle East. The Catholic Church has sometimes played a part in Venezuelan politics, particularly when its interests there are somehow threatened. Relationships with President Chávez reached an especially low level with sharp interchanges between local bishops and the president, who accused the Catholic hierarchy of political preferences. The Catholic Church is clearly a transnational actor with moral weight in countries like Venezuela, whose population largely considers itself Catholic.

For the purposes of this volume, it is important to determine what role NGOs may play in the relationship between the United States and Venezuela. The Catholic Church responds to its leadership in Rome, and most priests and missionaries in Venezuela come from Spain. On the other hand, the growth of Protestantism in Venezuela tends to bring more Americans to Venezuela in the cause of religion, as Mormons, evangelicals, and other sects make incursions on the traditional Catholic turf. On the whole, however, such trends have had little or no impact on international affairs.

Perhaps the most influential American NGOs in Venezuela are rarely heard from, even though they may affect daily life without anyone giving them a thought. In the United States, many of the most important technical standards are set by NGOs. In many industries and professions, it is important that similar rules be applied for the production of goods and for standards of quality and service. In few cases does one set of rules or standards come to be accepted worldwide, even when efficiency would be gained. Countries that have intense exchanges among themselves benefit from sharing standards, since they facilitate trade and commerce. Often the adoption of common specifications depends on historical accidents or even colonial relationships from the past. Anyone who travels frequently will have had the unhappy experience of arriving in a country only to find that his electric shaver or her hairdryer cannot be used because the plugs are not compatible.

In Venezuela, American specifications and standards are often, but not always, the norm. This is certainly the case in the oil industry, where the American Petroleum Institute standards began to be applied from the early days of exploration and production. Examples can be taken from just about any industry, be it electricity, telephones, or television. Yet European traditions also coexist alongside American standards, especially where long-standing rules dominate. Such is the case of the metric system, where it is the United States that is out of line with the global (and Venezuelan) usage. Another exception is the legal system in Venezuela, which emerged from the period of Spanish colonization and follows the continental rule of civil law.[15] U.S. influence comes from the practical context of the way in which certain industries have developed, from the presence of American investment in a given area or even from the place where Venezuelan professionals have been educated. Little-known organizations can shape institutions in unexpected ways. For instance, the American Association of Collegiate Schools of Business is now acting as an unofficial body for the accreditation of master's programs in business (MBAs) in Latin America. Venezuelan students routinely study English in order to take the Scholastic Aptitude Test, which is offered through the Venezuelan-American Friendship Society. The Audubon Society, based in the United States, has an active Venezuelan chapter that is considered to be one of the more influential environmental groups in the country.

In the area of human rights, transnational relationships play an especially important role. Amnesty International, for instance, has grown to be an international organization with chapters in countries throughout the world, including Venezuela. Since human rights groups often enter into political conflicts with governments, Amnesty International has a special mode of operation, in which local members serve to supply information on possible abuses to the world organization but do not directly act in their own countries to press individual cases, thus protecting each member from persecution.

Human rights groups recognize the power they may exert by their international links, although their influence chiefly comes from their ability to publicize abuses and to call for action by governments or international organizations. In Venezuela, human rights organizations have actively protested poor prison conditions, police excesses, and other abuses ranging from limits on free speech to violations of local laws or personal privacy. Some, like the press, are associated with international NGOs such as the Interamerican Press Society, while others are local but linked to outside NGOs for funding. While the government may feel uncomfortable with such independent groups, it also recognizes the force that international membership and access to communications media accords them. Undoubtedly, the U.S. government depends on information from such groups when it prepares its annual report to the Congress on human rights in the world. No government wishes to find itself accused before the International Court of Justice for abusing human rights. The Venezuelan government has learned that complaints by such groups cannot be ignored without cost; when the new Constitution was drafted in 1999, human rights groups took an active part in drawing up the articles for protecting citizens from abuses.

Many other NGOs act in the complex of relationships among countries. Some maintain links to governments, while others are strictly independent. While governments are expected not to intervene in the internal affairs of other countries, NGOs make a habit of it. Even political parties establish international links, hoping to support parties with similar ideologies abroad. In the case of the United States, such efforts are almost official. The U.S. Congress provides financing for the National Endowment for Democracy, for instance, which in turn works with the National Democratic Institute and the National Republican Institute. These organizations sometimes provide help to similar foundations in Venezuela to further the development of a healthy political system, but usually with a bias toward political organizations that share their orientation.

Likewise, there are international links among labor unions, although in this case, Venezuelan unions tend to depend mostly on their relationship with the International Labor Organization. Many external labor unions made their presence felt in late 2000 in Venezuela at the time of a national referendum designed by the government to remove the current union leadership on the strength of the popular vote. A strategy so at odds with the ideal of labor union autonomy called forth criticism from abroad, including from American labor leaders, and their visits undoubtedly contributed to reducing the legitimacy of the referendum, forcing the government to opt for a negotiated settlement. Thus the diffuse links between governments and NGOs may sometimes place the NGOs in a position of "making foreign policy," particularly where governments cannot so easily tread. Foreign-government criticism of this sort of domestic problem might smack of unjustified external meddling, but such strictures are more difficult to apply against the International Federation of Free Trade Unions, which commonly acts to support its affiliates throughout the world.

Today, the lines between governments, citizen groups, and even individuals tend to fade. Seemingly unremarkable activities of some prestigious organizations may influence the climate of bilateral relations even when they are not specifically aimed at this objective. Nonprofit think tanks, for instance, routinely carry out comparative studies of countries which are avidly consumed by potential investors looking for information. One example, already mentioned, is the World Competitiveness Report issued annually at the World Economic Forum of Davos and published by Imede, a Swiss business school. Another is the Economic Freedom Index calculated by the Heritage Foundation in the United States as a country rating of friendliness to investment. Such studies are complemented by companies such as Standard & Poor's and Moody's that rate the riskiness of investments in different countries.

The global reach of some news media also affects the climate of relations between countries. An editorial in the *Washington Post* may have more impact in Caracas than the positions taken by the local press. Sometimes Venezuela and other developing countries perceive coordination among all of these actors, be they banks, NGOs, or private firms, contributing to the widely held view that they operate in collaboration, implicit or explicit, with the U.S. government.

To sum up, common people are making foreign policy every day. Governments work to improve their images abroad, they negotiate to find common areas of collaboration, and they contribute to the ability of their citizens to enter into a wide variety of interchanges. These very real contacts form opinion and condition the popular attitudes that enable or retard the relations between countries.

SEVEN

CONCLUSIONS

A T LEAST UNTIL RECENT TIMES, BILATERAL RELATIONS BETWEEN Venezuela and the United States could generally be classified as positive, both in strategic and in tactical terms. Both in the long term and even on specific issues, no significant problems emerged over almost two hundred years of contacts, within a simple and relatively controlled agenda of common interests. With the end of the Cold War, a certain readjustment was in order, to the extent that the United States would necessarily redefine its role in the world and in Latin America in a new hemispheric policy with a clear regional and commercial orientation. Just as inevitably, Venezuela would also reassess its position until a new equilibrium could be found.

The roots of the adjustment of the relationship between the United States and Venezuela can be found in various factors, whose characteristics have been analyzed in this book. We have seen a process in which new areas of confrontation have emerged, both strategic and tactical, that naturally concern decision-makers and analysts, although they also generate opportunities to develop a new bilateral agenda, of greater complexity perhaps, that will reflect the significant transformations that have occurred in the structure of the contemporary international system.[1]

In the first place, on the world scale a series of interrelated problems requires new interpretations and even new theoretical tools to understand them. Rosenau said not long ago: " . . . the enemy was known, the challenges were clear, the dangers appeared obvious," so that it was possible to plan public policies with a certain degree of certainty.[2] In a bipolar world, the international agenda was determined principally in terms of geopolitics, or "high politics." Economic development was seen as a lineal historical process that proceeded in only one direction, and global security depended on the "balance of terror" established between the United States and the Soviet Union. While aspects of the great-power debate have not altogether disappeared—there are still nuclear warheads in Russia and elsewhere, and changes in China, southeastern Europe, or Asia could still alter our view of the world—today there seems to be reason to think that the post–Cold War world is substantially different. Economic issues have come to the fore, granting greater importance to what we formerly classified as "low politics."

Beginning in the 1970s and intensifying in the 1990s, a profound transformation of the world became evident, projecting the international structure toward a more fractured configuration. The breakdown of bipolarity, the growth of world commerce, the complexity and importance of communications and information flows in general, combined with the growing role of nongovernmental actors, tended to generate turbulence and a heterogeneous international agenda in which economics took a seat next to geopolitics and governments were forced to assume new behaviors in order to adapt to the moment—to the climate of the times.

An important ingredient in the new international context was an increasingly dominant trend to accept the principles of liberal economics—called neoliberalism by its detractors—which privileged economic openness, deregulation, reduction of the size of the state and the breadth of government activity, the pursuit of efficiency and quality in both the private and public sectors, the value of the "virtual" economy based on services, communications, and information, and new themes related to the environment, culture, labor conditions, and technology.[3]

All of these changes implied that governments would have to formulate and implement foreign policies in various dimensions, not only at the level of interstate relations but also on the planes of quasi-governmental relations, multilateral organizations, and transnational relations.[4] The new diplomacy required a simultaneous change away from inward-looking economic strategies and in favor of liberalization of trade, privatization of state-owned enterprises, greater foreign investment, and the incorporation of new standards, regulations, and international regimes. Pressures in these directions were augmented by international organizations such as the World Trade Organization, the World Bank, the International Monetary Fund, and the Interamerican Development Bank, which had gained considerable influence over the construction of the global agenda.

Among developing countries facing an asymmetrical power relation with the rest of the world, the adjustments required by the new international structure implied costs in terms of their loss of autonomy, insecurity, impacts on their domestic power relations, and pressures for adaptation to scientific and technological transformation. Trade liberalization created tensions between both the requirements of economic openness and harmonization of policies and their tradition of protectionism; between globalization and local interests; and between macroeconomic policies designed for domestic needs and the discipline required for stable exchange rates and the balance of payments. At the same time, worldwide trading arrangements developed side by side with the promotion of regional and subregional trading blocs without parallel in past times. The world moved from relative international anarchy toward complex interdependence in which the domestic and the international became inextricably intertwined as "intermestic."

The United States, as the primary world military power and one of the three pillars of the world economy, defined its global role according to three specific objectives: promoting democracy and human rights across the planet; influencing multilateral and transnational organizations in favor of its own initiatives and interests; and ensuring the terms of the new economic and political agenda of good government and openness. This set of policies is fully illustrated by the nature of Washington's hemispheric policy toward Latin America and the Caribbean, which underwent a significant change over a period of about twenty years.

The United States became more regional and more multilateral, with fewer special privileges assigned to individual countries and more insistence that all adopt open policies and transparency in democratic processes, develop community organizations, combat narcotics trafficking, and defend human rights and the environment. Of course, the changes in world politics and in U.S. policy were not so complete as to mean the disappearance of old and recurring themes on the American agenda. There was still room for concerns about political stability, the weakening of states, corruption, international terrorism, and other problems that new approaches could hardly ignore. And there was still room for special relationships, such as the closer links that the United States forged with its closest neighbors, Mexico and Canada.

For Latin America in general and Venezuela in particular, these global changes sometimes appeared to have a double impact. Not only do these countries have to adjust to alterations in the international rules of the game, but they must also respond to the exigencies imposed by the United States, which seem ever more diverse and complex. Each Latin American country sought its own solution. Brazil, as the largest country in the region, seemed to prefer a more autonomous stance balanced by relative cooperation, while Chile tended to seek out a special relationship with the United States. Venezuela's closest neighbor, Colombia, emerged from a period of conflict marked by disagreements over the drug trade and its repression to a move toward greater collaboration with the United States. Central America, once its internal civil wars and conflicts came to an end, sought both regional integration and accommodation to the liberalizing agenda. Argentina also put aside its traditional distance from the United States in favor of policies more closely aligned with U.S. interests. Mexico did the same, achieving the closest relationship with the United States among all the countries of the region.

In this context of closer American ties to many countries in Latin America, Venezuela's relationship with the United States tended to be less consistent, wavering over a decade between acceptance of a liberal international order and efforts to eke out an independent and more autonomous position. By the end of the 1990s, however, the drive for autonomy was predominant. Venezuela nevertheless tried to maintain a good relationship with the United States, despite some specific conflicts over trade and a certain deterioration in the strategic coincidence that had been traditional during much of the past century.

At least since 1958, Venezuela and the United States have shared a strategic vision that required the full democratization of Latin America. This strategic coincidence ensured excellent relations, especially during periods when dictatorships were the rule in the region and communism was perceived as a threat to hemispheric stability. Equally, Venezuela never wavered from its commitment as a reliable supplier of oil to the United States, a position that weathered every crisis, including two world wars and many lesser ones, as well as the oil boycott by Arab members of OPEC in the 1970s, in which Venezuela did not participate. With such a strong shared strategic vision, lesser conflicts had little effect on the overall relationship.

Venezuela nationalized foreign oil and iron ore companies, including important assets of American companies, in the mid-1970s, for instance, but this act was carried out with full respect for the rules governing indemnification. By the 1980s, however, certain underlying tensions began to emerge. Venezuelan democracy was no longer exceptional in the Latin American region; indeed, some democratic practices in Venezuela looked increasingly rigid and fragile; when economic difficulties hit the country, its response tended to go in the direction of statist solutions just when other countries were trying out liberal remedies.

Entering the 1990s, despite a short attempt at adopting market-oriented policies, Venezuela's full political and economic crisis became evident, and no politically acceptable solutions were found, at least until the consolidation of the Chávez government at the end of the decade. Yet the new regime hardly ensured longer-term stability. It enjoyed high levels of popularity mixed with significant minority opposition, especially from the traditional elites and the educated classes. It was precisely these opposition groups that distrusted the efforts of the Chávez administration to distance itself from the United States in favor of a more autonomous stance. They feared the effects this might have on investment and trade and, in the long run, on the oil exports of Venezuela to the United States.

The breakdown of the domestic consensus in Venezuela coincided with the fall of the Berlin Wall and the emergence of new patterns of international relations associated with that event. A relationship that had been perceived as stable and easy to manage both in Washington and Caracas turned volatile, perhaps shaken by the global transformations, the new hemispheric agenda of the nineties, the regional and global requirements of American foreign policy, and the bureaucratic complexity that it implied, including the insertion of new items on the bilateral agenda beyond the simple goals of democracy and energy security that had heretofore concentrated attention.

For reasons having little to do with international politics, Venezuela was undergoing its own domestic revolution at the end of the 1990s, giving rise to an inability or unwillingness to assume the convenience of the new trends toward globalization, openness, and submission to world rules for trade and investment. President Hugo Chávez interpreted the situation as one in which Venezuela should emphasize its autonomy and its own approach to economic development, a model that questioned the tenets being promoted by the United States, such as the virtues of globalization. While even in the United States the virtues of globalization met resistance from many domestic groups, the government's foreign policy seemed to be increasingly at odds with that of Venezuela, despite their long history of strategic consensus. Venezuela seemed to be distancing itself from the traditional Western outlook that had been its central tendency for at least half a century, although the pull of its traditions would be likely to come to the fore again.

The United States is learning to deal with the greater complexity of the post–Cold War world, experimenting with different approaches to engagement and distance. International organizations provide a way to act in the world while avoiding charges of unilateral intervention. On the other hand, the varieties of situations throughout the world also require specific responses. The disintegration of the Colombian government's control over its own territory in the face of increasingly powerful rebel groups and drug traffickers led to the U.S. decision to intensify engagement there in 2000, although encouragement was also given to European and Latin American countries to support peace negotiations among the warring groups.

Greater involvement in Colombia was matched by greater distance from Venezuela, at a time when the Venezuelan government was particularly sensitive to any sign of incursions on its sovereignty and autonomy on the part of the United States. U.S. diplomacy became almost passive, despite the fact that Venezuela increasingly found reason to complain of excessive American pretensions to influence events on its border and elsewhere. This passive approach seemed effective in dulling the criticisms and even in making the Venezuelan government look excessively thin-skinned.

It can no longer be claimed that "nothing happens in Venezuela" as the traditional saying had it. As the pages of this book show, the transition from an old agenda to a new one, both in Venezuela and the United States generated tensions beyond the mere tactical differences of the past. It was once a simple task to align the two countries on the two axes of democracy and oil, but a more complex set of goals also makes agreement more difficult. Yet if history is any guide, the long-term tendency of the two countries to perceive fundamental agreement should tend to reemerge. Old friendships sometimes pass through periods of stress, only to reappear later as if nothing had happened. For this reason, perhaps, both countries also make efforts to preserve their mutual respect in times of change.

Venezuelan foreign policy toward the United States, seen in historical perspective, achieved a certain success in ensuring the permanent support of Washington for its democracy and for democracy in the whole region, as well as the smooth and untroubled nature of its oil relations with the United States, even taking into account Venezuela's membership in OPEC. As Venezuela appeared to diverge from its long-term style of foreign policy, emphasizing relationships with countries in other regions from China to the Middle East and marking its distance from the United States, the United States refrained from strong reactions. This might be seen as a natural way of awaiting the reassertion of the structural forces that had always acted in favor of friendly and trustful relations. Indeed, the United States could also count on the fact that in the complex world of foreign affairs, with multiple issue areas and interests, the dance of nations is always in movement.

Some questions remain. To what extent can Venezuela expect continued tolerance in the United States for the political changes that began in the nineties and intensified with the inauguration of President Chávez? Might not the new administration in the United States show less tolerance and passivity should Venezuela again encounter domestic political conflict? And to what extent will Venezuela accept transformations in the world economy that imply a greater application of liberal economic policies and openness to trade and investment? Will the tradition of seeking excellent relations with the United States create political pressures within Venezuela to reestablish its normal strategic coincidences?

At the start of the new century, changes are under way that will continue to shape bilateral relationships between the United States and Venezuela. In the United States, presidential elections at the end of 2000 brought a new president to the helm, and as this book has shown, every administration puts its own mark on foreign affairs. In Venezuela at the same time, President Hugo Chávez was consolidating his government, with ambitious plans to revolutionize his country, to create justice, and to participate actively in the world. It seemed that U.S.-Venezuelan relations had entered another phase, perhaps more difficult and certainly more complex.

Venezuelans still have "suspicious minds" about U.S. interests in their nation, while the American government also seems to have doubts about the course of events in Venezuela, where revolutionary rhetoric and nationalistic tendencies might promise either a true turn toward modernization or the intensification of conflict, both domestically and internationally. It is fair to say that both nations are learning to meet the challenges of global society with a more multilevel and complex bilateral agenda. Venezuela is no longer perceived by the United States as a special country, although every country is important in its own way and Venezuela is more important than many. In regional matters, the United States follows its own lights and on few occasions has it listened especially to Venezuela. Yet, when they think about it, Venezuelans would also admit that they too seek to decide their own international policies, often challenging American positions. As long as no strategic issues are at risk, the complex world of the beginning of the twenty-first century would appear to accommodate a relationship that has shown itself to be solid in the face of both global and domestic changes.

PRESIDENTS OF THE UNITED STATES AND VENEZUELA: 1900–2001

1899–1908	Cipriano Castro	1901–1909	Theodore Roosevelt
1908–1913	Juan Vicente Gómez	1909–1913	William Howard Taft
1913–1914	José Gil Fortoul	1913–1921	Woodrow Wilson
1914–1922	Victorino Márquez Bustillos		
1922–1929	Juan Vicente Gómez	1921–1923	Warren G. Harding
		1923–1929	Calvin Coolidge
1929–1931	Juan Bautista Pérez	1929–1933	Herbert Hoover
1931–1935	Juan Vicente Gómez	1933–1945	Franklin Delano Roosevelt
1935–1941	Eleazar López Contreras		
1941–1945	Isaías Medina Angarita	1945–1953	Harry S. Truman
1945–1948	Rómulo Betancourt		
1948	Rómulo Gallegos		
1948–1950	Carlos Delgado Chalbaud		
1950–1952	Germán Suárez Flamerich		
1952–1958	Marcos Pérez Jiménez	1953–1961	Dwight D. Eisenhower
1958	Wolfgang Larrazábal		
1958	Edgar Sanabria		
1959–1964	Rómulo Betancourt	1961–1963	John F. Kennedy
1964–1969	Raúl Leoni	1963–1969	Lyndon B. Johnson
1969–1974	Rafael Caldera	1969–1974	Richard M. Nixon
1974–1979	Carlos Andrés Pérez	1974–1977	Gerald R. Ford
1979–1984	Luis Herrera Campins	1977–1981	Jimmy Carter
1984–1989	Jaime Lusinchi	1981–1989	Ronald Reagan
1989–1993	Carlos Andrés Pérez	1989–1993	George Bush
1993	Octavio Lepage	1993–2001	William J. Clinton
1993–1994	Ramón J. Velázquez		
1994–1999	Rafael Caldera		
1999–	Hugo Chávez Frías	2001–	George W. Bush

VENEZUELA AND THE UNITED STATES: A COMPARISON, 1997

	UNITED STATES	VENEZUELA
Population (millions)	288	23
Territory (1,000 sq. kilometers)	9,364	912
Growth of population (%)	1	2.4
GDP ($ millions)	7,834,036	87,480
GDP per capita ($/year)	27,202	3,803
Manufacturing (% GDP)	18	16
Agriculture (% GDP)	2	4
Exports of goods (% GDP)	8	25
Imports of goods (% GDP)	11	19
Food as percent of imports	5	16
Fuels as percent of imports	9	1
Youth illiteracy (% Males 15–24)	—	3
Life expectancy (years at birth)	76	73
Infant mortality (per 1,000 live births)	7	21
Tax revenues (as % of GDP)	19.8	17.5
Telephones (fixed lines per 1,000 persons)	644	116
Daily newspapers (per 1,000 persons)	215	206
Personal computers (per 1,000 persons)	407	37
Women in workforce (%)	46	34
Inbound tourists (1,000 per year)	48,409	796
Human development index (UN 1995)	943	860
Higher education (% of age group enrolled)	81	25
Education expenditure (% GDP)	5.8	4.1
Armed forces (% of labor force)	0.9	1.2
Military expenditure (% GDP)	3.9	1.1

Source: World Bank, *World Development Indicators* (Washington, DC: World Bank, 1999).

NOTES FOR INTRODUCTION

1. Carlos Romero, "Las relaciones entre Venezuela y Estados Unidos: Realidad históri-ca u opción política?" *Política Internacional* I, No. 2 (April-June, 1986): 11–14.

2. Judith Ewell. *Venezuela and the United States: From Monroe's Hemisphere to Petroleum's Empire* (Athens, GA: University of Georgia Press, 1996); Aníbal Romero, "La situación estratégica de Venezuela," *Política Internacional*, 1, No. 1 (1986): 6–14; Carlos Romero, "Las relaciones entre Venezuela y Estados Unidos: Realidad histórica u opción política"?

3. Gene Bigler, *La política y el capitalismo de estado en Venezuela* (Madrid: Editorial Tecnos, 1981); David J. Myers, "Perceptions of a Stressed Democracy: Inevitable Decay or Foundation for Rebirth?" in *Venezuela: Democracy under Stress*, ed. Jennifer Mc Coy, Andrés Serbin, William C. Smith, and Andrés Stambouli (New Brunswick, NJ: Transaction Publishers, 1994), 107–138.

4. Elsa Cardozo de Da Silva, "Repensando políticamente el Mercosur desde Venezuela," *Política Internacional*, X, No. 12 (1996): 9–13; Carlos Guerón, "La doctrina Betancourt y el papel de la teoría en política exterior," *Politeia* 1 (Caracas: Instituto de Estudios Políticos), Universidad Central de Venezuela, 1972): 231–243; John Martz, "Venezuela's Foreign Policy toward Latin America," in *Contemporary Venezuela and Its Role in International Affairs*, ed. Robert Bond (New York: New York University Press, 1977).

NOTES FOR CHAPTER ONE

1. Alfredo Toro Hardy published the book *El desafío venezolano: Cómo influir en las decisiones políticas estadounidenses* (Caracas: Instituto de Altos Estudios de América Latina, 1988) as a way of convincing his country that the best way to gain influence in the United States was to know its institutions and penetrate its network of lobbyists, con-gressmen, and other organizations. He was named Venezuelan ambassador to the United States in 1999.

2. Benjamin Frankel, *Venezuela y Los Estados Unidos, 1810–1888* (Caracas: Fundación Boulton, 1977).

3. Judith Ewell, *Venezuela and the United States: From Monroe's Hemisphere to Petroleum's Empire* (Athens, GA: University of Georgia Press, 1996).

4. *Caudillo* is the word commonly used in Venezuela and other Latin American coun-tries to refer to powerful leaders whose domination is often of a personal nature.

5. Sheldon Liss, *Diplomacy and Dependency: Venezuela, The United States, and the Americas* (Salisbury, NC: Documentary Publications, 1978).

6. President Hugo Chávez attended a meeting of CARICOM (the Association of Caribbean Countries, comprising ex-colonies of the United Kingdom and other Caribbean nations, of which Guyana is a member) in July 1999, an unusual act of friendship, since he was the only head of state from a non–member country attending. At the meeting, Chávez made the generous promise to extend the benefits of the San José Agreement, granting oil discounts to countries in the Caribbean, to the members of CARICOM not included to that date. Although the gesture was appreciated, the group ended its meeting with the traditional vote of support of Guyana against Venezuelan claims over Guyanese territory.

7. The reader will find a useful table of the presidents of the United States and Venezuela and their terms of office in Appendix I.

8. The approach to Venezuelan-U.S. relations that puts oil at the center can be seen in Robert Bond, ed., *Contemporary Venezuela and Its Role in International Affairs* (New York: New York University Press, 1977); Ewell, *Venezuela and the United States*; and Carlos A. Romero, "Las relaciones entre Venezuela y Estados Unidos: Realidad histórica u opción política?" *Política Internacional* I, No. 2 (April-June, 1986): 11–14.

9. In this book, we follow the U.S. tradition of calling its own citizens "Americans." It should be noted, however, that this practice is often frowned upon by Latin Americans, including Venezuelans, who also consider themselves to be Americans. In their own language, they tend to refer to citizens of the United States as "North Americans," although this practice also leads to confusion, since Canadians and even Mexicans are located in the North American continent.

10. For an excellent history of oil in Venezuela, see Franklin Tugwell, *La política del petróleo en Venezuela* (Caracas: Monte Avila Editores, 1975).

11. Carlos Rangel, *The Latin Americans: Their Love-Hate Relationship with the United States* (New York: Transactions Publishers, 1982). This book was published in Venezuela with the title: "*Del buen salvaje al buen revolucionario*" (From the noble savage to the noble revolutionary), which also conveys the sense of the conflicting image and mixed feelings that dominate in U.S. relations with Latin America, and particularly with Venezuela.

12. Jonathan Hartlyn, Lars Schoultz, and Augusto Varas, *The United States and Latin America in the 1990s* (Chapel Hill, NC: University of North Carolina Press, 1992), 13.

13. Tomás Polanco Alcántara, Simón Alberto Consalvi, and Edgardo Mondolfi Gudat, *Venezuela y Estados Unidos a través de 2 siglos* (Caracas: Cámara Venezolano-Americana de Comercio e Industria, 2000).

14. Carlos Guerón, "La doctrina Betancourt," 231–243.

15. Guido Grooscors. "La política internacional de Rómulo Betancourt y la defensa de la democracia en América." *Venezuela Analítica*, July, 1999, vol. 3, No. 41. Available at http://www.analitica.com/.

16. John Martz, "Venezuela's Foreign Policy toward Latin America," in Robert Bond, *Contemporary Venezuela and Its Role in International Affairs* (New York: New York University Press, 1977).

17. A cartel is an agreement among producers of a product to control supplies to the market in order to maximize the prices and extract the maximum benefit from consumers. Cartels are thought to work only when the number of important producers is relatively small and when sufficient authority exists within the group to decide production quotas for each member and to enforce them.

18. David Blank, *Venezuela: Politics in a Petroleum Republic* (New York: Praeger, 1984), 140–145.

19. Later events would lead to a quicker takeover by 1976.

20. Rómulo Betancourt, *Venezuela: Oil and Politics*. Translation of 2nd ed. by Everett Baumann (Boston: Houghton Mifflin, 1979).

21. The gas industry had already been reserved to the state in 1971, and the local commercialization of hydrocarbon products followed suit in 1973, indicating that Venezuela was accelerating its plans to take over the oil industry even before the Arab-Israeli War.

22. SELA, based in Caracas and backed by Venezuela, had ambitions to compete with international organizations that were seen to be dominated by the United States and that excluded Cuban membership, such as the Interamerican Development Bank. While SELA still exists today, reduced circumstances have limited its ambitions.

23. For example, the average price of Venezuelan oil in the first half of 2000 was about $28 per barrel, which appears to be almost as high as the prices of the peak of 1974. Because of inflation, however, this price represented only 57 percent of the purchasing power of a barrel of oil in 1974 and could be considered about equivalent in real terms to the price of 1985.

24. The relationship between economic problems and resource-based income is complex, but one phenomenon associated with high export earnings from a single product is the "Dutch disease" by which a very strong sector in an economy tends to weaken other sectors, thus reducing a country's competitiveness. High income from oil also creates an atmosphere of "easy money" that shapes decision-making and can contribute to corruption. Violent price fluctuations, common in oil, create volatility and interfere with investment and smooth development. As will be seen below, the oil boom had many negative effects on Venezuela and would leave its economy and society in worse shape by the 1980s. See Terry Karl, *Paradox of Plenty: Oil Booms and Petrostates* (San Francisco: University of California Press, 1997).

25. One well-worn but cynical joke that reflected the U.S. blind eye toward human rights offenses in governments such as that led by President Somoza in Nicaragua is the quote attributed to a high American official: "He's a son of a bitch, but he's our son of a bitch."

26. Romero, "Las relaciones entre Venezuela y Estados Unidos: Realidad histórica u opción política?" 11–14.

27. Venezuela responded to Chamorro's request for support when President Carlos Andrés Pérez applied the president's discretional fund for national security to that objective. This fact became notorious when Pérez was investigated for misuse of the fund for personal purposes. The case formed the central basis for his impeachment in 1993.

28. Laura Rojas, "Aspectos económicos de la política exterior de Venezuela," in Carlos Romero, ed., *Reforma y política exterior* (Caracas: Nueva Sociedad-Invesp, 1992), 145–172.

29. Excerpts from White House tapes released by the National Archives and published in *El Nacional*, December 5, 1999, H6–7.

NOTES FOR CHAPTER TWO

1. Robert Kagan, "The Benevolent Empire," *Foreign Policy*, (Summer 1998): 24–35.

2. Samuel P. Huntington, *The Clash of Civilizations and the Remaking of the World Order* (New York: Touchstone Books, 1998).

3. Thomas Carothers, "The United States and Latin America after the Cold War." Working Paper No. 184. (Washington, DC: The Woodrow Wilson Center, Smithsonian Institution, 1990), 2.

4. Joe S. Nye, Jr. "Redefining the National Interest," *Foreign Affairs*, vol. 78, No. 4, (July/August, 1999): 22–35.

5. The International Bank for Reconstruction and Development (IBRD) has come to be commonly known as the World Bank (WB). On the role of international institutions in shaping bilateral relations, see Chapter Three.

6. Cole Blasier, *The Hovering Giant: U.S Responses to Revolutionary Change in Latin America* (Pittsburgh, PA: Pittsburgh University Press, 1976).

7. Samuel Huntington, *The Soldier and the State: The Theory and Politics of Civil-Military Relations* (Cambridge, MA: Harvard University Press, 1957).

8. Deborah L. Norden, "Democracy and Military Control in Venezuela," *Latin American Research Review*, vol. 33, No. 2 (1998).

9. The different political strategies of the two coup leaders led to conflicts between them that would eventually come to a head when Arias declared that he would run for president against Chávez in 2000.

10. Strictly speaking, the objection of the United States was not simply that Chávez had led a coup attempt, but that he had not proven that he would accept democratic mechanisms for change in the future. The United States did award a visa to his comrade in arms Francisco Arias Cárdenas after he joined the government of Caldera and then went on to compete for and win the governorship of Zulia state. Chávez had criticized Arias for participating in the system that he saw as irretrievably corrupt. When Chávez changed his strategy and competed for the presidency, the United States admitted unofficially that Chávez would be granted his visa should he win in a fair election and did grant one immediately after this occurred.

11. "Neoliberal" is the term widely used in Latin America to refer to economic policies based on market solutions and favoring privatization, elimination of subsidies, and dismantling of state control of the economy. Most Latin American governments also avoided accepting the "neoliberal" label, which had come to be associated with insensitivity toward the problems of the poor, although they did increasingly accept the tenets of market-oriented policy.

12. See Michael Shifter, "Colombia on the Brink: There Goes the Neighborhood," *Foreign Affairs*, vol. 78, No. 4 (July/August, 1999): 14–21.

13. Paul Krugman, *Pop Internationalism* (Cambridge, MA: MIT Press, 1996).

14. Kenneth Waltz, "The Myth of Interdependence," in Charles P. Kindleberger, ed., *The International Corporation: A Symposium* (Cambridge, MA: MIT Press, 1970).

15. Paul Krugman, "Los ciclos en las ideas dominantes con relación al desarrollo económico," *Desarrollo Económico*, vol. 36, No. 143 (October-December 1996): 715–731; Andrés Serbin, Andrés Stambouli, Jennifer McCoy, William Smith, *Venezuela: La democracia bajo presión* (Caracas: INVESP, North-South Center, University of Miami, Editorial Nueva Sociedad, 1997).

16. Paul Krugman, "Los ciclos de las ideas dominantes con relación al desarrollo económico," 730.

17. Sistema Económico Latinoamericano (SELA), *La ayuda de los países industrializados y los organismos económicos internacionales: OMC, Banco Mundial, FMI* (Caracas: SELA, SP/DRD,1997), No. 16.

18. Rogelio Queijeiro, "El tratamiento multilateral de las políticas comerciales y el derecho de la competencia." *Revista de la Facultad de Ciencias Jurídicas y Políticas* (Universidad Central de Venezuela), no. 104, (1997): 307–378.

19. Manuela Tortora, "Manual del negociador económico de la próxima década," *Capítulo del SELA*, no. 49, (January-March 1997): 8.

20. Queijeiro, "El tratamiento multilateral de las políticas comerciales y el derecho de la competencia," 307–338.

21. Jorge Domínguez, *International Security and Democracy. Latin America and the Caribbean in the Post–Cold War Era* (Pittsburgh: Pittsburgh University Press, 1998).

22. Mitchell Seligson and John Passé, *Development and Underdevelopment: The Political Economy of Global Inequality* (Boulder, CO: Westview Press, 1998).

23. Janet Kelly, "Venezuela Foreign Economic Policy and the United States," in Jorge Domínguez, ed., *Economic Issues and Political Conflict: U.S.-Latin American Relations* (London: Butterworths, 1982), 107.

24. Original members included Colombia, Peru, Ecuador, Bolivia, and Chile. Venezuela ratified the Andean Pact in 1973. Chile retired from the group in 1976 during the Pinochet period.

25. The numbers should be viewed carefully. The increase in direct exports to the United States reflects a decrease in oil exports that formerly passed through refineries in the Netherland Antilles. PDVSA had changed its export strategy from one of depending on the channels that the foreign oil companies had built before nationalization in 1976; in the succeeding years, PDVSA bought numerous refineries in the United States (and in the Antilles), as well as its own commercial outlets through the purchase of the large American gasoline chain Citgo. Such a strategy, however, did serve to intensify the trade relationship with the United States.

26. Based on data from the U.S. Census Bureau, Foreign Trade Division, Data Dissemination Branch, February 18, 2000.

27. Michael J. Enright, Antonio Francés, and Edith Scott Saavedra, *Venezuela: The Competitive Challenge* (New York: St. Martin's, 1996).

28. Petróleos de Venezuela, S.A., *Informe anual 1996* (Caracas: PDVSA, 1997).

29. IMF, *International Financial Statistics Yearbook* (Washington, DC: IMF, 1998).

30. "Rechazan presión parlamentaria de Washington contra países OPEP [OPEC]," *El Nacional*, March 24, 2000.

31. For a discussion of ongoing negotiations on the Bilateral Investment Treaty with the United States, see Chapter Three.

32. Laura Rojas, "Aspectos económicos de la política exterior de Venezuela."

33. See Daniel H. Levine, "Goodbye to Venezuelan Exceptionalism," *Journal of Interamerican Studies and World Affairs* (Winter 1994): 145–182.

NOTES FOR CHAPTER THREE

1. Hans Morganthau, *Politics among Nations: The Struggle for Power and Peace*, 5th ed. (New York: Knopf, 1972).

2. This argument has been made by very different observers of the international scene. See for instance, Walter Wriston, *The Twilight of Sovereignty* (New York: Charles Scribner's Sons, 1992) for the view of a well-known private banker, and Jacques Attali, "The Crash of Western Civilization: The Limits of Market and Democracy," *Foreign Policy* 107 (Summer 1997): 54–65.

3. For a contemporary treatment of the problems of sovereignty and its different meanings, see Stephen Krasner, *Sovereignty: Organized Hypocrisy* (Princeton, NJ: Princeton University Press, 1999).

4. Susan Strange, *States and Markets: An Introduction to International Political Economy* (New York: Basil Blackwell, 1988).

5. For information about how the IMF enforces its rules, see John Williamson, ed. *IMF Conditionality* (Washington, DC: Institute for International Finance, 1983).

6. Jane Perlez, "U.N. Rights Commission Foils U.S. Effort to Condemn China," *New York Times*, April 19, 2000. Venezuela voted with a not-very-democratic group: China, Bangladesh, Bhutan, Botswana, Burundi, Congo, Cuba, Indonesia, Madagascar, Morocco, Nepal, Niger, Nigeria, Pakistan, Peru, Quatar, Sri Lanka, Sudan, and Zambia, as well as Russia and India. Abstainers included Argentina, Brazil, Chile, Ecuador, and Mexico, while Colombia, El Salvador, and Guatemala voted with the United States.

7. The U.S. Ambassador to Venezuela, John Maisto, had two problems during the scandal over the suspension of the elections in May, 2000. On the one hand, election observers from the Carter Center were in Venezuela, and their public doubts about whether the elections could be carried out in a transparent manner were causing some irritation on the part of the Venezuelan government. At the same time, one of the private firms hired by the Electoral Commission to carry out the automatization of the process was an American company called Electoral Systems and Software (ES&S), which was being blamed by the Electoral Commission for the whole fiasco, even though it was obvious that ES&S could hardly carry out its job without a good list of candidates supplied by the commission. The ambassador quietly tried to lower tensions and contributed to protecting both the company and the electoral observers from undue criticism.

8. *El Nacional*, July 29, 2000.

9 . The Andean Community, including Venezuela, Colombia, Peru, Ecuador, and Bolivia, was originally referred to as the Andean Pact, resulting from the Cartagena Accord signed in 1969. Originally, Chile was also a member, but the Pinochet dictatorship chilled relations and the liberalization strategy pursued by his government made continued membership impossible. Peru also distanced itself from the pact after President Fujimori violated the constitution, but later resumed its participation.

10. "Chirac está dispuesto a conversar con Chávez sobre caso del Chacal," *El Nacional* (Caracas), June 26, 1999.

11. Joseph Tulchin, "Reflexiones sobre las relaciones hemisféricas en el siglo XXI," Síntesis (Madrid), no. 25, (January-June, 1996): 125–132.

12. United Nations, Economic Commission for Latin America (ECLA-CEPAL), *Panorama de la Inserción Internacional de América Latina y el Caribe* (Santiago de Chile: CEPAL, 1996).

13. Cardozo, "Repensando políticamente el MERCOSUR desde Venezuela," 10.

14. Juan Mario Vacchino, "Las negociaciones hemisféricas: Interrogantes y opciones," *Capítulos del SELA*, no. 49 (January-March, 1997): 99–109.

15. Jorge Castañeda, "Razones para el escepticismo," *El Nacional* (Caracas), April 18, 1998, A/7.

16. Janet Kelly, "Algo más que un tratado bilateral," *El Universal* (Caracas), April 4, 1998.

17. See, for instance, Stephen J. Kobrin, "The MAI and the Clash of Globalizations," *Foreign Policy* 112 (Fall, 1998).

18. Under the Andean Pact, restrictions on foreign investors were extensive during the 1970s and 1980s, although eventually these were removed as members adopted liberal economic reforms in the 1980s and 1990s.

19. Dani Rodrik, *Has Globalization Gone Too Far?* (Washington, DC: Institute for International Economics, 1997): 4–6.

20. Eduardo Galeano, "Los trabajos y los miedos," *El Nacional* (Caracas), March 8, 1998: A4.

NOTES FOR CHAPTER FOUR

1. James Q. Wilson, *Bureaucracy: What Government Agencies Do and Why They Do It* (New York: Basic Books, 1989).

2. Douglass C. North, *Institutions, Institutional Change and Economic Performance* (Cambridge, UK: Cambridge University Press, 1990).

3. For an overview of the current trend to synthesize the neorealist approach that stresses relative power with theories of bureaucracy and interest group politics, see Gideon Rose, "Neoclassical Realism and Theories of Foreign Policy," *World Politics* 51, No. 1 (October, 1998): 144–172.

4. Strobe Talbott, "Globalization and Diplomacy: A Practitioner's Perspective," *Foreign Policy* 108 (Fall 1997): 75.

5. See Federal Reserve Bank of New York, "Treasury and Federal Reserve Exchange Operations," January-March, 1995 (New York: Federal Reserve Bank of New York, 1995).

6. See the report on "The Future of the International Financial Architecture" by a Council on Foreign Relations Task Force. *Foreign Policy*, vol. 78, No. 6 (November-December, 1999), 169–184. The conclusions of this report bear a striking resemblance to those of the United Nations, *Towards a New International Financial Architecture: Report of the Task Force of the Executive Committee on Economic and Social Affairs of the United Nations* (Santiago: Economic Commission for Latin America and the Caribbean, January 21, 1999).

7. Ruth de Krivoy, *Collapse: The Venezuelan Banking Crisis of '94* (Washington, DC: The Group of Thirty, 2000).

8. FARC refers to the Revolutionary Armed Forces of Colombia, the most important guerrilla group in that country, which entered into fitful peace negotiations with the Colombian government that intensified for a time with the election of President Andrés Pastrana in 1998.

9. In one of the stranger incidents of Venezuela's modern diplomacy, Virginia Contreras's mistaken view of the requirements of her job would lead her to refuse to vacate her office and residence on receiving news of her dismissal. Eventually, the locks were changed, and she had to go.

10. President Pérez would pay later for this unexpected ploy. The Congress named Escovar Salóm attorney general during Pérez's second government (1989–1993), when the job of preparing the president's impeachment fell to Escovar. He assumed the task with enthusiasm.

11. Some analysts claim that the 1999 Constitution accords a more political role than did the 1961 Constitution to the military, since it no longer contained a specific reference to "obedience" to civil authorities and for the first time allowed the vote for military personnel. Article 322 calls for a National Defense Council formed by the president and ministers of security-related areas, including the defense minister—not necessarily a military officer—as one among the group. Article 328 defines the (single) armed force as a professional body, with no political activism . . . and in no case at the service of any person or political grouping. Internal regulations of the military continued to require a strict adherence to the tradition of military obedience and the chain of command. The greater role given to the armed forces in national development by President Chávez did tend to raise the political temperature of the military, however, and many retired officers, as well as the president's former allies in the coup attempt of 1992, complained of excessive politicization.

12. Carlos Romero, "Las relaciones cívico-militares en Venezuela desde una perspectiva comparada," *Politeia* (Caracas: Universidad Central de Venezuela, no. 29, 2000).

13. "Invito al pueblo a que investigue y se ponga en pie de lucha" (Interview with Joel Acosta Chirinos), *El Nacional*, February 13, 2000.

14. Central Bank presidents enjoy a fixed term, but since the early 1980s few have finished their five-year periods without having to resign. The longest-sitting president of the bank, who lasted from 1993 until early 1999, was named as a substitute.

15. Richard Neustadt, *Presidential Power: The Politics of Leadership from FDR to Carter* (New York: Macmillan, 1980).

16. "Support" is a diffuse concept as used here. Venezuelans have an expression that refers to a person's attitude toward another, saying they would or would not like to be seen together in a photo. Support on a given question is often as subtle as that: who is seen where, who accompanies whom to meet the president or minister, how heavily the press covers a problem, etc. Such messages are read without much difficulty to measure the strength of business representatives and ensure that they indeed represent their members.

17. *El Nacional*, March 8, 1997: A/3.

NOTES FOR CHAPTER FIVE

1. *El Universal* (Caracas), September 1, 1992: 26.

2. Carlos Romero, "Dealing con cualquiera," *El Diario de Caracas*, September 20, 1992.

3. César E. Baena, *The Policy Process in a Petro-State: An Analysis of PDVSA's Internationalisation Strategy* (Aldershot, UK: Ashgate, 1999).

4. Among these agreements were those related to double taxation, investment promotion, the system for regulating subsidies, copyright rules, tuna exports from Venezuela subject to a U.S. embargo, and disputes over trade in steel, cement, aluminum sulfate, and iron silicates. Venezuela, Ministry of Foreign Relations (MRE), *Libro Amarillo* (Caracas: MRE, 1992).

5. William Smith and Jennifer McCoy, "Venezuelan Democracy under Stress," in Jennifer McCoy, Andrés Serbin, William Smith, and Andrés Stambouli, eds., *Venezuelan Democracy under Stress*, Miami, FL: North-South Center, University of Miami Press), 1–12.

6. William Smith and Jennifer McCoy, "Venezuelan Democracy under Stress," 1–12.

7. *El Diario de Caracas*, March 19, 1993.

8. The president of the Venezuelan Senate, Octavio Lepage, served briefly as president until the Congress named Velásquez as the president for the remainder of the term.

9. *El Diario de Caracas*, September 3, 1994 .

10. *El Diario de Caracas*, December 2, 1993: 51.

11. Speech at the Venezuelan-American Chamber (Venamcham) conference by assistant secretary for inter-American affairs of the U.S. government's Department of State, Caracas, on December 2, 1993.

12. Speech at the Venezuelan-American Chamber (Venamcham) conference by President-elect of Venezuela Rafael Caldera, Caracas, December 15, 1993.

13. *El Globo* (Caracas), January 23, 1994: 7.

14. Venezuela, MRE, *Libro Amarillo* (1994), 181.

15. Judith Ewell, *Venezuela and the United States*.

16. *El Nacional* (Caracas), September 6, 1996: A/2.

17. Venezuela, MRE, *Libro Amarillo*, (Caracas: 1996).

18. *El Nacional* (Caracas), December 11, 1996: A/2.

19. After his election, President Chávez did reduce oil production, in line with agree-

ments made with OPEC and other oil producing countries. But the feared rollback in the contracts with foreign investors was not considerered; in fact, similar plans for opening up the gas industry were soon announced as well.

20. Carlos A. Romero, "EE.UU y Chávez: Una oportunidad." (Caracas: Mimeo, 1999).

21. Romero, "EE.UU y Chávez: Una oportunidad" (1999).

22. Romero, "EE.UU y Chávez: Una oportunidad" (1999).

23. When the treaty was being considered in Congress in 1999, the Chávez government once again started to have doubts about it. Attacks in the press by Fundapatria characterized the treaty as one-sided, and the government decided to study it again. Seven years had gone by since the treaty was first considered by the Pérez government. Despite the delay, Chávez finally gave the green light to the treaty.

24. *El País* (Spain), August 20, 2000.

25. "EE UU propone a Venezuela fortalecer inteligencia y entrenamiento antidrogas." *El Nacional* (Caracas), July 9, 1999.

26. "Chávez buscará apoyo en la ONU para evitar intervención militar de EE UU en Colombia." *El Nacional*, September 16, 1999.

27. One thesis heard among Chávez opponents who favored the relationship with the United States was that cooperation with the United States on overflights would involve the air force closely in joint operations in the air. The air force was considered to be a focus of opposition to President Chávez among the different forces, and according to this conjecture, was not trusted by the president.

28. *El Diario de Caracas,* August 10, 1993: 26

29. Venezuela, Ministry of Foreign Relations, *Libro Amarillo 1994* (Caracas: 1995), 181–182.

30. Bravo, "El narcotráfico en Venezuela." (Caracas: Mimeo, 1997).

31. *El Nacional*, March 13, 1996: A3; *El Nacional*, March 14, 1996: A2; *El Nacional*, March 16, 1996: D/1.

32. Some years later, Venezuela accused the United States of violating this agreement when a U.S. Navy ship supposedly entered Venezuelan territorial waters. The United States claimed that it was acting within the meaning of the agreement, but it was not clear if the protest was simply a statement of sovereignty by Venezuela with respect to disputed areas or if the United States was indeed sending a signal that it was willing to impose its greater power should the need arise. *El Nacional*, November 11, 2000.

33. Reported in José Vicente Rangel, *El Universal*, March 9, 1997; and Bravo, "El narcotráfico en Venezuela."

34. "Washington y Caracas acuerdan reformular convenios antidrogas," *El Universal*, July 10, 1999: 1–13.

35. *El Universal*, March 2, 2000: 1–6. Venezuela expressed similar criticism of the annual U.S. report to Congress on human rights. See "Venezuela rechaza evaluación de EE UU sobre derechos humanos," *El Nacional*, March 8, 2000.

36. The Venezuelan foreign minister at the time of the denial of the visa, Miguel Angel Burelli Rivas, deplored the sanction, saying that " . . . obviously, the denial of a visa is a matter of State sovereignty, and we should not pass judgment on it, yet we may lament what occurred with Colombia's President, since he is not a common citizen, but a Head of State." *El Nacional*, July 12, 1996: A2.

37. In addition to the amounts assigned to Colombia, a smaller amount of $300 million was to go to Bolivia, Ecuador, and Peru. Since these four countries are Venezuela's partners in the Andean Community, it seemed that the political unity of the community would be affected by the link with the United States that would exclude Venezuela. The package was

opposed by many Democrats in Congress on the grounds that it could involve the United States in a civil war similar to Vietnam.

38. Ewell, *Venezuela and the United States,* 85–87.

39. *El Nacional,* July 29, 2000.

40. *El Universal,* August 13, 1994.

41. *El Universal,* May 4, 1994.

42. A common measure of confidence in a government's economic policy is the "risk premium," which is the difference between the interest rate that the government of the United States pays for its borrowings in the financial markets and the interest rate charged to other governments. Latin American governments may pay much more than the United States to borrow, sometimes as much as 10 percent or more above the rate paid on U.S. Treasury bills.

43. *El Nacional* (Caracas), March 17, 1996: E8.

44. *El Nacional,* June 1, 1996: D3.

45. Luis Jorge Garay, "Regionalismo abierto e integración en las Américas. A propósito del caso del Grupo Andino," in Mónica Lanzetta, ed., *Agenda de largo plazo en las relaciones Colombo-Venezolana* (Bogotá: Tercer Mundo Editores, CAF, Cámara de comercio e integración Colombo-Venezolana, 1997): 472.

46. Albert Fishlow and James Jones, eds., *The United States and the Americas: A Twenty-First Century View* (New York: W. W. Norton, 1999), 26.

47. Juan Mario Vacchino, Las negociaciones hemisféricas: Interrogantes y opciones, 99–109; IRELA, "La Unión Europea y el Grupo de Río, La Agenda Birregional, Documento DB-GRIO 97 (Madrid, IRELA, 1997).

48. Manuela Tortora, *Política social y el ALCA* (Caracas: SELASP/DRE/D, No. 20, 1998): 1.

49. Venezeula intenta reinvindicar su política comercial ante la CAN," *El Nacional,* February 23, 2000: D5.

50. "Venezuela propondrá disolución del Tribunal Andino de Justicia," *El Nacional,* March 9, 2000: E1.

51. "Exigirán fuerte reducción de azufre en la gasolina," *El Universal,* July 9, 1999.

52. Elba Rossini Martin and Jaime Luis Socas, "La Orimulsion: Un complemento para la industria petrolera Venezolana," *Política internacional* X, No. 42 (April-June, 1996): 22–28.

53. MTC elaboró un proyecto que stá siendo revisado por la FAA: Reingreso a la Cetegoría 1 depende de aporbación de Ley de Aviación Civil," *El Nacional,* June 6, 1999.

54. As stated by Thaimyn Márquez, the newly designated head of SAPI in 1999. "Venezuela atrasada," *El Universal,* July 7, 1999.

55. On this point, some candidates for the National Constituent Assembly based their platforms on opposition to the validity of international agreements taken at the multilateral level without ratification by Congress for their legality in Venezuela.

56. United States Trade Representative, *1998 National Trade Estimate Report on Foreign Trade Barriers* (Washington, DC: USTR, 1998).

57. We use the word "regimen" advisedly. President Chávez had billed the new Constitution not as just the reform of the existing document, but as the basis for founding a new republic.

58. Carlos Romero, "Las relaciones entre Venezuela y los Estados Unidos durante la era Clinton: coincidencias estratégicas y diferencias tácticas." Unpublished manuscript, Caracas, 2000.

59. Joseph Tulchin, *Reflexiones sobre las relaciones hemisféricas del siglo XXI*, 125–132; Jorge Domínguez, *International Security and Democracy. Latin American and the Caribbean in the Post–Cold War Era.*

NOTES FOR CHAPTER SIX

1. On the role of NGOs in international politics, see P. J. Simmons, "Learning to Live with NGOs," *Foreign Policy*, no. 112 (Fall 1998):82–96.

2. Andrés Oppenheimer, "Y quién certifica al certificador?" *El Universal*, March 12, 2000.

3. This paradoxical position comes from the analysis of the economics of the drug trade. Economists argue that investment is attracted to those industries with the highest rates of return. A higher-risk business typically requires the highest rates of return to compensate for the risk. Government suppression raises the risks to those who would enter the drug business, but also raises the rate of return to those who are successful.

4. Later testimony showed that a U.S. agent entered Venezuela under a false passport.

5. Esmeralda Garbi, ed. *La fuga de talento en Venezuela* (Caracas: Ediciones IESA, 1991).

6. This was the figure estimated by the president of the Venezuelan-American Foundation. *El Universal*, January 3, 2001.

7. Bravo, *El narcotráfico en Venezuela.*

8. *El Nacional*, March 21, 1997: A2.

9. In 1977, 796,477 tourists arrived in Venezuela, of which 185,746 came from U.S. point of origin. Excluding arrivals from nearby islands, the most important origins for tourists were: Canada (71,872), Italy (52,891), and Spain (33,756). Venezuela, Ministry of the Interior, National Office of Identification and Immigration. Reported in Consejo Nacional de Promoción de Inversiones (Conapri), *Venezuela Now* (Caracas: Conapri, 1999).

10. Fundación Gran Mariscal de Ayacucho, Vice-presidencia de Operaciones, Gerencia de Apoyo. Caracas: March 18, 1999.

11. Domenico Chiappe, "Fundayacucho muestra los dientes y obliga a una repatriación forzada," *El Nacional*, March 12, 2000: H1.

12. Elena Granell, *Managing Culture for Success: Challenges and Opportunities in Venezuela* (Caracas: Ediciones IESA, 1998.

13. Universidad Católica Andrés Bello, Informe de Avance del Estudio de Pobreza. Presented at the meeting of the Santa Lucía Group, Caracas, June 24, 1999.

14. Even new technologies that would seem to dissolve borders follow the asymmetric pattern. According to a director of StarMedia, a company organizing Internet sales in Venezuela, some three quarters of the $170 million in Internet purchases made by Latin Americans in 1998 went to U.S. suppliers (and most of the rest went to Brazil). *El Universal*, July 7, 1999. In the United States, there has always been awareness of the way in which foreigners may react negatively to American power and American values, a phenomenon that fluctuates over time. See for instance, a review of anti-Americanism published in *Newsweek* (International Edition), January 31, 2000.

15. While Venezuela's legal system undoubtedly follows the European tradition, there is a tendency to adopt some aspects of the Anglo-Saxon tradition. A reform of the criminal code carried out with support from the World Bank instituted the new practice of oral hearings and the use of small juries.

NOTES FOR CHAPTER SEVEN

1. Carlos Romero, *La descentralización política en Venezuela y su impacto en la política exterior* (Caracas: Universidad Central de Venezuela, 1997).

2. James Rosenau, *Too Many Things at Once: The Theory of Complexity and World Affairs* (Burbank, CA: The Rand Corporation, 1996).

3.   United Nations, Comisión Económica para América Latina (CEPAL), *Panorama de la inserción internacional de América Latina y el Caribe* (Santiago de Chile: CEPAK, 1996).

4. Richard Cooper, *Economic Policy in an Interdependent World* (Cambridge, MA: MIT Press, 1985).

6-5/05